# PIANO VARIATIONS

by

## FRED KRONACHER

# DEDICATION

I dedicate this book to my mother Gretel, who loved music deep in her heart and sang to me when I was a baby. And to my father Gerald, who wouldn't let me quit when I wanted to as an adolescent. I also dedicate this journal to all the students I've had the opportunity to work with over the years; among them, those that presently grace my home by their weekly visits — Kate, Lewis, Henry, Kwang, Elle, Julian, Patrick, Iona, Nina, Tia, Shigeko, Casey, Aida, Selene, Munya, Gwen, Chelsea, Nancy, Karin, Dani, John, Yann, Sally,Madeleine, Mathew, Zhemin, Arnav, Sana, Yurina, Krithi.

Acknowledgements:
Cover Art- Cal Hynes-Hoffman
Editor- Charles Smyth
Photo- Megan Stacker

*"After silence, that which comes nearest to expressing the inexpressible is music"*

*—Aldous Huxley*

# TABLE OF CONTENTS

# FOREWORD

I have long believed, and have spent a long life seeking evidence for, the proposition that Life and Art are inextricably linked, and that a true and balanced success in either one is impossible without the other. In fact, we might say that one teaches, or informs, the other. Robert Henri, the great American Art Teacher, who had so much to do with connecting American artists with the Impressionistic movement in Paris, "demanded from his students a firsthand emotion received not from art but from life."[1] He also said that "the subject is beauty---or happiness, and man's approach to it is various," which also, in an ideal sense, can be said of both Art and Life.[2]

Fred Kronacher, in his "PIANO VARIATIONS: A musical voyage of self discovery" takes us on that voyage with him, in a series of twenty-two vignettes drawn from his life, from early childhood when he discovers at the same time the wonders of piano playing and baseball, to his maturity as Pianist, Teacher, Lecturer, and Director of the Musical Experiences Foundation.

His admiration for great baseball players is comparable to his reverence for great pianists he hears and describes to us. The New York tabloid, THE DAILY NEWS, is a favorite newspaper because of its coverage of the Mets and Yankees games in New York. He perceives baseball in musical terms, in his description of hearing "Mickey Mantle make that special music that comes from a perfectly timed powerful stroke of the bat, colliding with an oncoming baseball. The clean, fortissimo crack that ensues, and the rapidly rising legato flight of a small white ball against a blue, cloudless sky is a thing of beauty; one might call it lyrical." With only slight alteration, this could describe a virtuoso performance by Vladimir Horowitz.

We travel with him from his earliest experiences at the piano, which until college was simply a great love, through his decision to become a piano major at Ithaca College, through graduate study in New York at The Manhattan School of Music with Robert Goldsand, to his first steps in a career as a performing pianist and teacher. His in-depth discussion of his teaching is a "how to" book for ambitious young teachers. How does a sensitive mind with a formidable talent learn to focus on the sometimes reluctant student in a piano lesson? He learns, and promises himself that in future his students will "have his complete presence" in every lesson. This could be a description of how an actor prepares his performance for the stage.

He explores the universal themes of growing up, brushes with tragedy, the formation and loss of beautiful friendships, disappointments, human relationships, and the inner quest for understanding and harmony in life and art, all through the vehicle of the confrontation of Life and Self. It is at once an unabashed valentine to the art of Music, and to the mystery of Life itself.

The idea of "presence" is a theme throughout the book, whether in himself as teacher and performer, or experiencing it in other great artists he hears and describes in detail, baseball players he admires, friends who grace his life, or students who require his undivided attention. As he says so eloquently in the book, "To light the lamp in the soul of one's neighbor is a privilege not given to everyone. A good teacher, once ignited himself, may pass the flame to another."

Reader, it comes to your hand

Jess Smith
Executive Director Emeritus
Brooklyn Conservatory of Music

# PRELUDE

I am a piano teacher. There are many thousands of us. We are found in the cities, towns, and villages of diverse lands, spread over the wide world. Musicians and teachers, we serve as links in a chain, keeping the melodies unfolding from generation to generation.

Most of us don't get rich or achieve great notoriety. We work in relative anonymity. Yet, we may make a deep and lasting impression upon our students. The motivated teacher-musician reaps a rich reward, not easily measured in a money–driven society. To light the lamp in the soul of one's neighbor is a privilege not given to everyone.  A good teacher, once himself ignited, may pass the flame to another.

Whether musicians or not, it seems we all strive to be in greater harmony. We all prefer to play in tune. Now, I realize that Music is not the sole opening to the light. *Harmony* may be sought for down many of life's myriad avenues. But what finer way to seek it than in music, the very "art of harmony".

I recognize too, that music exists as part of life, not as the whole of life. It exists as a particularly luminous gem, capable of reflecting our ever shifting moods; even mirroring our aspirations to proceed from rivulet, churning torrent and rolling river– to the vast, open sea. It is a universal language open to us all. Though harmony must necessarily be sought in music, it can also be sought in our other pursuits.

This memoir is not meant to be a comprehensive and revealing overview of my life. Instead, these pages are devoted to the musical trek I have embarked upon.  My aim is to limit this set of variations to a single motif: that of music.

And as I am a man first, then a musician, I hope this book speaks of more than just the specific art of music. For while music is the special art of tones, rhythms, timbres, and harmonies, it is also the inner song of the soul, and as such it sings of all human experience.

# Music Dawns

The music started early. Though no single memory presents itself as being the very first, a distinct few stand out clearly. I know I was playing tunes with chordal accompaniments on the piano by the time I was five. In one vivid, early memory, I'm playing the piano at some type of preschool in New Jersey. I remember playing songs by ear with pleasure and facility, surrounded by the presence of other five year olds. It felt like the most natural thing in the world. Finding melodies, feeling the rhythms, and searching out basic harmonies all came of itself. No one taught me.

I retain a host of early memories from my fifth and sixth years, playing an old upright piano at home in New Jersey. To the best of my recollection, the German folksong *Mussi Denn* was my first success as a pianist. This was my father's favorite tune. I played it in C Major; the right hand took the melody, the left covered the harmony, employing basic I, IV, and V chords. It excited my father to no end that I could play this song.

Strauss waltzes soon followed. My mother Gretel, who lived the first 18 years of her life in Vienna, adored the Waltz King. Before long I was playing an assortment of pieces on the piano and receiving effusive praise from my parents, neighbors, and relatives. The accolades swelled my little head. Gerald and Gretel were thrilled by my nascent musical bursts. My Aunt Litzi pronounced me a genius. How was I to know that she was wrong? Music was so much fun. It moved and delighted me so. Maybe I was something extraordinary.

Gerald Kronacher had grown up in Munich. In 1933 he left for Zurich to study engineering at the Swiss Polytechnic School. That, of course, was the year that Hitler came to power in Germany. Being in Switzerland, which remained neutral throughout the tumultuous years to come, proved crucial as it concerned the fate of the entire Kronacher family. My father, safely out of Germany, was eventually able to secure visas for himself, his parents, and his brother Hans, to immigrate to Bolivia. He had gone to Paris in 1938, and there from consulate to consulate, desperate to win removal from Germany for his family of German Jews. After being turned away by country after country, he finally succeeded, with the aid of a small monetary bribe to an official at the Bolivian consul, and secured the visas that saved his family's life. Fortuitously, the training and degree he received at the acclaimed Zurich Polytechnic held him in good stead for the rest of his life, permitting him to make a decent living as an engineer.

As these lines are being written, he stands three weeks shy from celebrating his 99th birthday. He has always been a generous, good-hearted, supportive father to both my sister Erica and me.

Shortly after my sixth birthday, our family took a two week summer vacation in the Catskills. The Catskill Mountains of New York State, sometimes referred to in those days as the "Jewish Alps" or the "Borscht Belt," lie about a two hour drive northwest of New York City. "Alps" they are not, but rather a picturesque series of wooded hillsides and smaller mountains. Back in their heyday they were dotted with grand old hotels.

Our family stayed at an unpretentious, modest sized place called Hotel Star, which was frequented by a mostly Jewish clientele. Though we stayed there only once, I still remember this old hotel with fondness. It was something of a faded rose, a wee bit dilapidated, a little frayed at the edges, but still managing to retain an old world, dignified eloquence. To my six year old mind it was quite glamorous.

I played games with other children, Ping-Pong with my father, took walks with my family, frolicked on the ample, green, gently sloping lawn, and sat on the comfortable front porch at dusk, listening to adults tell jokes I couldn't understand. It made no difference that I couldn't comprehend the jokes. Just being out on that open air porch, after dinner on beautiful summer evenings, surrounded by hardworking people who were relaxing and laughing together on their summer vacations; this made me happy.

But most special of all was being permitted to stay up well past my bedtime to play the piano for the guests in the lounge. Mr. Frölich, the house musician and an Austrian immigrant who entertained most evenings on the piano, had invited me to play a few numbers. I had not yet had any piano lessons and played solely by ear. Thus it was a scant repertoire that I carried with me up to the Catskills that summer. I'm sure I played *Mussi Den*, my warhorse, and I recall knocking out a version of *Yankee Doodle*. I probably played one of own creations as well, a piece I called *March of the Dwarfs*. Beyond that my recollection goes hazy. My strength was being able to give a decent rendition of a piece once having heard it. The most lasting memory of these early performances is that it caused me to be kissed by some ladies who I had rather not have been kissed by. I remember the scent of perfume, the jangling of loose brace-lets, the red lipstick-lined mouths, and the snippets of—"What a bright little boy—how cute you are, let me hug you dear." This was something I realized had to be tolerated. It had been simpler entertaining my little peers in the nursery school.

Still, it was an honor to be up late in the lounge, sipping ginger ale while middle-aged men and women schmoozed over wine and cocktails. One night I had an unfortunate accident. After going to sleep, I wet my bed. This caused my father to declare that henceforth I would no longer be allowed ginger ale or any other beverage after dinner. I was not pleased by this new arrangement. I had grown extremely fond of ginger ale. Staying up late was not much fun unless I could drink along with the adults.

Now my father was a fairly strict, disciplined German, and it wouldn't do any good showing cranky petulance. I realized it would take some cunning on my part to savor the taste of ginger ale in the evening. Hence, I went to work on my mother. She was soft, yielding, and gen-tle; all heart, but no discipline. My supplications were rewarded. She brought the much prized elixir into my room on the sly, unbeknownst to her husband. I still see the loving gaze of her kind, brown eyes as she passed me the little cup of ginger ale. This remained our clandestine arrangement the remainder of the vacation.

Back home in New Jersey I discovered the joy of listening to great music on records. Mozart, Haydn, and Beethoven thrilled me. Their music more than merely pleased or entertained. It awakened something elemental in me. It made me love being *alive*. There is just no other way to say it. Magnificent music can do this, and it struck deep into my innermost self.

Bach soon followed. After receiving a recording of the Brandenburg Concertos from my Uncle Hans, I was quickly hooked.

My mother was the source of whatever musical gifts I was given. She was the musical one in the family. She listened to classical music with reverence and could quickly identify the great composers upon hearing segments of their work. The radio at home was always tuned to WQXR, the classical music station owned by the New York Times. When a favorite piece of hers, such as Beethoven's Third Piano Concerto was being played on the air, she would turn to me and sigh. "Ay, Beethoven—Gott, he's great, isn't he?—Ay, so beautiful." She would often sing at home, always in tune with a mellifluous voice. My mother favored light melodies from operetta when she sang. She sang with gaiety and charm, yet I could detect a hint of melancholy in her voice.

As a young child, I knew very little of the tragedy that had darkened her youth. She had lost both her parents in the Holocaust a decade or so before I was born. With her younger sister Litzi, she had gotten safely out of Europe, arriving in New York in November of 1938.

As a six or seven year old, I'm not quite certain which, I made a startling discovery. I learned that I could make my mother cry by playing a particular style of music on the piano. I had intuitively begun improvising and playing various types of music by ear, and when I stumbled upon the rich, emotional style of Hungarian gypsy song, it brought my mother to tears. I had imbibed a favorite record of hers which featured this bewitching, Middle European sound. I loved it! It was music that had been popular in Vienna and my mother had grown up with it.

Gretel Kronacher, née Berger, was a Viennese through and through. This meant that Strauss waltzes, as well as Hungarian dances, lit an immediate spark in her heart. The lilting, uplifting waltzes swept her along joyously, while the poignant gypsy melodies in the darker minor keys brought her to tears.

Sometimes she would ask me, "Freddy, will you make Mommy cry?" I knew what that meant. I would go over to our piano and begin to play the melodies and harmonies that would invariably press upon a deep and tender spot in her gentle, violated heart. My mom would cry. Tears just poured from her eyes.

I had only the vaguest notions about what she had been through. Still, I sensed that for whatever the reason, she just needed to cry. Somehow, it seemed all right that I play these heartrending, sad melodies which she had asked for, and which provoked such a strong emotional response. It created a kind of bond between us. Our special secret. I believe today, that it must have been a type of catharsis for her. Hearing her firstborn child play music that she had grown up with in Vienna, and play it with an innate emotional understanding of its Hungarian spice and melancholic flavor; this just always made her weep. It undoubtedly took her back to Vienna, and conjured up images of her parents.

"Freddy, make mommy cry." She would say it every two or three months up until the time I was ten or so. I would always comply.

Gretel was eclectic in her musical tastes. She loved the great European masters, but she also embraced Ella Fitzgerald, Rodgers and Hammerstein, Gershwin, and other popular American musicians. She was always singing their tunes. In my teenage years she took a shine to the Beatles and Simon and Garfunkel, singing their songs with enjoyment, sometimes to my piano accompaniment. Music just seemed to ooze from her.

My parents had faced harrowing times and real hardship during their youths. They first met one another in New York in the early 1950s. After having both survived shattering events, they would sadly have one more great disappointment still to bear; their marriage. It was not a happy one.

I will make no attempt at describing their relationship here. It turned sour by the time I was six or seven, and a cloud was cast over the remainder of my childhood. Life became more complicated, more confusing and more unsettling. An uneasy, tense atmosphere often permeated our house throughout my school years. I lost my way.

Despite this, youthful ebullience never wholly abandoned me. And my parents, their lives troubled by an unhealthy relationship, still loved my sister Erica and me. We always knew this. The light of love twinkled in their eyes. Despite whatever mistakes they may have made with my sister and me, their intentions were always good. They gave us so much. I can appreciate today the stresses they were under, the wounds they carried within themselves, the obstacles put before them. They loved us and taught us to love. They were courageous in their persistent, hopeful optimism. They never bowed and surrendered to cynical callousness. They kept their hearts through all their considerable trials. And of course, they nurtured my love of music.

For my seventh birthday, my parents gave me a book that I still own today. Entitled History's 100 Greatest Composers, it is written for schoolchildren and includes sketch portraits of the composers. I had spotted this book at the Korvettes Department Store in West Orange, where our family sometimes shopped and browsed. I begged my parents to buy it for me. It appeared at home on my birthday and soon fired my imagination with the lives of Beethoven, Schubert, and the other greats. Today this book sits on a bookshelf in my home in Seattle. Now and then it gets loaned out to some of my students, and thus continues to inspire budding seven year old musicians.

I was never the genius that Aunt Litzi declared me to be, but I had been given a modest talent and a true love for music. The tonal art had now been established in my life. The beacon light had been lit, and its warm rays have emanated outward ever since. For this, I am ever grateful.

# TIA

Most of my lessons are given after 3; when school has let out. On weekdays, I typically do the bulk of my teaching between 3:30 and 9. Often, I'll have one or two adult students, mid to late morning. The early hours are reserved for my own piano practice. But today is Wednesday, and eight year old Tia will be here in five minutes. Tia is an early bird, taking her lesson each Wednesday bright and early at 7:30, before going on to school.

After savoring a last sip of coffee, I wash a few dishes, then responding to the knock at my front door, turn and walk through my living room to greet Tia and her mother Paula. Both enter my old Seattle bungalow radiating warmth and good cheer. Tia immediately fills me in about a play that she's to be in at school. She recites a few of her lines, which seem to be well-lodged in her memory. She frequently enthuses over the many passions in her young life while walking into my piano studio.

I used to resist teaching so early. I preferred keeping early morning for some quiet sitting, and especially for practicing. But I have become quite fond of my current Wednesday morning routine. Seeing Tia's fresh face and being infected by her high spirits is a fine start to the day. Our midweek rendez-vous at the piano helps bring my being into greater tune. It is time well spent, and has a value no less than whatever else I might do.

As she settles herself at the piano, she smiles and proudly informs me, "I made up a blues melody. I want to play it for you. Can I play it first today?" I was poised to ask her to start with some finger exercises and scales. Tia, like most young pianists, needs to acquire greater finger control.  However, I yield easily to her request, "Yes go ahead Tia, play it for me." She confidently plays a jaunty little blues tune with her right hand.  The left hand sits quietly on her lap, and so this tune lacks harmony.  It does however possess spiky imaginative intervals, and a jazzy, bouncy rhythm.  As promised, several pungent "blues" notes ring out prominently.  It's the real thing.

"I love it Tia," I exclaim.  Paula, who watches our lesson, is smiling now.  Tia's dark eyes glow as she turns toward me, her straight jet black hair glistens, radiating youth and health; her whole being enlivened by her embrace of creativity.

I decide to postpone the finger exercises and scales and stick with our foray into the world of blues and original composition.  "Tia, this tune needs a harmony," I say.  "Now you already know a lot about harmony.  Today we can learn some more.  You can give your blues piece a nice chord progression." "I know about seventh chords," she pipes up, "and look, I can play a blues chord progression." With that, she starts to show me a left hand progression of simple chords that she's learned from her father, Tao, who plays the piano.  It's a basic progression utilizing I, IV, and V chords.  Soon I'm teaching her what a diminished chord is.  She understands quickly, and picks it up readily.

When I first started to teach children, more than three decades ago, I was less pliant about flowing with the needs and temperaments of individual students.  I still remember that very first lesson one Saturday morning in February many years ago.  I had just been hired at the Brooklyn Conservatory of Music.  My first pupil that day was a cute, chipper little seven year old girl named Stacy.  We had just gotten acquainted and I was eager to address the issues of hand position, rhythmic regularity, and note reading, when little Stacy chirped, "I'm going to a birthday party today!" Slightly thrown off stride, I replied, "Oh that's nice," or some words to that effect.  Stacy was quite animated telling me about the dress she was planning to wear, and which friends of hers were coming.  All this excitement over a birthday party was something of an unexpected roadblock thrown in the path of this earnest young teacher.

I remember being charmed by Stacy's warmth and energy, but also feeling anxious to get down to the business of being a piano teacher. After all, that's what I was hired to be, wasn't it?

Since then, I've heard my share about birthday parties, loose teeth, sleepovers, soccer games, math contests, spelling bees, family squabbles, divorce, personal dreams and hopes; a whole range of "non piano" subjects. I was certainly in no hurry to dampen Tia's youthful enthusiasm for the blues this fine Wednesday morning. Scales, arpeggios, Bach, Mozart—they could all wait. It works best that way with Tia. She's been my student for three years now, and we've learned to work with one another.

Tia is a musical, extroverted, smart, temperamental, strong-willed, creative, wonderful girl. She's a good piano student, though not an exceptional one, and doesn't practice with highly focused discipline—at least not yet. But she has talent, progresses surely and steadily, is maturing emotionally, and is just eight years old. She is becoming a musician.

When we do get around to Bach later in the lesson, she plays the G Major Minuet with felicity and assurance. "Tia, that's the best you've ever played this piece!" I praise her. "You didn't rush in the second half like you did last week. You kept your tempo even all the way through." "I used the metronome!" she tells me. "That's right," Paula's voice now chimes in, "She practiced with the metronome this week." It's been slow-going getting Tia to play along with the ever steady ticking of the metronome.

For many children, it takes a gradual maturation of the nervous system before they can gain the necessary coordination to play steadily, along with the insistent, imperturbable little time keeper. I once had a little seven year old girl become so flummoxed trying to keep up with my old German mechanical metronome that she ended by exploding in rage. Her cheeks turned beet red, smoke seemed to rise from her scalp, and she finally clenched both fists and screamed, "The metronome is wrong! It's not in time! It's wrong!" I could certainly sympathize. How many aspiring musicians have been frustrated by this blasted little device! Now, it does happen that metronomes malfunction and go awry—but rarely. Alas, it's almost always us piano players that veer off rhythm, unable to keep up with this smug, impeccable contraption.

Today represented a breakthrough. Tia had successfully employed the metronome and tamed the urge to rush uncontrollably through the second half of a Bach minuet. I exchanged a high five with my pupil. She beamed proudly.

Toward the end of our lesson, I tell her, "Tia, we need to pick a new piece today." She already had a Mozart piece in progress, so I thought we should do something from a different style and period, perhaps a 19th or 20th century work. "We'll pick something new today. I'll give you three choices and you pick," I say.

With most students, I simply assign the piece I think best for them. When I was a boy, neither Mr. Brent nor Mr. Chiapinelli, my teachers, would have ever let me choose my repertoire. But I have found that this approach really pays off with Tia. I know that if she has a say in the choice of music, she'll be more motivated. *She* has to like it.

I play a short work by Bartok, a toccatina by Kabalevsky, and a piece by Tchaikovsky. She looks pensive, grins, and says, "I'm not sure, I sort of like all three." Then suddenly, her eyes open wide, a look of wonder blooms on her lovely face, and she exclaims, "I know, another Bach minuet!" With that, she grabs the music book on the rack and excitedly thumbs through its pages. "Here it is!" she cries. "Remember? You said I could play this one too—remember?—Remember when we picked out the first Bach song?" My mercurial student smiles triumphantly. "That's right Tia, now I do remember." I had played two minuets for her a couple of months back. She had chosen the G Major Minuet with the understanding that the g minor would be waiting in the wings. She had not forgotten.

Though I had planned to assign something different, I wasn't about to cross Tia and dampen her youthful enthusiasm. She certainly knows her own mind, and if it's another minuet by an old timer named Bach that she wants, then another Bach minuet it will be. "Ok Tia, let's go for it—minuet in g minor." I begin to write some fingerings in her book, and Tia bounds happily over to Paula for a hug. After I play the first eight measures for her, our time is just about up.

"Now I'll play *You Gotta Have Heart,* she declares. Tia loves songs from old Broadway musicals, which she's come to know through watching some of them on DVDs. *You Gotta Have Heart* comes from the show *Damn Yankees* which dates from the fifties. She begged me to teach it to her, so I'm teaching it to her by ear; a little each week. She joyously plays what she's learned thus far. It's not perfectly smooth. She hesitates in a few spots, disrupting the rhythmic flow. But how she enjoys this song! Before she leaves, I play it and she sings boisterously along in full voice. She knows all the lyrics. "I dare say Tia," now switching over into my best British accent, "I dare say, I believe you've got it." I do this because I know Tia loves to show off her own British accent, gleaned from seeing films like My Fair Lady. She is quite a mimic. Now, as it happens, my British accent is not bad—but Tia's is spectacular, far surpassing mine. I'm agog at how dead-on perfect it is. Predictably, she takes my bait and gleefully puts on her smashingly brilliant British accent. "Why thank you sir, quite kind of you to say so sir, I shan't forget to practice well sir," I'm floored as usual, and look toward Paula with wonder. "She's going to wind up on the stage," I say. Paula nods, her eyes seem to acknowledge this thought, and if I read Paula's expression correctly, it's a thought tinged with apprehension.

As she gathers her books and prepares to leave for school, Tia informs me she has a new favorite classical piano piece. She then sings out the main motif of Mozart's great a Minor Piano Sonata. It happens to be a piece I myself am working on, in preparation for an upcoming concert. "My dad is practicing it," she tells me. "I love it!—it's my favorite!" "One day you'll play it too Tia," I respond.

Tia and her mother step out onto my front porch and we bid each other farewell. I feel energized and ready to play the piano. It will indeed be the great a Minor Sonata of Mozart that shall now be the object of my attention. Soon the great *maestoso* motif, the one Tia has just sung, is being propelled from the sound board of my grand piano, and vibrating through the house.

# Café Geiger

Café Geiger has vanished into the mists of history. It no longer stands between second and third avenues on East 86ᵗʰ Street. Along with most of the other German establishments that once graced Manhattan's Yorkville neighborhood, it is gone. I remember it wistfully.

From the age of five, I enjoyed the mocha torte, the piano trio that once performed Strauss, and Schubert, and the company of family and friends, all in the cozy yet stylish ambiance of this German restaurant/café.

By the time I turned five, my family had moved to a house in New Jersey. Occasionally, on Sundays, my parents, my sister Erica, and I would make the drive into the city, and meet Uncle Hans or Aunt Litzi at Café Geiger. I had already discovered my love of music by then. We had a second hand, dark brown upright piano at home, and I would play it by ear, picking out the melodies and harmonies from waltzes by Strauss, German folk songs like *Mussi Denn* (my father's favorite) or Haydn, Mozart, and Beethoven symphonies I had come to know through recordings.

My uncle Hans, the brother of my father, always brought me a new record when he came to visit us. I couldn't wait to un-wrap each new disc and place it on the turntable, and drink in the marvels of these orchestral works. The three Viennese classical giants, Haydn, Mozart, and Beethoven became my musical Gods. Their music shined a warm, luminous light on my early childhood. This music awakened my youthful soul, and revealed a wonder and depth of feeling, that has stayed with me through all the years.

I was lucky. My mother was very musical. My father, though not so musical, respected music, and encouraged me to follow the clarion call of this ethereal art. My Uncle Hans and Aunt Litzi both also loved music. Only my sister Erica seemed impervious to the classical masters.

Back in the late fifties and early sixties, Café Geiger still presented a trio of musicians who played a kind of background music on a small stage at the far end of the restaurant. My parents explained how it was customary in the cafes of the great European cities for there to be some live music. The very name Café Geiger has musical connotations, as Geiger is the German word for violin. The trio that played Sunday afternoons at Geiger consisted of three middle-aged émigres who spoke German, and English with pronounced German accents.

The pianist was the most gregarious of them. He also showed the keenest interest in my musical progress. My memories of the violinist and the cellist are less clear, but I do remember the violinist had a debonair, stylish bearing, and the cellist often appeared lost in thought. My father and I referred to him as the "thinker." I loved this trio.

Up until the age of nine or ten, I was always urging my parents to make the drive into New York, and to Café Geiger. I succeeded in this mission maybe seven or eight times each year.

We would usually meet Uncle Hans there, and sometimes Aunt Litzi as well. And we would always ask for a table as near to the musicians as possible.

This German trio specialized in what is known as "schmalz", the type of light, sentimental, accessible, melodic music that pulls at the heart. I readily confess to having a weakness for well-played schmalz. Yes, schmalz can be played well, or it can be played poorly. The musicians must understand the subtleties, and feel the unique charm of this music to do it justice. Even as it requires a certain feeling of "soul" to play the blues well, or a rhythmic, earthy sensuousness to play Spanish music well, it takes a certain Viennese sophistication and charm to get the Merry Widow Waltz just right. When it is played properly, I am utterly captivated by its lilting rhythms, melodious curves, and simple, rich harmonies.

It was at Geiger that my lifelong appreciation of European café culture was born and nurtured. Although I was too young to be allowed the coffee that my parents and Litzi would always drink, or the glass of beer that Uncle Hans liked so much, the mocha torte was my specialty. The food, drink, and music were mingled with convivial conversation. Despite the unfortunately troubled nature of my parents' marriage, I can only remember everyone being happy and in extremely good spirits when at Café Geiger. We sat together, under the glimmering chandeliers, our round table covered by white linen, surrounded by the European atmosphere of this always crowded New York haunt. One heard a lot of foreign accents, a lot of German, as well as an assembly of other languages.

When the musicians took a break, the loquacious pianist would sometimes stop at our table and talk with us for a few minutes. I don't remember his name, but I remember the rich timbre of his voice, his accented but very clear English, his mostly bald head, bordered by neatly trimmed dark hair, and his amiable sociability.

He invited me up on the small platform stage to play the piano. I must have been six years old when I played my first solo at Café Geiger. He told me "Freddy my boy, when I was a lad in Germany, I played too much soccer. I was crazy for soccer, you know, and I really didn't practice the piano enough." "So you see" he told me "the result is I have to play here in Café Geiger every Sunday."

As a young child, I couldn't possibly fathom what could be wrong with performing at Geiger on Sunday afternoons. What could be better than that! Well, by the time I turned eight, there was one other prospective activity that could rival the dream of playing schmalz at Geiger. And that was the dream of playing second base at Yankee Stadium for the New York Yankees. I had been stricken with baseball fever, and Mickey Mantle, Roger Maris and Whitey Ford now rivaled Haydn, Mozart, and Beethoven for my attention.

"I know you like baseball" said my café pianist, "but you must not neglect the piano. That's what I did, playing soccer for hours on end with my friends. Remember my example Freddy, don't go overboard playing baseball and neglect your piano practice!"

As things turned out, he was proven prescient. I did play a lot of baseball, and became stubbornly lazy about regular piano practice. But that is another matter, its reasons complex and not the subject of this writing.

I wonder about this gentleman and his two colleagues. "They are real trained musicians" my father would say. "I'll bet they've been to music conservatories."

In later years I came to know something of the insecure, hard scrabble life of the free lance musician in New York. Perhaps my Café Geiger pianist did some accompanying, vocal coaching, and gave some lessons. Perhaps the two string players did some studio recording, or played occasionally in the pit at Broadway shows, and did some teaching. Or maybe, worked jobs completely disconnected to music. I wonder how the Nazi upheaval of their young years may have impacted their career possibilities.

I had been told that I didn't want to end up playing piano in a restaurant. But for a wide eyed six year old, these three German immigrants were stars.

Eventually, the trips to Café Geiger became more infrequent. By the mid sixties, the restaurant stopped presenting live music. My father never cared for the big, crowded city, and in time, we stopped making Café Geiger a Sunday afternoon destination.

By the time I turned twelve, though I continued to play the piano, my practicing was undisciplined and not particularly inspired. Mozart was now competing with the ball field, the television set, the Beatles, and the desire to fit in at school. American popular culture had gripped its talons round my juvenile mind. Serious piano practice was sporadic and my indolence continued through most of my teenage years. Yet, I never really stopped loving the classics.

Time passed, I moved away to attend college, and my latent love for great music surged anew. I decided to throw myself in completely, and be a musician. Five hour practice days became the norm. A real inspiration and love for music fueled my efforts at Ithaca College. For the first time in my life, I began to develop some discipline, which I had always hitherto lacked. After completing my Bachelor's Degree in Applied Piano at Ithaca, I moved to New York to attend the Manhattan School of Music, to pursue a Master's, and more importantly-- to continue to develop as a pianist and musician.

So it was as a young twenty-two year old fellow that I walked in to Café Geiger one Sunday afternoon in October of 1975. I hadn't been there for maybe nine or ten years, and can't say that I'd thought of it much during the intervening period. But my heart jumped when I walked in that afternoon. The magic of those childhood days with my family flooded my surprised soul. There was no music; that had been dispensed with years ago, but my eyes strained to find the spot at the back of the restaurant where that marvelous trio had once held court, carrying my youthful spirit aloft on the wings of melody.

And then I walked past the pastry and bread case, the tortes and strudels still elegantly displayed, just as I remembered them. The staff was still dressed as before, in the formal European livery of white and black. The head waiter who showed me to my table wore a black bow tie and spoke with a German accent. I was shown to my table, covered with the familiar white linen table cloth. A strong emotion, which I hadn't expected, welled up within me. A few tears escaped from my eyes. I controlled myself to order mocha torte from the German waitress who came to wait on me. And now that I was a young man, it was accompanied by coffee. It was on that day that I discovered the strong, wonderful coffee offered at Café Geiger.

In the following decade, as a New Yorker, I regularly enjoyed my visits to Café Geiger. Sometimes I'd meet my mother and Aunt Litzi there for lunch. They both lived in New York during those years, my mother having moved back to the city after her divorce from my father. Sometimes I would meet my father for lunch or dinner. He loved the bratwurst they served, and so did I, until I became vegetarian. I was also an enthusiastic ambassador for Geiger, introducing all my good friends to this *gemütliches deutches* restaurant on the Upper East Side.

As it had been in childhood, Café Geiger continued to be that special cavern full of simple, glorious delights. It was old Europe, dark woodwork, elegant chandeliers, excellent food, the best German bread, the best German beer, my favorite coffee, and the delectable *konditerei*, from mocha torte to apfel strudel and beyond. I remember it as always being crowded, and the hum of conversation, forks clinking on plates, the snatches of German phrases intermingled with English and other European languages, all singing in a most pleasant counterpoint. It was a place to be happy, a respite from one's worries and troubles. I always felt it was something of a little gala to walk through the doors of Café Geiger.

But those days have come and gone. On one of my return visits to New York after having moved to Seattle, I learned that Café Geiger had closed its doors. Little by little the entire Yorkville neighborhood had changed. It had been a vibrant German middle class and working class neighborhood since the early years of the twentieth century. As such, it was still a thriving community in the late fifties when I was first introduced to this middle European milieu. Germans, Poles, Czechs, Austrians, and Hungarians lived in and around this quarter. It was home not just to Geiger, my place, but also to the Kleine Konditerei, the Bremen Haus, the Czech restaurant The Ruc, the Hungarian restaurant the Budapest, about which Litzi raved "Ach Freddy, such a goulash they make!", the Heidelberg, Café Mozart, Die Lorelei, and many more places I can't remember. All but one or two are gone now. That's the American way. The children that grew up in Yorkville moved to the suburbs, or to far off places like Seattle. Rents were raised, big developers moved in, and as has always been the case in New York, ethnic communities assimilate and disperse.

Although I lament the departure of Café Geiger and its European cousins on or near east eighty sixth street, I suppose I should realize that when German Town began its ascendancy, circa nineteen ten, some long dead man or woman must have similarly mourned the passing of a favorite café or shop. And let us not forget the native peoples of this island, who lived once in a pristine wilderness of green forest, surrounded by two pure, majestic rivers.

Transience is life. And in a relatively young country of immigrants like this one, it molds its transformations fleetly, even if it carries off a jewel like Café Geiger, and a whole neighborhood; a whole culture, leaving some of us feeling abandoned.

In Italy, I saw a production of Verdi's *Rigoletto* at a nearly two thousand year old arena in Verona. Here in Seattle, where I live today, the Kingdome, a stadium built for sports, was demolished after having served the city's baseball and football teams for all of twenty years.

A person can have a drink in Paris at La Closerie des Lilas, where Hemingway quite often did in the twenties, or drink coffee in Tommaselli's in Salzburg where the Mozart family dined in the eighteenth century. But I can't go back to East Eighty-Sixth Street and find those favorite European establishments. That's too bad for those of us who value tradition. New York doesn't stand still for very long. It is a perpetual swirl of shifting peoples, cultures, and neighborhoods.

When I visit my family and friends in New York, I still enjoy the city's streets and its energy. So far, at least, I can count on finding the Metropolitan Museum of Art firmly anchored on Fifth Avenue and Eighty-Sixth Street, and Carnegie Hall clinging to its foundations on West Fifty-Seventh Street. But I no longer journey over to Yorkville. Not since Café Geiger and its colorful neighborhood faded into the gritty, thin, city air.

I miss it, and it still glows in my memories. I still see the incandescent light flicker off Uncle Hans' amber glass of beer; still see the impressionistic swirl of waiters with trays held high, the milling of patrons— the smiles on my parents faces as my sister and I pick out our cake. And if I close my eyes and strain my ears just a little, I may even catch a snippet of a Brahms Hungarian dance, or an ever so faint strain of the Merry Widow Waltz, still floating gently in the breeze high above the remnants of a time and place gone by.

# A Vacation

Another working day has drawn to a close, much of it spent like so many before it; teaching and playing the piano. Kate's lesson has just finished up, and I walk her to the door. Kate is a happy, attractive girl of fourteen and a half. She's becoming a fine pianist. Her Schubert impromptu bubbled along today with impressive clarity and real panache. Some years earlier when she was eight or nine years old, Kate instructed me to cease calling her Katie, the name her parents called her. She was quite particular on this matter, saying that either Kathryn or Kate would be acceptable. Kate had self esteem as a little girl, and she has it today. She's studying Spanish in high school, as I once did a long time ago; and we have fun spending a portion of each week's lesson practicing our *Espanol*.

As she steps out onto the front porch of my house, I remind her that I'll be gone next week. *"No estoy aqui la proxima semana."* Tomorrow morning I leave bright and early for the Canadian Rockies and a ten day holiday. *"La proxima leccion sera en dos semanas Katarina."* Kate smiles and replies *"Me recuerdo, tenga una buena vacaccion." "Adios."*

The door closes behind me, and I spot the backpack and overnight bag sitting on the sofa, beckoning anxiously for my attention. I'm glad to have a vacation. I adore hiking in the mountains and I've never before been to the Canadian Rockies. I look forward to the coming adventure. And yet, I feel no pressing need to take a break. Teaching piano has become so natural and invigorating to me. I never feel at all burdened by time spent with my students.

It hasn't always been so. It's taken time to learn how to be more fully present, and hence more fully engaged while teaching music.

Additionally, fortunate circumstances now favor me with wonderful students. Taking a break from practicing is an altogether different matter. That is more appreciated and always helps me. Coming back to the piano after a bit of a lay off never fails to ignite the old passion for making music.

As I go about packing and readying myself for tomorrow morning's departure, I fall in to a contemplative review of the three concerts programs I gave this season. My mind scans back through these performances. How close, I wonder, did I come to attaining my goal? The hunger to play great repertoire has remained strong. I have yet to tire of the regular toil required in seeking technical and artistic excellence

The Bach program with my friend Dan Rouslin, an excellent violinist, was richly rewarding. We each played a solo partita, and then collaborated on the E Major Sonata. I played the great Second Partita in c minor, a piece I hadn't performed since my master's recital at the Manhattan School of Music, some thirty five years ago. I feel good about the performance. Having learned it so solidly in my student days made it relatively easy to bring back. The score was all there, dormant within me, and quickly reawakened by a couple of weeks study.

What a joy to play Bach on the piano; exploring the twisting, turning melodic lines, dancing in a most perfect counterpoint, and the ensuing rich, probing harmonies. I love it! My only trepidation in performing this music is the menacing possibility of the slightest memory lapse. Even the slightest memory lapse, easily overcome and negotiable in most other composers can be deadly in Bach. With Bach, it is perilous to get even the least bit lost. One can end up in a dense maze of contrapuntal lines and shifting harmonies, and struggle to find one's bearings and proceed gracefully.

After considering using the music, I chose to eschew the written page in favor of the freedom that comes from playing by memory. The piece was deeply enough embedded within me, and I'm glad to have gone ahead and performed it *par coeur*, I like that phrase 'by heart'. It is an apt and poetic description of playing music without the book. Like most pianists, I give my solo recitals by memory. There's a very simple reason why pianists play by memory — *freedom*. For once music is committed to memory, the musician is set free to concentrate solely on its beauty and meaning. No question remains as to what notes to play. A pianist may now lose himself more completely in the music, and liberated from reading a written page, he may soar high into the ether.

The Chopin, Liszt program in January came off well enough, but I feel I played Liszt's *Valle d'Obermann* a bit too fast. Some passages could have been more cleanly executed as well. It was the first time I'd performed this major work. I was more satisfied with the Chopin b Flat Minor Scherzo and the Liszt pieces *Au bord d'une source* and the etude *Gnomenreigen* which I feel were played with color, feeling, and clarity.

As I zip up my back-pack, I am suddenly overtaken by a feeling of nostalgia. It hits me squarely that for the past thirty five years now, I've done two things in particular with steady, persistent regularity, on a near daily basis— play the piano, or teach someone to play the piano. This thought makes me stop and sit down for a moment. A sigh of satisfaction, but also tinged with wistful nostalgia, seems to whisper, "thirty five years— has it really been thirty five years?" is followed by a few minutes repose. For me, music has always been much more than a profession. Getting back to my packing brings a resumption of my reveries.

The final concert, given in June featured works dating from the turn of the century. I titled it '*Fin de Siècle*- Music from 1890 to 1910'. It was held in an intimate chamber that held an audience of maybe one hundred people. I was satisfied with my playing of the late Brahms works, the Debussy preludes, and especially pleased with my Ravel Sonatine. But the Albeniz *Triana* got the better of me. Despite the roar of approval it elicited from my auditors, I knew better and left the stage disappointed. A rare memory lapse tripped me up about two thirds of the way through this delicious, sensuous evocation of Seville's old Triana neighborhood. Oh how I ache for another crack at this fiendishly difficult but marvelous tone poem! Not a touring pianist, my opportunities to perform are few. Yet I am resolved to surmount the challenges of

Albeniz' masterwork. I relish the old feeling stirring inside, the old fire of desiring to perfect and own a favorite piano piece.

I set the all important hiking boots out on the porch. On the cusp of ten days away from the piano, my excitement at heading for the mountains seems to be matched by an equally strong urge to assess the past year's musical voyage. As I roll up a jacket to place in my bag, my thoughts turn to the public piano recital my students gave in June. The kids exceeded my expectations this year by the poise and assurance they displayed in performing their pieces. Two of my most talented and accomplished students had graduated the previous spring, and had left for college. I wondered if this year's program might come across a bit flat, a bit less splendidly than last year's, what with the loss of my two 'stars'. On the contrary, this June's recital was on the whole, better.

Kate, to whom I just bid good bye, played her Mendelssohn Venetian Boat Song with soulful beauty, and her Haydn scherzo with playful zest. Lewis, another high school student, played his Bach gavotte accurately but cautiously, and then relaxed and rendered a Chopin prelude with strength and purpose. The little ones, like five and a half year old Aida, and two other six year olds pulled off their pieces successfully, albeit with varying degrees of confidence. Aida, an extremely timorous, cute Vietnamese girl, just finishing Kindergarten, has a good ear, a fine sense of rhythm, and good finger coordination. She is on her way to becoming a musician. Due to her shyness, she speaks sparingly and softly during our lessons despite the prodding of her parents. She played the big grand piano on the stage very quietly, as if in a whisper, without any major errors, but lacking in self assurance. Confidence will come to Aida later. Of this I am sure. Playing the piano will assist her.

Many children, quite naturally wrestle with nerves when stepping forth before an audience and performing an exacting piece of music on the big, black, shiny grand piano. Once a seven year old student of mine named Eugene was approached by one of his mother's friends just before the start of a piano recital. "Eugene" she addressed him, "you look very nice wearing that tie. Tell me, are you nervous, getting ready to play in your first piano concert?" Eugene, an honest and self aware little boy answered her in a stentorian voice full of conviction, "Well, of course I'm nervous! What do you think! What a question!"

There are some children, however, who seem to relish the opportunity to perform, and actually play better when under the spotlight. Little Iona, now eight and a half years old, seems to be one such child.

Oh how I enjoy Iona's lessons! She has a great big smile, an exaggerated yet most earnest little frown, and an elemental love of music and of life. She loves to play with speed and alacrity, and already possesses excellent facility on the keyboard. Her cute, expressive face reveals a wide open, bold, curious soul. Iona's mother is a vivacious, beautiful, multi-talented Japanese woman. Her father, an American, is more taciturn and calm. Luke, a police officer, is a proud and supportive papa. Rie, his energetic wife is more of the task master, but also loving towards Iona and her younger sister Nina. Nina, six years old, is another charmer, with a wholly different persona than her older sister. Something about this family touches me in a special way. I am fond of all of them as individuals, and appreciate the way they interact as a family. My job has allowed me to observe the inner workings of many families over the years.

Iona loves to perform, and this past June she announced to her mom on the morning of the recital, "Mom, I'm *so* ready!" Sure enough, that evening she nearly ran out to the piano onstage, and breezed through two Heller etudes and a Grieg lyric piece with precision and aplomb. Her concentration was unwavering; her enjoyment palpable. I myself was wholly captivated

Her friend Sana is another talented eight year old, also a child of a Japanese/American mixed marriage. They attend Japanese school together on Saturdays. Like Iona, Sana is musical, has an excellent attention span, intelligence, and a true love for music and the piano. She has a sweetness and a *joie de vivre* with very little of the moody obstinacy or bursts of irritability that sometimes accompanies vibrant, gifted children.

At the concert, Sana got a bit rattled and started her Kuhlau sonatina a whole octave too low. I felt terrible. How would she manage to extricate herself from this unfortunate gaffe? Amazingly, she kept her composure and just played through the entire movement; modulations, secondary themes and all, a full octave lower. Remember, this was done completely without music in front of an audience. My, did she show me something! She even laughed about it afterwards. "I'm sorry I started in the wrong place" she told me, "but I guess I had to keep going." She laughed and accepted this unplanned detour with grace.

Friedrich Kuhlau, whose sonatina had just been performed, albeit in a somewhat altered form, was a German composer and contemporary of Beethoven. He was among the first batch of composers to write music for the piano, just as it was bursting into prominence, becoming the most popular instrument in western music. Herr Kuhlau wrote his sonatinas in the early eighteen hundreds. Would he be surprised that they continue to be studied and brought to life in the twenty first century? I wonder.

Since I was a teenager, predictions of the piano's demise have been made. It would be replaced by electric keyboards. Classical music would meekly fade away under the onslaught of rock and roll. Mozart and Beethoven didn't stand a chance. I still hear similar prophecies of doom from time to time. But the piano hasn't gone away. Kuhlau sonatinas are still being played in student recitals all over the world. They are studied by young pianists in Asia, Europe, the Americas—I wonder how many Kuhlau sonatinas saw the light of day in Japan alone last year? Or Germany? Or the United States? Many thousands. Students like Sana apply their energies, learning to do justice to the arching phrases, the fleetly running sixteenth notes, the dancing rhythms and quick-changing harmonies of composers like Kuhlau, Clementi, Mozart and other early masters of the pianoforte, a now three hundred year old instrument. I'm sure Mr. Kuhlau, had he attended my student's performance last June, would have gulped hard when little Sana started to play a whole octave too low. And I'm sure he would have admired her bravery, as she forged on, all in the wrong register, still holding it together with unflappable poise.Sana is blessed with wonderful parents, talent, a kind heart, and a happy, even temperament. She's now working on a Chopin mazurka, her first work by the great Polish poet of the piano. She is in love with it. "I want to play more Chopin," she has announced. Once last year, when she was seven, she asked me "did you practice really a lot when you were growing up?" I felt myself put in a tricky spot. I didn't want to confess to Sana, to my piano student, that I really had not; that I practiced minimally and sporadically, and that only in my late teens did I begin to work hard. "Not overly hard, Sana," I answered gingerly, finessing her question, "I practiced all along, and by and by kept improving." How could I reveal to this beautiful little girl who admires me that I was a pretty lazy kid. Here I am, her teacher, pushing her to practice consistently. Though I shrank from full candor in my response, I at least let it be known that I was not an especially hardworking student in my childhood years.

My answer appeared to satisfy Sana. She seemed to turn things over in her mind. A pensive face gave way to a sly, private grin, then she looked at me brightly and said "you know, I think I'm going to be a pianist," adding "and a piano teacher!" I do believe Sana will be an excellent pianist, whether professionally or not.

The car is just about all loaded up now. I only need to check that I've got all the necessary road maps for tomorrow's long drive. Ah! And I mustn't forget my passport. These days a simple trip to and from Canada requires that I have it. I know I'll have some of the kids in my thoughts next week, hiking the trails of Banff National Park.

There's Henry, for example. Henry is the most talkative of ten year olds. When he sets foot in my teaching studio, he smiles, adjusts his eye glasses and begins talking. "Can I tell you something?" he starts in a high pitched, occasionally squeaky voice. "I think I had a little trouble learning the minuet. Sometimes my fingers can't find the low note. Can I tell you something else?" he continues. "I got most of it learned— I think." Henry's father is there for each session and he'll usually break in at this point, "Henry, don't talk so much." But Henry is all wound up and likes to talk. Throughout our lessons, he always seems to have a lot to say. I tell him not to talk while I'm explaining something, or demonstrating something on the piano. He acquiesces, as it is expected of him, but he's clearly chomping at the bit to resume being loquacious. His young, active mind is brimming over with things to say.

"I try not to play too fast," he tells me, "but can I tell you something? I kind of like to rush." He fidgets with his glasses and adds "I like playing fast— can I tell you something else? It can be kind of a pain to play slow." "Henry!" his father speaks more sternly now, "don't talk so much!"

In between the flurry of words, Henry plays the piano. He is musical and motivated, a good student. He is able to focus that teeming young mind on the music. I predict that he will be a fine pianist. Henry is full of life and youthful enthusiasm. It's a bit of a challenge to keep him focused on the task at hand, limit his verbal flights, and still leave room for this young personality to find expression. At the end of each lesson, I like to offer him the unfettered opportunity for his verbosity to flourish. "Henry," I ask, "do you have any questions?" "No" always comes the answer in a suddenly quiet, flat voice, with a now calm, stolid face. "Any comments or thoughts? Anything you'd like to say?" "No." Henry looks at me blankly through his glasses. It goes like this every week. Finally, at the conclusion of our most recent lesson, after the predictable pattern had run its course, I asked him, "Henry, why do you never have anything to say after our lesson finishes?" He thought this over for a moment, then replied, "Well, I guess your comments just don't inspire any questions." He smiled and added "they're not inspiring enough." He broke into a high pitched laugh. I laughed too, and so did Henry's dad, shaking his head.

Henry is not shy in expressing himself, and does so with a fresh, direct frankness that I find utterly captivating. Once I played a passage of his Mozart Fantasy, mimicking his style, accentuating the notes that he had played poorly or unconvincingly. I do this occasionally with my students. Afterwards, I asked him, "Henry, tell me what I did wrong. Explain to me what was not right about the way I just played that phrase." He responded, "Can I tell you something? Your examples are too obvious. Of course I can tell you what's wrong " His ten year old eyes twinkled mischievously. "Henry, if it's so obvious to you, why didn't you play it better?" "Because," he replied, "this passage is annoying!" "Come on Henry. You can do better. Concentrate your best and try again." Then he played the passage through another time and improved on his earlier attempt. Through all the notes, words, phrases, and sentences that fill our weekly lessons, he progresses steadily. Henry has his own special shine.

As I prepare to turn in for the night, I hope I can manage to get some sleep. My mind is oscillating between the excitement of tomorrow's trip, and a stream of oncoming reflections. Chopin's f Minor Ballade and Mozart's a Minor Sonata take turns whirring through me. They are the two new pieces I am just now in the midst of learning, both being prepared for next season's concert series. I'll carry them with me, hiking up the winding switch back trails out in the pure mountain air. Hearing music involuntarily, having come unbidden to one's inner ear while away from the piano, is a natural part of the learning process.

Not easily getting to sleep, I lie in bed with a host of images. First, I see fifteen year-old Selene playing a Debussy Arabesque with increased control, sophistication, and nuance. It brings me a smile. Then it's Zhemin's stoic, focused nine year old face as he performs a movement of Mozart. This is followed by eighteen year-old Sasha galloping brilliantly through the third movement of Beethoven's *Moonlight* Sonata. She really brought the house down at the conclusion of the Children's Recital. My mind seems bent this night on resisting sleep. My memory calls forth snippets of music, faces of friends, old and new, some now dead. Faces of past loves make their appearances before departing. One lovely face in particular persists in reappearing; pretty brown eyes glow with feminine radiance. This image too melts away. Many other actors from the stage of my life make their entrances, then take their exits. These remembrances, and the myriad thoughts they lead to, all appear, and in time, like a succession of musical phrases, fade away into silence. Finally, waking consciousness itself fades away.

When I awake, I'll be on holiday! Then it's north to the border, onward to the trans-Canadian highway, and the glorious rocky mountains. There will be music there too, and not just the music I carry within myself. There will be the music of the rushing streams, the powerful splashing falls, the sighing of the mystical mountain winds, the antiphonal songs of the birds, the swaying forest firs, and the thud of glaciers releasing chunks of ice. All this symphonic grandeur will serve as welcome nourishment to this lover of music.

# ITHACA AND A SPECIAL TEACHER

Saying goodbye to my parents and sister outside my college dormitory, one hot, late August day in 1971, I felt scared, alone, and exhilarated all at once. I see now what an immature, confused and undisciplined eighteen year-old boy I then was.

I was adrift. I hadn't worked hard in high school, nor had I applied myself musically. My consciousness was pretty well constricted to a limited world, where fitting in and finding a place in the narrow mainstream of American culture mattered most. The reasons which could help explain why I consider a portion of my youth misspent will not be explored in this journal. These years were not without their positive aspects, but on the whole they stand as opportunity missed; promise unfulfilled.

That first day at college, I wasn't clear about much of anything, including about what my major field of study should be. Music remained an opaque possibility in a cluttered, uncertain mind. Although I was not conscious of it, I was standing on the precipice of a new life.

I had left home in New Jersey and had propitiously found my way to Ithaca College, with its truly fine school of music; and was prescient enough to have signed up for piano lessons, and to have enrolled in a music theory course. These simple but fortuitous decisions set me on a path upon which I continue to tread today.

The theory class proved stimulating. The lessons with the young professor and pianist David Kelsey were engaging. Studying the Mozart A Major Sonata with him, I felt the stirrings of a life force from deep within. After two or three months, it became evident that music would be by my major field of study.

In the meanwhile, the process of self-discovery took its meandering course amidst the swirl of student life. With one eye always open to the beautiful girls on campus, and access to them mostly denied me by my painful shyness and insecurities, I formed friendships, played sports, learned to drink beer at parties, made my round of classes, soaked up the beauty of New York's lovely Finger Lakes region, and slowly started to find my way back to myself. A zeal for learning began to develop. A class in English literature and another in philosophy struck some sparks, and together with my musical studies gave my first months on campus some momentum.

In February, I announced to Mr. Kelsey that I wanted to major in music. He was delighted and told me that I really should study piano with his own teacher, George Driscoll, then the chairman of the piano department. "He really is the best teacher here, Fred. You must be placed in his studio. I will arrange for you to meet him and play for him." With these words, I was placed on the threshold of a pivotal piece of good luck.

George Driscoll was roughly sixty years of age when I became his student. His face wore the lines of a somewhat older man, but it was a kind face. He was quite thin, of medium height, and atop his head sat neatly trimmed and combed wavy white hair. He was a very fine teacher. He knew his way around the piano, knew how to teach technique. I was shown how to practice difficult études and complex passages with intelligence. He was patient and supportive. He believed in my abilities and potential, and told me that I would become an excellent pianist.

But there was something more. He was a genuine musician. Music was his calling, not just his profession. This struck me as evident at our very first session together. I somehow instinctively knew that this kindly, affable gentleman had come to this world from the sphere of music, and that only others who had similarly been brought here from that harmonious sphere could recognize him as a compatriot. From the first, I was inspired. My magical old mentor was showing me to my true self; to the world of artistic beauty; where I had come from, and where I now felt fervently compelled to return.

By the time I turned nineteen in the spring of nineteen seventy-two, I had fallen under Driscoll's spell, and so commenced a major turning point in my young life. Emerging from a dark age, I suddenly found the world rich with meaning. My personal renaissance had begun. I had purpose and I had passion. For the first time in my life, I became a genuine student. Practicing the piano became an obsession. Five hours were spent most days in the school's various practice rooms. Tired, worn out pianos suffered at the hands of my fellow students and me. I tussled with scales, arpeggios, chordal patterns, leaps, thirds, octaves, varied touches, dynamics, études; the whole regimen of acquiring good piano technique. Like a man enamored of the most alluring woman in the world, I was driven by a combination of despair and desire, in hot pursuit of my goal. Cognizant of the fact that I was working to make up for precious time lost, I forged ahead with determination. I simply *had* to become a pianist.

All this came together with a general awakening. Learning became my *raison d'etre*. Music history with Professor Swensen was exhilarating. Medieval and renaissance music with Professor Arlin provided an opening to another world. Professor Hoffman's philosophy class brought a first introduction to Socrates, Plato, and Descartes. English literature with Ms. Blanpied gave me my first taste of James Joyce. The excellent theory classes given by Mr. Broadhead and Ms. Lewis were as jolts of caffeine to an erstwhile lethargic musical intellect. These classes threw open the windows to structure, harmonic language, the intricacies of voice leading and counterpoint. I already had the instinctive love of music's essence, but now I was being shown inside the atelier, to learn the craft, the nuts and bolts, the intellectual mastery that lies behind the works of great composers.

These classes and experiences have stayed with me. The nourishment I was offered has provided ongoing sustenance. It was a new beginning; a big bang that has led to a still expanding universe. I was starting to receive an education. Learning was the new high.

All the while, the many yearnings, aches, exhilaration, and pain of impressionable youth shadowed those four years of growing up at Ithaca College. A cadre of friends helped me fend off a persistent loneliness that frequently threatened my equanimity. The sweetness of solitude was yet unknown to me in those days.

There were comrades to share many of the drives and impulses that coursed through me. Firstly, the fellows in the dorm, with whom to play ball outdoors, and with whom to discuss and analyze the mysteries of human sexuality indoors. Young men between the ages of eighteen and twenty-two seem to have an unending fascination with sex. So it was with my dorm-mates and with me, the only music major in the group. We were driven not only by Nature's hormonal workings, strong as they are, but also by the need to prove one's manhood and hence feel like a success. This we all learned from our enveloping culture and society. We were expected to be winners in the game of love. We were expected to "score." It was to a degree a matter of self-esteem; a matter of assuaging large but insecure egos. No one wanted to be left out. It was essential to have some experience.

Now there were some impediments to my achieving greatness in the arena of romance. Firstly, my extreme shyness and insecurity. Another was my choosiness; a trait, that for better or worse, has stayed with me. A certain sensitivity also precluded the quick, easy, impersonal type of encounter.

Nonetheless, the sixties still permeated the air in the early seventies, and promiscuity abounded on college campuses all over the country. "Make love, not war" was a political and social rallying cry of the day. Determined to gain some experience, I ultimately found my way to the promised land with the help of a potent ally; the piano. I learned that I could woo a woman with Chopin, or if need be, with Paul McCartney, Paul Simon, or Led Zeppelin: whatever worked. I could always play popular music without needing to practice. Happily, the type of woman that attracted me was generally more prone to melt under the affecting tones of Chopin's soulful poetry or Beethoven's masculine grandeur. Music helped endear me to the objects of my desire, as it provided an insecure young man with some self-esteem.

It was an intensely political time. The war in Vietnam was debated over bitterly in the dorm, as it was all over the country. Ithaca had an especially active political scene. Although a town of only about thirty-thousand inhabitants, it is home to Cornell University, the venerable Ivy League institution, to the smaller Ithaca College, and to a generally eclectic and well-informed citizenry. It was, and still is a green, hilly, picturesque old college town; a seat of learning, and a comfortable enclave for free thinking individuals unafraid to try the path less traveled.

There were demonstrations, rallies, and teach-ins. We all engaged in the debates concerning civil rights, women's liberation, gay liberation, psychedelic drugs, and more. A large anti-war movement pervaded on campus and in town. All of this political ferment informed my friendships and formed a palpable backdrop to my student years.

In the winter of seventy two, my friends Bruce, Ed, and I joined a busload of other students from both Cornell and Ithaca College for a long weekend in New Hampshire. This was just in advance of the nation's first presidential primary, and we were there to advocate on behalf of the candidacy of George McGovern. He was running for president as a dark horse on the pledge to end the American involvement in the Vietnam War.

There were maybe fifty of us, and we rang door bells and handed out literature at shopping plazas. I remember our group spending the nights sleeping on the cold stone floor in an old New Hampshire church, with just our sleeping bags.

McGovern unexpectedly won the nomination of the Democratic Party, but then lost decisively to Richard Nixon in the presidential election. Nonetheless, I am still glad, nearly forty years on, to have worked for his campaign.

Through the swirl of experiences, ideas and fluctuating moods, swinging from buoyant optimism to melancholic despondency, the daily sessions with the pianos in the school's practice rooms remained the fixed star around which all else revolved; the lessons and master classes with George Driscoll the highlights of each week.

I developed a whole set of friendships at the school of music. There was a highly accomplished young pianist named Michael who impressed me; not just for his musicianship but also for his philosophical leanings and other worldly air. His mother was Japanese and his father an American Jew from New York, and he seemed to embody some of the finest traits associated with these two races. They were traits that I was becoming receptive to in those days; discipline, intellectual rigor, and soulful longing. It was through Michael's fine live performance that I first heard Beethoven's great opus 109 sonata. We had engrossing conversations on topics ranging from Beethoven and Mr. Driscoll, to poetry, physics, politics, philosophy, meditation; and oh yes, lest I forget; women. Michael may have read the Bhagavad Gita and meditated regularly, but he was still a young man between eighteen and twenty two, and made very much of flesh and blood. We were both in agreement that our fellow piano student Jayne, or Jaynie as she was often called, was a beauty. She became another of my friends.

Indeed, Jaynie did have a special radiance. Her face appeared angelic to me, and seemed to be lifted from an Italian renaissance painting. She had lovely long, straight, light brown hair, beautiful skin, and brown eyes which revealed a gentle, earnest goodness. I was always a little in love with her, and also a little intimidated by that very quality of earnest goodness. She seemed just a little too good for me. At any rate, by the time our friendship began to blossom, I was already in love with another girl, and involved in a meaningful relationship.

Both Michael and Jayne spoke of the lectures and meditation retreats that they attended at a spiritual center located near town. They simply referred to this place as "the center." It was a place I never visited, but it represented something vaguely mysterious and foreign, to my still provincial, circumspect young mind.

What was this "center" that they spoke of? Did one need an invitation to attend? Or was a rite of initiation required? My young mind was simply too narrow to permit further exploration. Reflecting upon the Huxley quote "After silence, that which comes nearest to expressing the inexpressible is music", it is clear to me that as a young college student, I was ready to embrace music, but not yet ready to explore silence. "Meditation is more difficult than playing a Chopin, or Liszt étude." Michael had told me. Jayne and Michael symbolized something vague, spiritual and alluring to me. I respected them and felt drawn to a type of calm yet vital energy, and seriousness of purpose I had not encountered in any of my peers before. A nascent spiritual yearning began to develop under the influence of these new friends.

The musician's path lends itself to the spiritual journey. Deep, focused concentration at one's instrument is a type of meditation. Playing a Chopin Nocturne or a Bach Fugue requires complete attention; holding the mind in the present moment. Art does not yield its exquisite beauties to the distracted mind.

Like the religious life, the musician's life asks much from its disciples. It is a practice, like prayer, yoga, or meditation. It is not merely intellectual, although the intellect plays its role in music making. No, it is a practice— not speculation, not an idea, not a concept, but rather full participation of one's being. It demands complete, undivided concentration, a sensitive, finely-tuned ear, an excellent memory, a heart full of love for the music with which you are participating. It demands an insight of the subtle emotional states revealed by the melodies, rhythms, and harmonies unfolding under the fingers. It demands a lucid overview of the work's architectural design. It asks the musician to show taste, to make decisions in balancing and shaping of voices, or in moving rhythms forward here, and pulling them back with ritardandos there. It asks for virtuosity of technical execution; that special ear, hand, mind, and heart coordination necessary to make one's musical intention an aural reality. And in performance, it requires steady nerves in the face of an audience that can hear, observe, and judge.

Great music is not interested in mediocrity. From its aspirants it asks a lot. The great violinist Jascha Heifetz was once approached after a concert by an admiring lady who gushed "Mr. Heifetz, your playing is sublime. It is beyond belief. I would give my left arm to play like you." Heifetz' reply was simple, "madam, I have given my life."

Like the monk sitting in meditation, the musician must center the mind and attain deep levels of concentration. And like the nun kneeling in prayer with hands clasped and eyes raised towards heaven, the musician must bring forth a heart of love and devotion. Music is a mysterious language, something meta-physical, ineffable; is it not?

With my friends in the dorm I moved amidst the world of convention. With Professor Driscoll, Michael, and Jayne, I felt myself moving in a different world; the world of the artist, the poet, the seeker. The call of this latter world would prove impossible to resist. When such wondrous horizons come into view, they can't be ignored. I learned that striving for musical excellence was intertwined with spiritual seeking.

Over the years I've also learned something else. Music alone is not enough. It is but one route to a Peace that seems to truly passeth intellectual understanding. Even then it is not enough. I have met superior musicians who lacked peace and basic happiness. I have met outstanding musicians who are selfish, arrogant and callous. Music is a beautiful part of life, but only a part. I didn't quite see this clearly, consumed as I was by youthful, zealous passion back in those magical student years. Music had slapped my face and tapped my heart. It had awakened me. In my gratitude I ascribed unlimited power to this holy art. I knew so little about the beauty of silence; the beauty of just being present. No, I was a man on the run in those days.

George Driscoll guided me through Bach fugues, Beethoven sonatas, Chopin études, Debussy preludes, Brahms intermezzi et al. He believed in me, and his encouragement helped to sustain my own innate belief in myself. "Fred, you need to play some major works now." I remember him telling me one fine day. "How would you like to learn the Chopin fourth scherzo in E major?" He smiled and his eyes filled with delight as he spoke those words. "Fred, you have the technique, you will play it very well," he said, anticipating my slight trepidation. I was thrilled to tackle a Chopin scherzo for the first time, and I immediately tore into learning it the very next morning. Having neglected the piano through my adolescent years, I was keenly aware of the need to play catch up. I took to Chopin's sophisticated and difficult fourth scherzo right away; practicing its intricate passages repeatedly. Driscoll really understood Chopin, and studying this piece with him was a joy. It became a kind of war horse for me, and I've performed it many times over the years.

On another occasion, he looked at me seriously and said "You know, I think you should study the Schumann *Etudes Symphoniques.*" George Driscoll was a Francophile who never missed an opportunity to speak French. He would never refer to this piece by its English name, *Symphonic Studies,* or the German name that Schumann gave it; *Etuden Symphonische.* Hence it's always been Etudes Symphoniques to me. I dove into this set of études with a zest that I recall so vividly. I was young, and I was in love with music.

At Ithaca, I gave two public piano recitals and learning to overcome my nerves was quite a challenge. Performing by memory before an audience is a daunting undertaking. The first time I played at one of Mr. Driscoll's playing classes I was overcome by such nerves that I could barely deliver the Beethoven sonata I had learned so well. What a shock that experience gave me! Gradually the ability to stay calm and focused while performing improved.

By my junior year, my lessons were occasionally given at the home of George Driscoll, instead of his studio in the music building. The remembrance of both these places stirs up precious memories. The studio with its two, black Steinway grands sitting side by side, is where most of the lessons were given. I still recall Driscoll, dressed in a black suit, running his fingers up and down the keys, illustrating an arpeggio pattern he wanted me to learn. It is an exercise I have given to several of my own students.

And I can still see him cautioning me against rushing Debussy's Homage a Rameau, and the beauty of tone and line that he drew from the piano illustrating this piece.

But the lessons and conversations that transpired in his house in town were even more special. George Driscoll lived only a few blocks from Ithaca's center, on West Seneca Street in an older, white clapboard home. The large open living room that took up most of the main floor was dominated on the left hand side by two Steinway grands; a sitting area with an older sofa and chairs, and an array of well-tended plants, the greenery of which enlivened the overall atmosphere, took up the other side of this large room.

It was in this house that I felt the privilege that comes from inhaling the rarefied air of Art and of Beauty. So, at least, was often my perception when seated at one of the two pianos, or on a chair in the sitting area where my professor and I talked about music, art, philosophy, life.

As a pianist, Driscoll's greatest strength was his way with phrasing, the beauty of his melodic line. His demonstrations of Chopin, Brahms, and Debussy were very beautiful. He had stopped playing in public when I knew him. There was talk among the students that he had had a flagrant memory lapse in one of his last concerts and that had caused him to retreat from performing. He was not practicing regularly anymore, but his intimate knowledge of the piano literature was impressive. He knew the scores. He once told me, "Fred, once you've truly learned a piece, memorized it thoroughly, you should be able to write it, it should be in you completely, and then you stand side by side with the composer when you play it."

Driscoll was fond of me and said nice things about my playing, but I think the highest compliment he ever paid me was when he told me, "you understand the music Fred, when you play Mozart, it's real Mozart, when you play Chopin, it's real Chopin, and so on. The composer is brought to light."

He encouraged me to follow my bliss and be a pianist without filling my head with delusional dreams. When I once asked him if there was any chance that I might one day make my living performing as a concert pianist he was blunt. "No" was his forthright and succinct response. I had waited much too long in getting around to serious study. Any slim possibility of becoming one of the fifty or so classical piano players that earn a livelihood just by touring the world giving concerts had already been forfeited.

There were whispers that Mr. Driscoll was gay. Gay wasn't yet the word used much back then. The atmosphere surrounding the whole issue of sexual orientation was rather different forty years ago. A homosexual man was more commonly referred to as a faggot, a fag, a fruit, a queer, or simply a homo. These words were often spoken with derision, or a wink, a nod, and a knowing grin that conveyed a sense of bizarre oddity or illness. Few felt the freedom to be at ease and open about their homosexuality. Being open risked severe consequences. What did I care whether my teacher was gay or not? Even as a pretty sheltered kid, I had no trouble accepting that some people are sexually attracted to members of the same sex. This never bothered me. On maybe five occasions I was George Driscoll's dinner guest at his home. How I enjoyed the conversations we shared on those special evenings!

I don't know the secrets of my professor's private life, nor does it matter to me. I only touch on this issue because it illustrates so well how the times were just then changing. Something that today can be discussed more openly and intelligently was still cloaked in a vale of dark secrecy. The times really were "a changin'" during those four formative years spent at Ithaca College.

A couple of Driscoll's other students insinuated that he had a drinking problem. Now this rather did jolt me. I was not at all keen to hear of it. To this day, I don't know to what extent there was any truth to it. I also am not even sure what constitutes a serious problem. I myself drink alcohol only occasionally, and then sparingly. But I have friends who imbibe two or three glasses of wine every evening. Is that too much? Driscoll was fond of martinis. Perhaps he drank one every evening before dinner. Whenever we dined together, he had a martini before dinner and one glass of wine with the meal. He was never inebriated at any of these occasions. I saw him tipsy only once, at a faculty party I was invited to. In any event, though I question the veracity of the accusations brought to my ears, the point is this: I was simply annoyed to hear any criticism of my teacher. I was always quick to rush to his defense. I was a quite naïve young fellow, and looked to my heroes to be pure, beyond reproach, unblemished by any trace of human complexity. But never was I shaken in my respect and love for George Driscoll. No one could cast aspersions on him in my presence without facing a fierce volley in return, advocating for his character.

Naturally my perception of my dear old teacher has evolved. I am no longer the inexperienced, quixotic youth that had the extreme good fortune of coming to Ithaca, and to the piano studio of George Driscoll nearly forty years ago. And though I didn't know him, as would a long standing close friend, I know he was a kind, well-respected, well-liked, talented, generous, good man.

Two years after I graduated and moved to New York, he retired from the college. He took some private students with promising ability gratis. I returned to play a piano recital on campus in honor of his retirement and his many years of service. The program I performed included the Bach Partita in c Minor, the Beethoven Opus 110 Sonata in A flat, the Chopin g Minor Ballade as well as some Schubert and Debussy.

We went out to a restaurant the following evening and had a penetrating and passionate conversation about music. Specific measures from my program were highlighted in our conversation. He was happy and proud of me, and full of encouragement as always. "Fred, they really understood the Schubert, I saw the smiles on many faces!" "And oh' the Beethoven, how about that spot in the fugue, where we get the subject inverted in G major, pianissimo! Ha! What a moment that is! It can give you goose bumps." On and on we went, my professor and I having become colleagues and friends, exchanging our ideas and musical concepts with ebullience.

Some years later, I visited Mr. Driscoll in Ithaca for the last time. At his home, I played a program for some people he had invited over. My program included Schumann's *Etudes Symphoniques,* the big piece he had once steered me towards. How I loved that old house! His guests that evening included my old friend Michael and other musicians. After the recital, we all talked. The atmosphere in this salon that I knew so well took on that magical glow I loved. Once again came the sensation of inhaling a rarefied air. I was with kindred spirits. I was in my professor's home. And I was back in Ithaca; *Ithaca,* where I had experienced my personal renaissance; where I had begun the rest of my life, setting out on the journey to return to my true self.

George Driscoll passed away a couple of years later. He's been gone now for some time. I can no longer visit him at his house in Ithaca.

He was the special teacher that touched the right lever at the right time. Nary a day goes by that his influence doesn't color my world. How I wish I could yet again visit him in the old white house on West Seneca Street; to play piano, talk about music and life, and to express my heartfelt gratitude.

# Iona and Nina

I'm glad it's Tuesday. It means that Iona and Nina will be coming for their lessons tonight. Their appearance will be much appreciated. I just looked over the newspaper and it didn't paint a very pretty picture of things. Tales of war, street violence, political corruption, environmental degradation, racism, intolerance, unemployment, poverty, and greed have left their mark. My spirits begin to sag.

It can make one wonder if any light at all is filtering through, still able to reach and brighten our troubled world. Yet I know that goodness persists and is pushing up through the cracks. There's as much light available to us now as there ever has been. My students teach me this truth every day.

The whole family shows up today. Iona, Nina, with their parents Rie and Luke appear at the front door. I count them all as friends. Iona, now nine, wears a beautiful smile, and announces, "I'm going first today." She hoists her canvas bag of music books over her shoulder and walks into the piano studio.

She's prepared today, and plays her trill exercise with speed and precision. Her finger coordination is excellent, and executing trills, scales, and ornaments *prestissimo* comes easily to her. Iona loves playing the piano. Every morning she gets up by seven to practice forty five minutes before going to school. Her parents don't make her do this. It is something she's decided on her own. She has other passions as well, among them rocks, skiing, reading, eating sushi, her friends, her family. She's told me that when she grows up she'll either be a pianist, a doctor, a geologist, or an FBI agent.

Today she plays the Chopin *Minute* Waltz in D Flat Major, a sophisticated piece of music, and quite advanced for a nine year old. She had fallen in love with it after hearing it on a recording, and begged me to let her study it. I was hesitant to agree, thinking it was a bit over her head. However, her impassioned pleas and solemn promises to practice hard, together with her irresistible, heart meltingly cute smile washed away my reservations.

Iona has made good on her promise to practice hard and she's playing it quite well now, though not yet at the highest level. Today we work on articulating the quicksilver ornaments that must be played well to do this elegant waltz justice. After making some progress in this, I challenge her to keep the chords in the left hand more *piano,* and put more life and spark in the quick right hand runs.

"Iona, it's not that the melody should be louder, but there should be more depth in the tone, more spark, more life—understand?" Her big brown eyes shine with intelligence and focused concentration. She slowly nods her head in agreement, then eagerly plays it. Voila! The balance is better! The right hand's melodic tones now shine forth with greater warmth. This nine year old musician is not fooling around. She's learning to make music on a high level.

Next, I challenge her to a round of "Match me or beat me." This is a game I play with all the kids. I play a passage of their piece, then ask them to play it, hopefully as well or even better than I have. Iona breaks into a robust smile and a trace of fire shows in her eyes. The prospect of giving "Match me or beat me" a go pleases her. She exudes confidence. I play first, hoping to illustrate how to properly balance the hands, and maintain a steady flow of rhythm. I achieve this goal, but I slightly fumble one of the ornaments. Iona catches it, and out of the corner of my eye I spy a gleeful smile. "Okay Iona, I've given you an opening, let's see if you can beat me now," I tell her. She takes her place at the piano and plays. Her balance is fine, the scale passages flow smoothly; she's cruising towards victory when she smudges one of the ornaments and then skirts over a couple of notes in a scale passage, slightly muddling the articulation. She looks at me with a sheepish smile. "Darn!" is all she says.

Last Saturday, Iona had a surprising pratfall at a playing class held at my house. I organize these classes periodically, at which groups of five or six students can perform for each other. Iona had her first ever memory lapse. She got stuck in the middle section of the Minute Waltz. A few notes into this buoyant melody, she forgot a bass note. Badly surprised, she froze, unable to continue. She floundered for maybe ten seconds, unable to restart this passage correctly or to proceed. Finally, I had to intercede and help her, getting her back on track.

After everyone had finished playing their pieces, the children and a few parents were munching cookies and socializing. But Iona sat alone, disconsolate, her head bowed, a big brooding frown on her still adorable face. Her arms were folded together; she sat motionless, impervious to the soothing words that Luke spoke to her. Luke smiled at me. He knows his daughter well, and realized that she just needed to be left alone for a few minutes. One of the other students' mothers leaned over to Iona and gently told her, "Iona, you're such a good pianist. Don't feel bad, everyone can make a mistake." That did it. Big drops of tears began to slowly trickle down the cheeks of my distressed student. She wiped them away, arresting the urge to break into an audible sob.

Ten minutes later, the cloud had passed. Iona, her little sister Nina, and two of my other young pupils were shouting and laughing, frolicking about in my front yard, engaged in a boisterous game of tag. This was shortly followed by an equally spirited game of Hide and Seek, played both outdoors and indoors, resulting in screaming kids charging both in and out of the house.

Now at her Tuesday lesson, there would be no memory lapse! The lyrical middle section of the "Minute Waltz" was firmly etched in Iona's capable young mind. She played it through without a hitch, infusing its well-known tune with youthful brio.

Iona is happy. She is having a wonderful childhood; a real childhood. She is not jaded as some children sadly are. Iona does not wear the mask of false sophistication or worldliness. She works hard and she plays hard, and is open to the wonder of being alive right now, right here, in this world. She is an inspiration.

Her sister Nina's lesson follows on this evening. Nina has a charm all her own. Almost seven, she is not quite as musically precocious as Iona was at a similar age, but she's plenty intelligent. Like her sister, she's totally present, unaffected, and a breath of fresh air.

She walks determinedly to the piano and hands me her piano books, brimming with eager confidence. She sits down at the piano and quickly informs me, "I practiced. I got real good at 'The Owl's Question,'" she smiles, revealing several gaps where her baby teeth have recently fallen out. "I'm perfect at it," she continues. Iona would never have made such bold pronouncements as a six or seven year old. Nina is not shy. She presents herself with fresh, crisp optimism.

She's all business playing her exercises. Her concentration is unwavering as she succeeds in running through her technical drills in good order. Next, I ask her to play 'The Owl's Question' by John Thompson. She attacks it with earnest focus, and plays it pretty darn well. "Nina, that's really good," I tell her. "Now remember the drop-roll touch on the second line? Remember how I showed you to play it? The first note is the louder one; the second is the soft roll-off. More-less, remember?" I demonstrate, singing along "more, less." "Oh yeah!" she responds. "I forgot!" " Okay, now go ahead and show me these measures. Use the drop-roll touch Nina; more-less."

She sits, looking intently at the spot on the music being studied. She appears to be surveying the situation with deadly seriousness. She then turns toward me and asks, "Do I have to make it more-less? It might be hard." "Just try Nina," I answer. She struggles the first few attempts, playing *piano-forte* or less-more. "Nina, that's less-more. That's the opposite of what it should be," I tell her and laugh. She laughs too, then tries it again and nails it. "There! Perfect!" I call. "Do it again." She knocks it out splendidly three or four times in succession, then looks at me directly with clear, alert eyes, glowing with life. "It's easy!" she asserts happily, breaking into a huge, semi-toothless smile.

"But you know what," she says, "you should clean these keys." She motions to the last few seldom used white keys of the high treble.

"They're dirty!" I notice the undeniable dust accumulating on these keys. "You're right Nina," I concede. "I'll clean it off right now." I get a damp cloth and wipe the keys clean. "You should keep your piano clean," she scolds me.

"Nina, let's do a note drill now," I say. "Oh?" her voice rises in a whining lament. "Oh—do we have to?" "Come on, you know how to read notes. Let's do it," I tell her. She braces herself bravely as I place the page of notes on the music rack. She knows that she hasn't drilled much on notes this week and stands vulnerable, about to be found out. "My mom didn't help me on note drills this week, and neither did Iona," she informs me. Sometimes Nina condescends to allow her older sister to help her with piano practice. Other times she rebels and banishes Iona from the piano. Nina struggles through a lackluster note drill, but I can't help but be touched by her steadfast effort and dogged determination. She is really present! I gain much from being her teacher.

"Nina, did you ask Iona to help you with note reading this week?" I ask. "Well—um, not exactly," she responds haltingly. I step out of the studio and call Iona, now in the living room, to come join us. "Iona, did you help Nina study the notes this week?" "I tried," she explains, "But she fired me. She just pushed me away and screamed 'You're fired!'" Iona shrugs her shoulders and continues, "I was fired, so there was nothing I could do." I can't suppress a smile. Iona smiles too. Nina sees the two of us smiling and breaks into laughter. "I like firing people!" she shouts, then laughs harder. Soon she goes into wild, unbridled laughter as only young children can. A gale of uncontrollable laughter shakes her little body. Her hilarity is infectious, and I now lose myself in the humor of the moment.

We all move out into the living room where we are joined in merriment by Rie and Luke, who have overheard us. Rie tells me, "Nina likes to fire Iona." Luke then adds, "Earlier today, I fired Rie when she offered to help me with something." Now all five of us laugh heartily.

I have to be careful in provoking Nina's laughter during a lesson. When she takes to laughing, there's just no stopping her;

her concentration disappears, and the lesson goes down the drain. But now, with the lesson at its end, what the heck? Why not have some fun.

These girls are growing up straight and tall. A happy family is a wonderful sight to behold. We sit in the living room and spend twenty minutes talking and laughing together. They may be my students, but I count Nina and Iona as two of my teachers as well. Indeed, I have many teachers: Tia, Selene, Yann, Zhemin, Elle, Gwen---Beethoven, Bach, Shakespeare—Sana, Henry—far too many to name.

# Pianos I Have Known

My first piano was a tall, battered, hulking old upright. It appeared one day in the living room of our house on West McClellan Avenue, in the suburban New Jersey town called Livingston. I was five years old when making the acquaintance of this imposing structure of wood, iron, felt, and strings.

I had sufficiently impressed my parents, by picking out tunes on children's toy keyboards at department stores to motivate the purchase of this old piano. The two of us, aged instrument and little boy, became instant friends. It was on this dark, worn out old clunker that I discovered how to play the German songs my father liked, the Viennese waltzes my mother adored, and the tunes and harmonies of symphonies by Haydn, Mozart, and Beethoven, after hearing them on records.

This was not a good instrument, or at least not at this advanced stage of its life. The keys did not all work properly, and the damper was weak, so tones lingered longer than they were meant to. But it wasn't without some virtues. I remember a fullness of tone that though not exactly beautiful, rang out with a stentorian, hopeful voice, avoiding the harsh, metallic sounds of so many older, worn out pianos.

Playing by ear came naturally, and I spent many hours of my early childhood exploring the world of melody, harmony, and rhythm, on this instrument. The one thing that I never did, however, was to practice on those clumsy uneven keys with discipline and guidance.

My parents got me some lessons by the time I turned six, but my first two teachers weren't very good, and I resisted real practicing. I was content to be left alone to my own devices; playing by ear and delighting in this intuitive, haphazard, and untrained approach to music-making.

It wasn't until I was 11 years old that we found a good teacher, but by then I had turned into a baseball fanatic and was even harder to motivate as a serious music student. Though I never ceased to enjoy playing the piano, I wouldn't submit to the discipline of earnest practice. This of course, has extracted a certain price.

John Brent became my piano teacher in my eleventh year. He was the first accomplished, competent teacher I had encountered. He was a tall, impressive-looking man in his early sixties with silvery grey hair combed straight back, and a pair of alert, searching eyes. He always looked me straight in the eye when addressing me. Unfortunately, I just refused to work hard for him, sliding along and doing the minimum; just enough to tease Mr. Brent with flashes of inspiration, but with generous portions of indolence as well, to disappoint and frustrate him. The old, dark upright on West McClellan Avenue got played regularly but was rarely practiced diligently.

One day Brent suggested to my father that I needed a better instrument. He took my family on a tour of a piano store in the town of Elizabeth, where he would sit and try snippets of pieces on various new vertical pianos. My father seemingly had ruled out the notion of buying a grand piano; a judicious decision considering my lackadaisical approach towards practicing.

"Tinny, too damn tinny," Brent would pronounce frequently after running a passage of sixteenth notes, or a series of chords. "Freddy, try this one over here," he told me, motioning to a particular piano. After I dutifully played a passage of Mozart he would again proclaim, "Tinny! You see what I mean?" looking at my father. "Ach, I don't have a good ear for music," my father would reply. My father was born and raised in Munich, and though he spoke excellent English, he retained one favorite word from his Bavarian youth—*ach*. Many of his English sentences began with this favorite utterance. "Ach, I trust your knowledge of pianos Mr. Brent." In the end, my father purchased me a new Cable Nelson studio piano with a smoothly finished light brown cabinet and a tone that John Brent declared to contain warmth and depth, and wasn't so damn tinny.

The big, old, weathered upright was sold, and its place in the living room was taken over by the handsome, gleaming new studio. I now had a new piano. All the keys worked, and the damper pedal did its job reliably.

Despite my anathema to serious study, I did learn some things from Mr. Brent, especially on the subject of various staccato touches and phrasing. And I liked the new Cable Nelson. It was a respectable, solid little piano. The lessons with Mr. Brent continued their uneven course. He was a talented, prickly, frustrated man and prone to outbursts of anger. He would fly into a terrible rage from time to time, which only lessened my desire to continue with piano lessons. He was frustrated by my listless work ethic, and also with a whole set of disappointments and complex issues. He had entered the Julliard School in his youth, but for reasons unknown to me, did not finish. He was clearly a serious musician, a fine amateur painter, (two of his oil paintings hung in the little waiting room of his home) and a strong-willed, formidable, artistic person. But a person whose artistic goals had been thwarted. He clearly liked me, notwithstanding his occasional bursts of temper. I can't blame John Brent for having been impatient with me. I always felt his underlying affection.

He had to endure many other students whom he found trying. Quite a few of the children brought to him for lessons were not only lacking in zeal, but also in talent. If he was in a bad mood, you never quite knew when an explosion might be imminent. When he'd ask me a question concerning the name of a touch that he expected me to be able to identify, he seemed verily to crouch in a predator's pose, awaiting my potentially fatal response. He taught me a common touch used for playing two-note slurs, which he referred to as a "down, up" touch. I usually call it the "drop, roll" touch now with my own students. I remember once when he asked me to identify this touch. "What's the touch you just used for those last measures Freddy? What is it called?" I sensed a hint of menace in his voice. Knowing a wrong answer would precipitate a vitriolic outburst, I became flustered and nervously blurted out, "up, down" instead of "down, up." Brent pounced. "How can it be up, down?" he cried. "For God's sake, show me how in the world it could possibly be up, down!" "Down, up," I managed to meekly reply. "I meant to say down, up Mr. Brent." But my words were too late. Brent had now become apoplectic and he vented his fury on me for another minute or so.

John Brent could be volatile and stormy, but he could also be warm and supportive. After my lessons with him came to an end, I learned a bit more about some of the demons which assailed him. Nothing more needs to be said of this, except that I now understand that my teacher was a passionate, talented, accomplished, frustrated and troubled man.

When I was 14, he died suddenly after suffering a massive stroke. So ended lessons with John Brent. I retain a certain fondness for him.

I thought I was finally free of lessons. But no, my father insisted I shouldn't completely give them up. So it was on to Mr. Chiapinelli, a short, stocky, energetic white-haired man in his late seventies or early eighties. Chiapinelli was an Italian from the old country whose accent was fairly pronounced. He badgered me with persistence and patience, but with none of Brent's foul temper.

It was during these years, my high school years, that I discovered the popular music of the sixties. The sturdy little studio in our living room, ever receptive to my youthful moods, poured out the music of the Beatles, Simon and Garfunkel, Peter, Paul, and Mary, and other folk and rock musicians. I retain an appreciation for these singer-songwriters to this day. The music and lyrics of their songs touched on the salient issues of this pivotal, tumultuous period. But none of this music would I dare present to old Chiapinelli. Amazingly, he coaxed some respectable performances of Bach and Brahms out of me. Beneath my obstinacy remained a still lightly, flickering flame for the great music which had first opened my heart to wonderment during my first years of life.

Once, Chiapinelli organized a lecture-demonstration by the brilliant pianist Rosalyn Tureck. She was one of the greatest Bach interpreters in the world; a supreme artist, a formidable intellect, and a marvelous speaker. I still remember her presence, her manner of touching the keys and producing tone, the timbre of her voice, her distinct diction, and even much of what she said. Some years later, after I had fully awakened from my adolescent hibernation, I saw her play book two of Bach's Well Tempered Clavier in New York. It was a memorable performance.

Chiapinelli was an extremely animated, industrious old fellow, always organizing competitions and pianistic events of various sorts. He was much in demand, had a full slate of students, was anything but lazy, and a friendly man. I can't say that I found him to be a superior teacher, or an outstanding pianist, but he was sincere and dedicated; a professional.

In the spring of my junior year of high school I took a part-time job on Saturdays. I became a Fuller brush man, going door-to-door in the suburbs, selling vacuum cleaners, utensils, and assorted household cleansers to housewives. I was no salesman. Once however, in the wealthy town of Short Hills, I hit the jackpot when an elderly, affluent, cultured couple came to the door and invited me into their beautiful home, where sat a Steinway grand. After delivering my uninspired, standard introductory pitch, I mentioned that I was a piano student. The lady and gentleman of the house became extremely attentive and ended up inviting me to play something on their wonderful piano. As I've stated earlier, Chiapinelli had worked patiently and persistently with me on some Brahms; specifically the g Minor Rhapsody, a piece I now love thoroughly and have performed many times through the years. I played it through with enough competence and élan to charm my kind host and hostess and precipitate the best day of my short-lived career as a salesman. They bought just about every item in the Fuller brush catalog. I didn't need to say a thing about the products. They fussed over me, insisting I sit with them in the kitchen and have a piece of pie and cup of tea. They were delighted to simply be able to help out a young high school student who could play a Brahms's rhapsody. This kindly couple surely had no need for most of the merchandise they ordered that day.

The little Cable Nelson continued to be *played* regularly, and *practiced* sporadically, until I left Livingston to go off to college. At Ithaca College, I came alive, and almost overnight became a disciplined, impassioned piano student. My little piano must have barely been able to recognize the young man that came home on vacation breaks. Its hammers, strings, keys, and dampers were suddenly put to the test. Much would now be asked of this instrument. My willing but challenged studio was pushed to hitherto unknown heights. Chopin études resounded through the house on West McClellan Avenue. Beethoven, Brahms, Ravel, Schumann; they were all hurled at this unsuspecting piano, which had previously known such an easy, comfortable life. The erstwhile lazy boy had been transformed into a demanding task master. Now our poor little Cable Nelson had its work cut out for it.

The overmatched piano strained to keep up. It couldn't quite do justice to the work being assigned it. I was now pushing myself, as well as my ever loyal companion to achieve new sounds, new colors, bolder fortissimos, withering decrescendos, more sublime legato; in short I was steering my ship through the portal of Art. The piano, despite its limitations served me faithfully. I spent some exhilarating hours practicing Liszt's marvelous étude, *La Campanella* on my breaks in Livingston. The Cable Nelson really outdid itself with the bell-like skips and rapid repeated notes that this jewel of an étude calls for. And it strained valiantly to sing out the voluptuous lines and poignant harmonies of Chopin's Barcarolle. We had our special moments, the two of us. I remember evenings where that rarified, mystical air of real Art wafted through our suburban home.

No one was more pleased or supportive of this turn of events than my father. And no one prouder than my mother. They had mercifully divorced after I had left home. My mother had gone back to New York, while my father remained at the house in Livingston. He would remain there alone, long after my sister and I had left, for another 27 years. Hence it was he that heard my musical efforts take flight whenever I was visiting.

After graduating from college, I moved to New York. The little studio that John Brent had picked out some 10 years earlier stayed put in New Jersey, with no one to stroke its keys and excite its soundboard.

As a graduate student at Manhattan School of Music, I made do without a piano of my own. I practiced mostly at the school, rotating through its various practice rooms with its assembly of much put-upon grand pianos. Not owning a piano, I became quite resourceful about finding additional places to practice. For example, a good friend and fellow piano student who was studying at Julliard snuck me into their building at Lincoln Center on Saturdays. There, we'd both practice for six hours. I had never practiced more than five hours in a single day at Ithaca. Six hours seemed like a lot. Yet, we were both easily surpassed as marathon pianists by some of the other students at Julliard. It was in that cool, modern, rather antiseptic building that I first encountered the true champions of marathon piano practice. Eight hours or more were spent daily by members of this rare species, attacking the myriad, complex passages of the most formidable works of piano literature. I distinctly recall entering a practice room at 8:15 one Saturday morning, adjacent to another room where a young female student was already immersed in Rachmaninoff's challenging third concerto. The same difficult measures were being played repeatedly, slightly under tempo, with exactness of rhythm and bold crisp attack. A cursory glance through the little glass window in the door revealed an austere, concentrated face. Practicing five and only occasionally six hours per day, was my limit. This young lady was still there as I took my leave late that Saturday afternoon, wearing the same determined, serious face, indefatigably attacking the Rachmaninoff Third.

Studying music in New York had its unique rewards. Among them, was that it brought me a realistic consciousness of the high level of talent and dedication of my fellow pianists. Young musicians flocked from all over the world to study at the city's three conservatories. In New York, one couldn't avoid or ignore the prodigious talent and the sometimes fanatical devotion found amidst this club of highly-driven young people.

Still without a piano, I struck a deal with a Presbyterian church in my neighborhood on the Upper West Side. The minister there allowed me to practice three hours every morning on the grand piano in the church's downstairs community hall, in exchange for my playing Bach, Handel, and Mozart at occasional Sunday morning services. Still, the need for a piano in my apartment was evident. I summoned the loyal Cable Nelson, which crossed the Hudson from Jersey to join me in my Upper West Side flat. This little piano gave me all it had, but the pressure was mounting on me to finally go out and buy a grand piano.

Here, I must introduce Todd Rice, a wonderful friend and most excellent fellow. Todd was a young pianist like me, but also a composer, a piano technician, and a young man of eclectic interests and boundless energy. He was just then apprenticing at Dietrich's piano shop on West 58th street. Todd tuned pianos all over the city, and was privy to whenever a good bargain on a decent instrument turned up. He was a wonderful friend. We laughed together, took long walks in Riverside Park, shared stories about our youthful adventures with women, lifting each other's spirits whenever fickle love's sting pierced the heart. We smoked cigars and discussed the vicissitudes of romance one whole summer evening on the campus of Columbia University. We played the piano for each other, hiked in the White Mountains of New Hampshire, and the Adirondacks of New York State. We analyzed the writings of Plato and discussed the spiritual and political teachings of Gandhi. It was high energy. Todd also gave me a first instruction in sitting meditation, and even introduced me to the Japanese tea ceremony. His nickname for me was "Rico." At first he called me Federico, the Italian version of my name. That eventually was shortened to simply Rico.

One fine day I answered the telephone and heard Todd Rice's voice full of excitement. He was almost breathless. "Rico! I found you a Steinway!" "A Steinway?" I replied incredulously. "How can I afford a Steinway?" "Rico listen," he continued. "I just tuned it. It's five foot seven, a beautiful mahogany grand. It's being sold for 3,500 dollars by a Swiss couple. They are leaving New York in a few weeks to return to Switzerland. The man who owns it is a diplomat at the United Nations. He's been transferred back home on short notice. He wants the piano to go to a serious young musician. He wants it put to good use. That's why he's only asking 3,500!"

A Steinway grand for $3,500 was a real bargain in 1978. But I only had 3,000 dollars in the bank, and a limited income from accompanying ballet classes, and giving a few lessons. I had just graduated the Manhattan School with a master's degree, but was living a bohemian lifestyle. Not quite the starving artist, but the economically hard-pressed struggling musician. Life was inwardly rich, but I was getting by on a very tight budget. "Rico, come on, I told them all about you. They'll hold it a few days for you," Todd implored me. "This is your Steinway! You must not pass this opportunity up."

The thought of finally owning my own fine grand piano, and one with the prestigious Steinway logo emblazoned across the fallboard to boot was tantalizing. "Rico, I played it. It's got a rich, singing tone and is in excellent shape. It dates from the 1940's, a good era for Steinways. Rico, let me tell them you'll come to play it and then buy it."

"Todd," I felt my heart beating faster as I clasped the phone receiver more tightly. "Tell those people I'll be there in two days. I'll have 3,200 dollars in cash with me." I couldn't quite believe it was my own voice saying this. Somehow I decided to draw a line at 3,200 dollars still knowing I'd have to completely deplete all my savings, and then still come up with a couple hundred additional dollars. "You'll love this piano Rico," Todd exuded. "I'm excited for you!"

In the end, I borrowed 200 dollars from my mother, and 200 from Bruce, my old friend from college. My bank account dwindled down to one or 200 dollars, but I jumped aboard the cross-town bus one fine, sun-dappled spring morning with 3,200 dollars in hundred dollar bills swelling the pockets of my pants. I suppose this would have been the worst possible day to get mugged, in what in those days was a fairly crime-ridden city. But no one was going to rob me that glorious morning. No one was getting that piano from me.

When I entered my hosts' apartment on the eastside just blocks from the U.N., I was dazzled. And not just by the promised piano, lovely in its stately, poised grandeur. But also by the young Swiss-French couple, perhaps in their mid-thirties; elegant, polished, and possessed with exceptional beauty. The Madame of this home was simply stunning. The monsieur was handsome, elegant, convivial. I almost completely forgot about the piano whenever his gorgeous wife glided into my view. Her husband, the polished diplomat of his country, quickly put me at ease with his welcoming smile and refined Gallic manners.

We took turns playing the piano. It had a warm tone and a solid action, and had been clearly well-maintained. The beautiful mahogany case shone proudly, unblemished. My offer of 3,200 dollars had been agreed to. I emptied my pockets of hundred dollar bills, aligned them all in neat, crisp stacks on a small table and asked my host to count out the sum. We were soon shaking hands. "You play well," my host pronounced. "I hope this piano will give you great joy." His wife appeared with wine glasses and the three of us shared some Burgundy to seal the transaction. I was now poor as a church mouse, but sipping wine with a dizzy euphoria, being toasted by a beautiful, sophisticated couple, and suddenly the proud owner of a fine Steinway grand piano.

Two days thereafter, my piano was delivered, and took its place in my rent-controlled, basement apartment, at 114th street and Riverside Drive. I shared a three-room flat with a roommate in those days. Thanks to the city's laws governing rent control at the time, I owed 400 dollars a month for this roomy apartment. My housemate contributed 200, so it was a quite manageable situation. The living room, which one entered from the foyer and was enclosed by French doors, served as my bedroom. It was in this rather large room that my Steinway would take its place, just across the way from my bed.

The first night that we shared this room together, I was too giddy to get much sleep. Every hour or so, I would wake up and look across the room to gaze upon my prize possession, which now represented the entirety of my financial assets. My heart would soar and take to beating faster, and after finally falling back to sleep, the same process would be repeated again, all through the night. Each time I awoke, I would look again —and there it was! The large, finely-crafted, beautiful mahogany instrument stood motionless before me. It was really there, not some dream or hallucination.

Eventually, after an intoxicating honeymoon ran its course, we became solid friends and good working partners. Just as its previous owner had wished for, this 1940 vintage Steinway was put to good use. Day after day, its hammers, strings, and soundboard propelled the musical thoughts of the great composers upward to reverberate off the high ceilings of my old New York dwelling. Having a basement unit was really a blessing. No neighbors beside or below me, and in the apartment above me, quiet inhabitants. I was unburdened by unwelcomed sound, and in turn could play the piano without causing any disturbance.

The arrival of the grand piano coupled with my depleted bank account necessitated the sale of my faithful little Cable Nelson. An advertisement in the New York Times produced a happy result. A nice younger couple, both Polish immigrants, appeared with their seven year old daughter to look at the studio. They were pleased to purchase this tried and true instrument for their eager, little, musical novice. I bid farewell to the Cable Nelson some 33 years ago, with a feeling of nostalgia. My childhood companion was now off to a new home, where it would feel the touch of tender, hesitant little fingers upon its now experienced, tested keys. Hopefully it gave nourishment to this attractive child. And may it yet live today, more than four decades since John Brent picked it out of a large, crowded showroom of instruments.

The Steinway was a fine piano. I practiced it regularly four to five hours most days over the next six years. The piano's strength was the tone of its bass and middle registers. The treble was its weakest aspect. It just didn't sing out the way it might have. The upper register was not shrill or harsh. That was not the problem. It simply couldn't soar easily over the bass. No matter how I had Todd voice it, the balance never fully satisfied me. The treble, though not unpleasant, was just a bit too thin. It neither sang nor soared like a bird.

The action was fine, reliable and slightly stiff. I tend to prefer a slightly stiff action to one that is too light. The action of my Steinway could have been more receptive to very light touches. Taking a decrescendo down to a real pianissimo was a challenge on this instrument.

Nonetheless, it was a valued friend. No person is perfect, and no piano is completely perfect either. Though my fine piano fell short of perfection, it brought much beauty into my life.

Beyond the regular practice sessions, my Steinway allowed me to open my home to musical salons with other musicians. Piano works, chamber music, and song recitals, coupled with poetry readings, lively conversation, and an inspired ambience all found a home round my piano. My basement residence received my friends and colleagues, and bore witness to some wonderful performances.

I began teaching full-time at the Brooklyn Conservatory of Music. I worked at both the Brooklyn branch in Park Slope, and the Queens branch in Flushing. I continued to practice steadily and give sporadic piano recitals. I enjoyed the company of wonderful friends, and as a New Yorker, took advantage of the unique cultural opportunities of the city. I was fortunate to hear some of the great musicians of the day, from Rosalyn Tureck, Vladimir Horowitz, Emil Gilels, and Henryk Szyring to Leonard Bernstein and Luciano Pavarotti. The Metropolitan Museum of Art became a favorite destination. My friend Todd and I established a Thursday morning routine at this palatial repository of great art. We would rendez-vous Thursdays at 11, out of doors on the expansive front steps, and then explore a specific room for an hour. We were very strict and specific about this. One room per visit was our limit. We would then have lunch in the museum's spacious, open café. We both brought our own bag lunches, but ordered coffee or tea at the café. It was during lunch hour that we enthusiastically discussed and analyzed the paintings we had just viewed. After lunch we returned to the exact artworks for another look. We always made it a point to separate and remain silent for the second experience of drinking in these works. Then it was off for a jubilant ramble through Central Park and back to the West Side; the vow of silence now lifted.

At this point, I must pull myself back to the business of pianos, tempting though it is

to relate the many adventures I experienced living in the greatest of cosmopolitan cities.

In the spring of 1984, I made an impromptu visit to Dietrich's piano shop on 58th street. There I found Todd, along with Mr. Dietrich himself. Dietrich was a master technician who had emigrated from Hungary. His shop was just down the street from the Baldwin showroom, and around the corner from Carnegie Hall, Patelson's music store, and the Steinway showroom. A wonderful little shop situated happily in the hub of this musician's quarter. Dietrich always had a row of seven or eight reworked grands lined up neatly and taking up most of the front showroom. His workshop was in the larger room in back. Walking in and finding Todd there naturally put me in a jovial mood straightaway.

"Rico, nice surprise seeing you!" Todd greeted me. After shaking hands with Mr. Dietrich, with whom I was already acquainted, they both asked me to sit down and try the pianos out on display. There were eight grands, all reworked under Dietrich's expert supervision. Seven Steinways and one Chickering awaited a smattering of musical excerpts from Bach and Beethoven to Chopin and Prokofiev. After trying out the seven Steinways, I remarked to Todd that they were very good instruments. Inwardly I thought, "Nothing here that would make me trade my piano." Then Todd insisted, "Rico, play the Chickering. You never even tried it." I knew nothing about Chickering, but I sat down at this old 1923 five foot four inch piano and began to play the Schubert A-flat Impromptu, Opus 142 Nr. 3. It was love at first touch! The sound struck to the core of my heart in the opening measures. I looked up at Todd with stars in my eyes. "Beautiful tone, huh Rico?" he beamed. I tried some Bach and some Chopin. The sound was penetrating and richly hued. It sang like a bird. It soared like a bird; especially in the treble.

"Todd, you play it," I told him getting up off the piano bench. Todd played some Bach, a little jazz, and then some Beethoven. I was still enchanted. I had found my piano! This 1923 Chickering, lovingly and masterfully reworked by Kalman Dietrich was on sale for 4,500 dollars. After talking things over with Dietrich, I put a hold on it. I had nothing more to ruminate over. This really was "my piano."

With my modest earnings derived from teaching, I knew it would be necessary to sell my Steinway. But that could wait a month or two.

First things first. I purchased the Chickering and for two heady months, the large main room of my apartment held two grand pianos within its confines. I played and practiced both pianos, but the Chickering outshone the Steinway. All my friends were staggered by its beauty, which only confirmed the rightness of my impulsive decision.

The Steinway had a market value of perhaps $9,000 in 1984. But I had been reading Gandhi, the Sermon on the Mount, Thoreau, Tolstoy, and other writings that I found inspiring and insightful. People said that I was an idealistic person. In any event, I felt funny about selling the Steinway for top dollar after the very generous deal the Swiss diplomat had offered me. I had paid $4500 for my Chickering and so I determined to sell the Steinway for $4500 to a serious, worthy musician. This just felt right to me.

And this is just what I did. The Steinway went to my friends Hae Kyoung and Ink Young Kim for exactly $4500. Hae Kyoung was a marvelous violinist and musician, and her brother Ink Young, as well as her sister Yae Kyoung , were all good friends.

The Chickering is still with me here in Seattle many years on. No piano is perfect, but this is my sweetheart, a dark mahogany beauty with shapely, elegant Queen Anne legs and a rich enchanting voice. It has a quality of tone that speaks to me and that most much more expensive instruments can't hope to match.

The piano was manufactured in Boston in 1923. Since I've had it, the hammers have been replaced twice. It continues to sing its old heart out. From time to time I'll come across a beautifully-restored old Steinway and feel tempted to buy it. Recently it was a lovely small grand, a mere five foot one inch in length, a dwarf among grand pianos. It dated from the twenties and put out a rich, old world tone. It had sufficient power to fill my modest living room with the lid raised. This jewel of an instrument had nothing generic about it. Like my piano, here was an uncommon personality. It was priced just above $20,000. I gave some real thought to buying it. Only one thing stopped me. I came home and played my own treasure. The old Chickering, now going on 90 years, still sang with its unique, glowing voice.

I have the money now to buy the Steinway without trading away the Chickering. But I don't have the space in the main living room of my home to suitably situate two grand pianos. I need the space, partly to hold my periodic master classes and music history classes, where as many as 20 students must be comfortably seated. Additionally, I felt the layout of this room would be thrown out of balance by the dominating presence of two grand pianos. Let's just say I have a sensitivity to the room's aesthetic look, or perhaps the "Fung Shui" impact of such a change in the room's organization.

I can't leave off the subject of pianos I've owned without now making mention of my wonderful little Everett studio, on which I give many of my private lessons. This piano, which I purchased some 20 years ago second-hand, sits in a room adjacent to the kitchen. The room measures twelve feet by twelve, is fully carpeted and features high ceilings. I have taught literally thousands of lessons in this room over the 25 years that I've been in this Seattle bungalow. It has been necessary not to overwork my beloved Chickering, and consequently a good deal of my lessons have been given on this second instrument.

Shortly after relocating to Seattle, one of my students offered me the use of an excellent Steinway studio for two years. I accepted this kind offer and put it to use in the afore-mentioned space as a piano to give lessons with. After it was returned to its owner, I shopped around the classified ads in the papers and eventually came across this quite decent, perky little Everett. This solid, dependable instrument seems to never lose its tune. It has a fine "perky" voice which rings true, and is happily "not so damned tinny". I believe old Mr. Brent would have approved. It boasts a reliable action, and seems positively impervious to any kind of frailty or breakdown. This is my bulletproof piano.

More advanced students take their lessons on the grand in the living room. Sometimes a lesson may be divided between the two pianos.

Occasionally I wonder— how would a five foot one inch Steinway grand sound in my smaller teaching studio? I know that I'm a pretty lucky fellow with the two pianos I presently have. I also know it can be difficult not to become covetous when around a very beautiful piano.

And yet, despite this awareness, knowing full well that greed is the enemy of glowing contentment,– still, I wonder; how might that 1920's Steinway grand sound in my little teaching studio? That might yet be something worth thinking about.

# FLUSHING FAREWELL

It had come down to my last day of teaching at the Flushing branch of the Brooklyn Conservatory of Music, a cool, clear Saturday in December just before Christmas. My day of lessons began at 8.30, and involved a substantial commute. I had gotten accustomed to rising quite early on Saturdays, riding the subway out to Queens, then having breakfast and reading the newspaper at a favorite diner. The Daily News was typically my paper of choice. The New York Times would take too long to read, and the New York Post had become a cheap tabloid by this time. Perhaps most importantly, the Daily News covered the Mets and Yankees Friday night baseball results to my liking. Baseball was still my sport and persisted in holding a fascination for me. The game was in my blood. Even today, I still remember my eight year old heart beating with excitement as I cradled a shiny, white new baseball in my right hand, or slipped my left hand into my well worn Carl Yastrzemski model glove. I would then hold the glove up to my face and inhale the rich, leathery aroma. I thrilled to the explosive crack of hard wood against rock hard ball, another type of music to my young ears; a strangely lyrical music, produced by two percussion instruments.

I couldn't get enough of playing ball, or of watching my favorite big league players play it. They were the virtuosi of the diamond. Though I only got to see him play once in person at Shea Stadium, I'll never forget Willie Mays. He was the most electrifying presence on a ball field I ever witnessed. When he trotted down to first base after drawing a walk, some 40,000 or so vocal New York fans took up the chant " Go Willie go! Go Willie go!" Willie promptly complied, dashing for second and arriving barely ahead of the catcher's strong throw. He was called safe by the umpire amid a cloud of dust, and his loving fans thanked him with a full throated ovation. With Willie, it was more than his accomplishments, great as they were. It was his artistry, and his exuberant way of playing every facet of the game. Through his love for baseball, his very love for being *alive* shone through.

I was lucky enough to be in attendance at the old Yankee Stadium several times, to hear Mickey Mantle make that special music that comes from a perfectly timed, powerful stroke of the bat, colliding with an oncoming baseball. The clean, fortissimo, staccato crack that ensued, and the rapidly rising legato flight of a small white ball against a blue, cloudless sky was a thing of beauty; one might call it lyrical.

Music may be found down many walks of life, and so much of life is expressed in music. But getting back to Saturdays in Flushing; after finishing my eggs and perusing the Daily News, I would proceed to my day of teaching.

I liked Flushing. It was in transition, becoming a predominantly Asian neighborhood, mostly Korean, but was still a quite varied ethnic stew, home to East Indians, Chinese, Jews, African Americans, Irish, and smaller clusters of other people as well. It was a generally clean, comfortable, unpretentious, and vibrant neighborhood of hard-working people. To me, it was New York at its best. The students that I came to know there were drawn not only from Flushing, but also from the surrounding Queens neighborhoods which encompassed even greater ethnic diversity. I was hardly surprised when I recently learned that Queens today is the most ethnically diverse one hundred and fifteen square mile territory on earth.

I would be moving to Seattle in a month, and so it was a day of sad farewells to some wonderful students. Among them were three who had become pretty good pianists.

There was Theodore Cheng, at fourteen a charmer full of wit, broad intelligence, and an alert, ever cheerful presence that seems to have been partly born from coming from a happy family. To see Theodore in the school's lobby with his smiling parents and his little brother at his side was to see a happy family. Tolstoy started his great novel, Anna Karenina, with the observation that all happy families are happy in the same way. He could have had the Chengs of Flushing in mind. Their happiness was so apparent and seemed such a natural thing.

I remember how once as a ten year-old, Theodore arrived at the studio with a mischievous twinkle in his eyes and his right hand held behind his back, concealing a splint on his index finger. With an impish grin, he explained how a game of punch ball at school had derailed that week's practice. I recall how as an eleven year-old he would sanguinely tell me of his plans to become a "medical practitioner" and his hopes of providing for his parents in later years. I loved the way he threw himself into explaining what was "first rate", or what was "third rate", about the most recent science fiction film he had seen. And I loved the way he played Clementi and early Beethoven. He was not a prodigious pianistic talent, but he had discipline, curiosity, musicality, and he thoroughly enjoyed himself playing the piano. His Beethoven may have not been perfect, but it was satisfactorily clean and accurate. It had strong dynamic contrast and above all, an élan and earnest joy that emanated from the player. Theodore's embrace of life was infectious. Happiness, like depression, can be infectious. Theodore, by the very act of exuding happiness was passing along a great gift.

So now it had come time to say good-bye. Theodore's father graciously thanked me for the five years of piano lessons, presented me with a crystal paper weight, and had me pose for a photograph with his son. That crystal paper weight sits atop a desk in my Seattle studio today.

Stephen Lakatos was another extremely intelligent boy, then a senior in high school, and soon to be a student at Yale. He had a stolid persona, and though lacking the easy charm that Theodore so effortlessly sprinkled about, he was quite pleasant and amicable. He was becoming a fairly accomplished pianist. We worked together on Beethoven's difficult *Waldstein* Sonata, and he played it with a fairly high level of proficiency. Stephen was a serious young fellow and he played this major work with a direct, no-nonsense approach. Though he hadn't plumbed the depths of this piece, he played it with clear fingerwork, a strong ringing tone, and appropriate dynamic contrast. We had also studied Beethoven's *Pathetique*

Sonata together, and he once told me "I like the *Pathetique*, but I love the *Waldstein*." These words were spoken in his quiet, reserved manner, but revealed a deep personal feeling for the music.

I always encouraged Stephen to play with his heart, and not to fret if he dropped a note here, or slightly bungled a passage there. So, I suppose it was only fitting that after he had attended one of my concerts at the Conservatory, he told me "Fred, your performance had feeling and sweep; you really brought the music to life. And as for the wrong notes in Liszt's *Au Bord d'une Source*, don't worry, like you always say, it's the expressiveness that counts." Ah, but how it did rankle me that I had played wrong notes in the Liszt. Many years later, as I recount this story, it still rankles me! Try as I might to take my own advice, hitting wrong notes during a performance, after hours of practicing and perfecting all the intricate passages can bring a sudden jolt to one's musical sensitivities, to say nothing of one's ego.

I remember once that Stephen talked to me quite sensitively about the meaning of good friends, girls, and the uncertainty of his future plans. I liked him a lot, and I liked his parents, Europeans like mine. The Lakatoses were Hungarian, and I remember well Mr. Lakatos recounting the harrowing story of how in 1956, just after the Soviet invasion, he had, as a twelve year-old boy, fled Hungary with his family. As the son of a German Jew and an Austrian Jew, I was sympathetic to Mr. Lakatos's, ordeal which had been fraught with risk.

As a parting gift, Stephen and his family gave me, appropriately so, two lovely books of Liszt's Hungarian Rhapsodies, which I have put to good use since.

I certainly never wanted to say good-bye to Jee-Hye Park. After all, I was completely charmed by this slender, beautiful Korean girl, full of talent, joie de vivre, and a captivating combination of poise and innocence. Jee-Hye, then sixteen, had been my student for three years, and I had had the privilege of introducing her receptive spirit to the music of Chopin, who had quickly become her favorite composer. Jee-Hye, like Theodore and Stephen, was fiendishly intelligent. She had a sharp, focused mind, a capacity for wonder, and a soul eager to be nourished by learning. She was anxious to share with me her impressions of the books she was reading at school. We discussed Shakespeare, Tolstoy, and J.D. Salinger. She was hopelessly besotted with the latter.

I remember the particular morning when I showed her the book of Chopin Preludes and told her I wanted her to begin studying some of them. Her pretty face flushed with excitement, her eyes beamed, she jumped up and let out a shout of pleasure. If her soul was filled that particular morning, mine was doubly filled. I had my reward. To share something as beautiful as Chopin's music with this bright young girl exemplifies the joy of teaching.

Jee-Hye may have appeared a charming ingénue, but she was also ambitious, a student at Hunter College High School, the most prestigious in all New York, and fiercely determined to realize her dream of going to Harvard. She once told me that as much as she loved music, art, and literature, she had no desire to "go hungry", a phrase she used several times and which I suspect she learned from her parents. Mr. and Mrs. Park had come to New York from Korea and worked hard in the business of importing goods. She didn't practice enough to become the pianist she could have been, but she played several Chopin pieces with delicate clarity.

Do I paint too rosy a picture of Jee-Hye? Of Theodore? Of Stephen? Perhaps, but I enjoyed and appreciated them so much. They were at most precious moments in their life journeys; young, impressionable, sending out hopeful sprouts. I was given the privilege of witnessing these tender buds unfurl, petal by petal. It was my job to water with the rudiments of musicianship, weed out mistakes and bad habits, fertilize with enough encouragement and inspiration, and share in the marvel of sprouting melodies and unfolding harmonies that reach towards the sun. Though I wax flowery, I never felt impelled to steer these gifted children into considering music as a career choice. That must always come from the student alone. It was satisfying enough to assist them on their musical flights; to share in the joy of music making.

Sometimes I'm afraid that teachers strain to bend a student in a pre-conceived direction, too sure that they know what's best. I hope I haven't been too guilty of that error. The talented few that could become top pianists don't always choose to exert the time and effort needed to achieve such a goal. And who says that they should? Ultimately, the thirst for artistic excellence must come from within the individual.

Theodore, Stephen, and Jee-Hye were bright, musical, happy adolescents, easy to be around and inspiring to work with. Of course it was sad to say good-bye. But interestingly enough, it was a little eight year-old Chinese girl, who nature had refused to endow with musical gifts, that proved hardest to leave.

Melinda Chen was my last student on Saturdays. She had just turned eight years old, and had begun lessons only nine months earlier. How she struggled to play the piano! She just couldn't seem to play the simplest sequence of notes in a steady rhythm. At one of our very first lessons together, I was feeling particularly burnt out at the end of a long teaching day, and I let my impatience show. Melinda saw that I was tiring of her repeated and futile attempts at playing a series of notes steadily. I saw the hurt on her face. Now, Melinda had about as innocent and adorable a face as any seven and a half year old girl could have. And I saw the hurt on that beautiful little face.

That afternoon, walking through Flushing's busy streets, I couldn't get the look of that face out of my mind. I thought things over. Surely I couldn't always be expected to be perfectly patient. Children can't always be shielded from failure. Dealing with disappointment is part of growing up. Playing piano requires a modicum of both discipline and ability, even for a beginner with no intentions of achieving excellence. Teachers need to push students, they can't be dishing out false praise all the time. Expectations must be set. Piano lessons aren't for everyone, are they? And I'm a serious, dedicated pianist, why should I be stuck trying to teach someone so devoid of musical ability?

As I got to my seat on the IRT subway train bound for Manhattan, all these thoughts tumbled through my mind. And still, I saw that hurt little face. I wrestled with my conflicted feelings as the train rumbled past Shea Stadium, through Corona, on through Jackson Heights, on through Woodside, and finally after burrowing under the East River, arrived in Manhattan. And all the while, as my thoughts jostled restlessly about, two persistent little eyes and a distressed little furrowed brow rode the tracks with me. It was no use. The look of that face was haunting me. A new feeling began to take hold. Somehow, I had to do right by Melinda Chen. I had to at least try.

At forty-second street I switched to the Uptown train and the final leg of my commute back to my apartment on the upper west side. As the subway barreled along beneath Broadway speeding me uptown, my feelings began to crystallize. By the time I climbed up the stairs and onto the street at one hundred and sixteenth street and Broadway, I had formulated my plan. Emerging from the subway and eyeing the familiar, comfortable sights of Columbia University, sitting across Broadway, and the reliable Chock Full o Nuts coffee shop at the corner of one hundred and sixteenth, my spirits were buoyed. I knew what I would do.

I would embark on a simple but serious experiment. Although I was pretty sure that Melinda lacked the musical talent to progress very far as a musician, I resolved to make the last thirty minute lesson each Saturday, Melinda's time slot, a sacred time devoted to the practice of patience. I would attempt to cultivate patience and full attentiveness. As I walked down the hill on one hundred and fourteenth street between Broadway and Riverside Drive towards my apartment, I made a pact with myself. Melinda would have my complete presence for each session together. "Then" I said to myself, entering the apartment, "then let's just see if she learns to play a bit of piano."

I can honestly say that in the weeks and months that followed, I honored my pact. It turned out to be relatively easy for me. Not because Melinda became a good piano student, she continued to struggle– but because she was honestly trying her best. She was an eager pupil despite her natural limitations, and she seemed to truly enjoy our lessons. Of course the more kindness and attention I lavished on her, the more she liked me and the more she strove to please me.

It was also easy because I had made it a challenge. I'm not the most patient of persons. Not at all. But now I had created a challenge, and I had to see if I could rise to it. Those thirty minutes with Melinda, each Saturday, began to take on greater and greater meaning for me.

Musically, the main challenge was to help her play in rhythm. After a few false starts, we finally started to make progress by thinking of how steadily a clock ticks time. "Tick Tock, steady as a clock" became my mantra. I tapped rhythm. I gesticulated and swayed to and fro, clicked my tongue, snapped my fingers, stamped my feet—anything to impress upon Melinda the way a clock maintains a steady pulse. Sometimes I tick-tocked away in an exaggerated, uneven manner and got her to laugh. "Clocks don't tick like this, do they?" I asked, and then went into my wildly erratic broken clock impersonation. She would always laugh at that. And she got the point.

Slowly but surely she began to make progress. Little five finger exercises began to sound even. Scales became more regular, and eventually almost perfectly steady. First with me beating time, then all by herself. Then came the songs from Fletcher and Thompson. "Steady as a clock" I would tell her, and exhort her onward with my tick-tocking and tapping out the beat. From quarter notes and half notes to eighth notes and dotted quarter notes, we tick-tocked ever onward; ever onward through the thicket of three quarter, four quarter, and six eight time. We counted out loud, she tapped while I played, I tapped while she played, we played simultaneously while I called out the counts, and we joked, broke into laughter, and had fun.

The hurt little face had turned into a happy little face. Melinda was a sweet, gentle soul. She was also receptive to my instruction and touchingly dogged in her pursuit of playing her songs in steady time. She was learning the rudiments of music, and improving bit by bit when our time together ran out.

I told her shortly after Thanksgiving that I would be moving away in six weeks. She looked deflated. This time it was sadness that I saw on her face; not hurt, just sadness. I felt sad about it too. Melinda Chen had become very special to me. I wonder how much we could still have accomplished. She was progressing slowly, but she was *progressing*, and she was after all, just eight years old. Even though musical ability is quite easy to spot in young children, I have learned over the years not to prejudge children quite so quickly. Many have surprised me. I didn't want our lessons to end. I had set out to be totally present for out lessons together; to be patient and to be attentive. One thing I can say with certainty is that Melinda was always patient and attentive with me. She had been present! And she had proven to be irrepressible in her pursuit of playing as "steady as a clock".

I sensed her eagerness as she would arrive for each lesson. She was always sweet and cheerful, but it was a cheerfulness that was cloaked in a fragile vulnerability.

It pricked my heart when she told me that she would never like any other teacher as much as me. "You're the only piano teacher I ever want" she said. I assured her that she would find another teacher she liked, but inwardly I worried. Most of the teachers at the Brooklyn Conservatory were serious musicians and capable concert performers. Many of them came to teaching reluctantly, and chafed at the task of working with children who lacked real talent. Had not I myself entertained doubts about teaching Melinda? Now what would happen? Would Melinda's next teacher be impatient or indifferent? And if so, would that bring her enjoyment of the piano to an end? Such were the protective feelings I now felt towards this sensitive little girl.

So it had come to my last Saturday in Flushing. I had had my farewells with Theodore, with Stephen, and with Jee-Hye. There remained only the last lesson of the day, Melinda's lesson.

She arrived in a state of excitement carrying a bag holding her music books, which also contained gifts for me. Her parents did not stop by, and the gifts she brought me were home made. She presented me with her own drawing, a drawing of herself playing the piano, and me standing beside her, reminding her in a caption to play "steady as a clock". Underneath that was another drawing, this one of a large clock, beside which were written the words. "Tick Tock, steady as a clock" "I will never forget, Love, Melinda Chen" The drawings had all been brightly colored in. Additionally, I was given a photograph of Melinda sitting at her spinet in her apartment, a stuffed animal on her lap, with the heating radiator visible in the background. These two gifts struck me to the core.

We had known each other only for nine months, a short period of piano lessons, and she was not one of my better students, yet it was with Melinda that I had undergone the most memorable journey. It was with her that I had undergone the most deeply human experience.

I was the thirty one year old teacher and pianist, aspiring to perform the great works of the piano literature, and yearning to share my enthusiasm and insights with talented students. Melinda was the gentle, vulnerable eight year-old child who lacked the aptitude for significant progress as a musician. The little journey we shared together was one of genuine affection, and of finding that special place where the rhythm just beats along all by itself, never wavering— forever and ever steady.

Later that afternoon I made the familiar walk from the school to the subway, carrying away gifts and a swirl of emotion. I was saying good-bye to human beings whom I had grown to love. Furthermore, I was bidding farewell to a community, to a city, to a time and a place to which I knew I would never be able to return. It was a poignant ride home on the IRT that afternoon.

Only a few hours later, I was befallen by a small tragedy. I had gone out to meet some friends in New Jersey that evening, and as I had been so touched by Melinda's drawing, I decided to bring it along to show them. I carried my treasure in a small backpack on the bus out to Jersey. Somehow, in my dreamy, nostalgic state of mind, I alighted from the bus without my backpack. I had left Melinda's priceless artwork on the bus! Of course I called the bus company but was told that no backpack had been retrieved. I called every day for the next few days but had no luck. The drawing of Melinda and me, and the big clock, was gone; as was the photograph. I would never gaze upon them again. I would never know the pleasure of pulling out that drawing from the special desk drawer where I keep such mementos and letters, saved up over time. I would never in later years, be comforted by the unrolling of a certain faded paper, holding those dear pictures and words, put down so ardently by her juvenile hand. No, I would never look upon that clock, that marvelous clock, ticking undisturbed through time. Sadly, there would be no tangible evidence of this particular slice of this piano teacher's life. It would have to suffice that Melinda's drawing, her photo, her face, and our lessons together would live in my memory.

As I bring this tale to a close, Melinda Chen must now be thirty-five years old. I wonder about her. Is she healthy and happy? What type of work does she do? Is she married? Does she have children? Did she continue to play the piano? – Does she remember me?

Once as a child she wrote these words" "Steady as a clock, I will never forget"– Nor will I.

# Tori, Jack, and Musical Experiences

Musical Experiences is now midway through its 20<sup>th</sup> season. With help from a lot of supportive people, I was able to get this small non-profit organization up and running in 1992. The mission is to bring the combination of live performance and music education to the community. As a pianist, I naturally love the challenge of performing, but I've also long wanted to find a way of talking to people about music in an informative manner, which is both accessible and entertaining.

Sometimes I think classical music concerts are too cloaked in an overly serious and stodgy atmosphere, which can be intimidating and off-putting. I've often enjoyed the manner in which a good folk singer talks to the audience while tuning his guitar, preparing people for the next song. I seek this relaxed, casual style, but with real information, real music education; that was and continues to be my goal.

I have been giving classes and concerts for over 20 years now which combine musical and historical analysis with actual performance. Over these years, I've continually tried to fine-tune and improve my presentations. As with all my endeavors in music, the inevitable ups and downs of success and failure, trial and error, comedy and tragedy, have shadowed every experience.

It took a powerful infatuation to ultimately motivate me to stop procrastinating and actually start walking my chosen path. I was working as an accompanist with the Pacific Northwest Ballet here in Seattle, in the fall of 1988. This job helped to pay the bills while I developed my private teaching studio and gave sporadic concert performances. In September a petite, young ballerina appeared and the world stopped. Two translucent gems, in the form of beautiful blue/green eyes, turned my head and shook my heart. I was struck hard. Tori wasn't just another beautiful young dancer. She was a dazzling Aphrodite of enchanting beauty, filled with innocent wonder, an open inquisitive mind, and a virtuous soul, or so she appeared to the man I then was. This was all made apparent to me with great immediacy upon watching her waltz, *chassee*, pirouette, and *jetee* across the floor, all in rhythm to my piano playing; which became ever more sparkling and passionate when she was dancing. Despite the obvious fact that I was the only person in the world meant for her, I found it difficult to approach her. How does one approach a mythical princess? One that was at least partly created by my own exceedingly fertile imagination.

I resolved to teach a course in music history to the dancers. I would become her teacher and elevate myself from the role of mere accompanist. I would charm her along with the other dancers by gently leading them into the inner sanctum of the world's greatest music. I would show them how colorful, complex, and compelling the great composers are. It was the type of course I'd always longed to teach. Now motivated by love, it became the course I ached to teach.

I approached the company's director, Francia Russell, with my proposal. Of course I made no mention of my amorous desires. I convinced her of how wholly musically undereducated most ballet dancers are. Ms. Russell was and is, a highly cultured and musical woman. She had been an assistant to the great George Balanchine at the New York City Ballet, and was a superb director and ballet mistress. A true grande dame of dance, she certainly knew the worth of a musical education to a dancer. She readily agreed to let me have my class.

That is how I got started giving talk and play performances. I was nervous and apprehensive when the day arrived to stand before this group of dancers and begin my class. But not for long. They were a lovely, attentive group and my genuine love for music took over. The class became popular, Ms. Russell was delighted, and I got to know Tori. I had a wonderful time showing her Seattle, and we became friends. But that's where it ended. Alas, the great love of my life failed to see in me, the great love of her life.

It was just not meant to be the great romance of the 20ᵗʰ century. But much was gained. Though my disappointment had been great, my recovery was swift. Another romance was born in its place, rising with the smoke, billowing high above the charred remains of doused hopes. A romance that has endured and only grown stronger over time. The romance of sharing music with people through talk, piano improvisation, musical analysis, historical perspective, comparative recordings, and of course playing the glorious works of the piano repertoire.

As for Tori, who left Seattle that June, looking back with a now more sober, realistic judgment, I can relate that she was a lovely young lady in every way. Even as my more tranquil state of mind presently allows me to relent, and concede that she didn't prove to be my one true love, I can still declare that she was, and no doubt still is, a thoughtful, intelligent, curious, charming person possessing real character. Though unintended, she helped me find the way to one of my life's true loves and callings. Of this she could never have known. Sometimes life works in the most mysterious of ways.

Having discovered the joy of giving talk and play programs, I've never stopped. The following year I began offering a music history/appreciation course out of my home, and with no advertising other than word of mouth, I had a group of 20 people with whom to explore the saga of western music through the ages. From the haunting beauty of medieval Gregorian chant, on through to the jagged dissonances of Stravinsky and the syncopated rhythms of jazz, we studied the ever evolving musical styles of more than a millennium. By the end of 1991, I was able to resign from my job at the ballet and begin Musical Experiences. This allowed me to pursue my passion of giving concert programs which combine live performance with music education, as well as continuing my classes in music history, and more recently, visiting public schools to bring the stories and the music of great composers to young children.

Since the inception of Musical Experiences some two decades ago, I've had the good fortune of meeting and interacting with so many good and interesting people; musicians, colleagues, and music-lovers from all walks of life. I have been blessed with the support and companionship of some wonderful people amongst the community. Loyal encouragement given by the serious connoisseur is incalculable to any performer. Such a relationship was exemplified by my friendship with Jack.

It's almost eight years now since he died. As sturdy and indomitable as he was, Jack couldn't overcome the cancer that grew in his bladder, or the sadness that assailed his heart. He was 73 years old when he succumbed to death's inevitable embrace. It was the end of June and I remember it well, because it was just a couple of weeks after the Musical Experiences concert of that season. He was gravely ill by then and it was the first concert of mine he'd missed since becoming a regular.

Jack Hornung was a strong, robust fellow possessed with rugged good looks. He had a fine head of graying hair, and a handsome face which oscillated between being clean shaven and bearded. His beard, in turn, oscillated between being neatly trimmed and a bit scraggly. He was a passionate lover of life. He was also temperamental, highly and vociferously opinionated, keenly intelligent, warm, generous, obstinate, a fiercely independent thinker, and an ebullient advocate of all he considered worthy. He considered me to be worthy. Somehow, I could do no wrong in his eyes.

Jack made his entrance into my world via the first of several letters he would dispatch to me. He had attended the all-Schubert program that Musical Experiences had given in October of 1997. He showered me with encouragement in his hand-written, difficult-to-decipher note. My friend and colleague, Deeji Killian, a wonderful soprano, had joined me for this Schubert evening. Our concert mixed a group of songs and some solo piano works with my typical preliminary explanations and musical illustrations. My love for Schubert runs especially deep and I made a particular effort with this program. I even included one of my own creations; a pastiche of famous Schubert melodies, woven together. The program was enthusiastically received. It was the first time Jack had been to one of my concerts.

His post-performance missive was full of effusive praise. Jack didn't give praise or criticism in a measured, nuanced manner. He either liked something or he disliked something. If he liked something he was effusive in his praise. If he found a reason to be critical, he was likewise, certain of his critique.

The majority of his letter heartily praised the program; both the educational aspect and the music itself. Near the end, however, I was admonished for failing to run the English translation of the words of Schubert's lieder, side by side with the German on the audience program. This error, he stated, was the one flaw in an otherwise stellar concert.

I wrote Jack a response, explaining that I preferred the audience to listen to the music while watching Deeji's expressive style of delivering these songs; not to have their heads buried in the programs, rustling them noisily in their hands. This, in turn, elicited a phone call from Jack, and after graciously thanking me for the concert, and assuring me of his heart-felt appreciation, he took up the cause of how best to present the texts of German lieder with their English translations. I was soon to find out that it wasn't very beneficial to disagree with Jack. He would not yield an inch of ground on the matter.

When certain of the correctness of his opinions, which was nearly always, he stood in their defense with the force of a lion. I thanked him for his kind support and suggestions and he signed off by assuring me he would attend my next concert. I told him to be sure to introduce himself afterwards. Our friendship would grow progressively for the seven and a half years that remained in Jack's life.

True to his word, Jack made it to the next concert, and to all the others after that. He had a burning love for music, or more properly stated, a burning love for the music he deemed worthy of love. His pantheon included Bach, Mozart, Beethoven (above all), Chopin, Brahms, Tchaikovsky, Gershwin. He admitted that Schubert was growing on him. I'd like to think that I can take some credit for that. My efforts to elucidate the beauty of Haydn never got very far with him.

Jack Hornung was born and raised in Syracuse, New York. He went to Harvard, and there his love of music really blossomed. He roomed with an erudite New Yorker who introduced him to the great names of music's interpreters. Jack already knew that he loved Beethoven and Chopin, but it was his sophisticated college roommate who taught him to appreciate the subtleties of Bruno Walter's conducting of Mozart symphonies, or of the differences between Alfred Cortot's Chopin and Arthur Rubinstein's. Jack became a connoisseur.

By the time I befriended him in Seattle, he was married to Robin, his second wife, with whom he had a five year old daughter, Sarah, who was clearly the apple of his eye. Robin, a physician, was Jack's junior by more than 20 years. Jack was retired from a career in urban renewal. He and Robin had moved out to Seattle from Philadelphia and when Sarah was born, Jack became a haus frau. He took Sarah everywhere. He shared his unbridled enthusiasm for so many things with his little girl. They camped in the rich green forests of the Pacific Northwest, hiked in its snow-capped mountains, explored the Pacific Science Center, went to the Seattle Children's Theatre (about which Jack raved), visited the museums, watched the films of Charlie Chaplin (the Mozart of the cinema, according to Jack), read books together, watched the birds, and of course, attended concerts and listened to music.

They went to many Seattle Symphony concerts together until one of Jack's several letters to symphony maestro Gerard Schwarz was answered unsatisfactorily. Jack, an inveterate letter writer, had become disenchanted with the Symphony's "Young People's Concerts." He accused the symphony of treating their young listeners frivolously; of catering to the shallowness of our contemporary commercial culture; of dumbing down their product.

Jack was full of strong opinions and he wasn't shy about thundering forth his proclamations. The symphony had sold out! Charlie Chaplin was the greatest artist of the 20th century—well, alongside Frank Lloyd Wright. Moby Dick is the greatest of all novels. New York is the world's greatest city. The string quartet is an unfortunate concept. Haydn wrote empty, meaningless music. An open marriage is the best type of marriage. Finnish women are the most beautiful in all of Europe. Bernini was the greatest sculptor after Michelangelo. Stravinsky, after spending his genius on the youthful masterworks, Firebird, Petrouchka, and the Rite of Spring, wrote nothing else but dry, acerbic, inconsequential music. He even once instructed me on the proper way of slicing bread.

In the last year or two of his life he codified his opinions on music in a beautiful small book, written lovingly for the aspiring young music lover. He entitled it "Immortal Fire—Jack's guide to the would-be classical music lover." It is a charming book and transmits some of Jack's special combination of warmth, forthrightness and genuine ardor.

Jack Hornung showed fierce loyalty to those he loved. If you were one of his chosen ones, you couldn't find a stauncher ally. One of his all time favorite pianists was the late German master of Beethoven, Mozart, and Schubert, Arthur Schnabel. He idolized Schnabel. The following except from his book shows the full extent of his loyal support for my musical activities.

"My friend Fred Kronacher recently announced that he would play two late Beethoven piano sonatas [Not Jack's favorite Beethoven]. Alarmed, I got out my authoritative Arthur Schnabel recordings of the 1930s, listened to each four times and notified Fred that his audience would not like these rather austere late sonatas. Do you know what Fred did? He invited me over and by playing each sonata he converted me because he had developed a personal, different, and revised approach. Fred, a fine pianist, but an unknown compared to the great Schnabel, rendered for me a superior performance that made these pieces accessible and satisfying."

Jack made it known to his circle of friends that I was a terrific pianist and played late Beethoven better than Schnabel. This predictably led to some good-natured needling from some of my friends, who asked, "So Fred, how does it feel to have surpassed Schnabel's Beethoven?" etc. Well, that was Jack, and he was honest in expressing his sentiments. Don't think that Jack's warm support didn't gratify me or stroke my ego. I take piano playing seriously. Nonetheless, I know I'm not Arthur Schnabel. Once, after another of my concerts, he asked, "Fred, what happened in the Chopin Polonaise? You were off tonight." He had been right. I had been disappointed with the performance of the polonaise that evening. His praise was never given as manipulative flattery, nor was he reticent about offering criticism.

Jack Hornung's life began to spiral downward about a year and a half before he died. I remember the day he appeared at my house and told me that his wife had asked for a divorce. "If Robin wants a divorce, then a divorce it will be. Fred, I'm going to move forward. I'm not looking back." He spoke these words in a terse, stern tone betraying his anger. Shortly thereafter, he moved to a rental house, and then came the diagnosis of cancer. I felt impelled to spend more time with Jack, and his loyalty to me increased even more.

I gave a series of music history classes in Bellevue, the city across the lake, just east of Seattle. He insisted on riding out with me and carrying along his fine stereo system for each class. "You don't need to worry about having a good quality sound system for the recorded excerpts you choose to use. I'll take care of that."

He was wonderful to have in class; always nurturing his classmates along with his warm greetings, and picking up on their comments and questions concerning music. Once we studied Schumann's great piano work *Carnaval* and I had the class listen to the same exact excerpts with recordings of Rubinstein and Rachmaninoff. Jack felt that Rachmaninoff, great as he was, hadn't grasped the essence of Schumann's soul. "He is making it into Rachmaninoff" was his critique. This provoked a lively conversation among my students, inspiring them to peer more deeply into Schumann's rich, evocative masterwork.

We would always go out for dinner together before my Sunday evening classes, dining in Bellevue's Il Palino Pastaria. Entering the restaurant, Jack would pepper me with questions and comments about music. I would usually respond, "Jack, we'll have an hour and a half class right after dinner, let's talk about something other than music now." I learned that Jack's interest in music was rivaled by only two other subjects, the great outdoors and beautiful women. I was impressed with Jack's adventures and accumulated knowledge in these fields, both of which appealed to me as well.

As a teenager, before entering college, young Hornung had worked for a spell as a lumber jack in the Adirondack Mountains of upper New York State. He developed a life-long passion for this region, and was fortunate to be able to return to these beautiful mountains many times to hike and camp. Jack's elemental soul responded to the clarion call of wild, untamed nature. He rowed his prize wooden flat boat in lakes and rivers throughout North America; once even rowing the full length of the Erie Canal. He hiked and backpacked in the mountains; the Olympic and Cascade ranges here in Washington, the Sierras, the Rockies, the Swiss Alps; but none captured his very heart of hearts as the Adirondacks had. "Fred, when I lick this damned cancer, I want to make a hiking trip with you there," he said to me more than once.

These convivial early Sunday dinners, at the cozy Pastaria, would occasionally veer into darker territory when the subject of Robin was broached. They had both hired lawyers and a financial settlement was being decided upon. The much more incendiary issue concerning the custody of their daughter was soon to explode and ignite a raging wild fire in my good friend's soul.

Robin wanted to forbid Jack from being alone with Sarah, declaring him a risk to his own daughter due to his volatile temperament. The dispute would ultimately be decided in court and Jack was temporarily ordered to agree to see his beloved child only in the company of a third person, another adult. Jack who had been Sarah's constant companion and guardian over her eleven years of existence flew into a rage. He refused to accede to such an arrangement under any circumstances. War was declared, and Robin was now referred to only as "my sworn enemy."

He announced he would see the legal process through, but would never bow to any ruling that put restrictions on his being able to see Sarah alone. I heard Jack's anger, and stood with him as sympathetically as I could. I supposed that Robin had a story to tell too, but Jack was my friend and I tried to support him loyally without falling into a blind, one-sided judgment. I know he loved his daughter, and had never, ever been accused of any wrong-doing. He had been good enough to take care of Sarah for eleven years. According to Jack, it was only after the haggling over finances that Robin accused him of being too erratic to be trusted as a guardian. Again, in fairness, I must caution that I am responding to but one side of the story.

Despite grappling with this inner anguish, and a malignant tumor, he carried on as valiantly as he could. We saw each other at least once a week and he never missed any of my classes or concerts. I continued to learn more about Jack.

He had been a leader in establishing the Mountains to Sound Greenway, which preserves hundreds of miles of natural beauty between the Cascade Range, east of Seattle, and the Puget Sound, whose marine waters create the city's western boundary. He had put his professional expertise in urban planning, gleaned from his career in Philadelphia, and his fervent love of un- spoilt nature at the service of this project. With his boundless energy, charm, and sincere good will, he proved to be a formidable advocate for the protection of natural habitat.

Jack was much more than talk and bluster, much more than the opinionated armchair critic who only pronounces judgment. He was a man who knew how to roll up his sleeves and partake in the good fight. In fact, he was one who could not but throw himself into this mad, swirling dance of beauty and pain. Of this ineffable, fleeting dance of joy and sorrow, major and minor, consonance and dissonance, hymns and dirges, waltzes and tangos, Jack Hornung partook exuberantly.

One day over lunch together, I learned something else about my friend. "Fred," he told me, "the one thing I'm most proud of in my life is something I did about fifty years ago. I responded to a friend's suggestion, and went down south with him to participate in the struggle for civil rights." He had never spoken of it before, and he mentioned it with a simple modesty. "I'm glad I made my small contribution," he added. Here was another example of the Hornung approach to life, putting principle into action.

But the turbulence and despair he felt grappling with the legal fight over his daughter was searing deeper and deeper into his already volatile psyche. How shocking, humiliating, and galling it was for him to be asked to consent to regulations that he couldn't understand. He saw no room for compromise. The prospect of losing his daughter and being discredited in her eyes, by what he was certain were lies and nothing more, drove him into an unsteady state of serious depression. This, together with the questionable prospects of reclaiming his physical health, pushed him into ever darker regions.

Eventually came the November day when I answered the telephone and got the disturbing news that Jack had attempted suicide. He had climbed up a hiking trail in the mountains, an hour's drive from town. He'd taken a big dosage of sleeping pills and lay down towards evening, underdressed, expecting to freeze to death in the night. Another hiker came across his slumbering body and called for help. Jack was rushed to hospital and rescued. The following day I visited him in Seattle's Harborview Hospital. He claimed that he was prepared to die, and that he wasn't afraid of death. Mingled with his defiance and flares of temper was a lucid awareness of his shaky psychological state, and an acknowledgement that professional care might help him to regain his footing. There was a humility in his candid admission that he needed medication and therapy.

Was Jack's bungled attempt at suicide cunningly flawed? Was it a dramatic cry for attention and help? I don't know. But Jack rallied. Though he would undergo two surgeries, chemotherapy, and ultimately a great deal of physical and mental pain, he hung in. As his moods swung between sanguine optimism and dark depression, he showed his courage in the final months left to him.

He charmed his physician, Dr. Julie Carkin, whom he referred to as a great doctor, "the best doctor I've ever known." He charmed his psychiatrist, Dr. Berg, whom he also referred to as "a great lady". After his first surgery, when I called his hospital room and spoke to the nurse, she took note of my name and then said, "Oh, you're Fred, the best pianist in Seattle. I've heard all about you." Jack had bonded with all the nurses. When I got through to Dr. Carkin, she spoke in a similar vein, "so you're Fred Kronacher, the great pianist. Jack has spoken of you so much." Though embarrassed, as though my own mother had been bragging about me, I was able to sally, "And you're Dr. Carkin, Jack has told me all about you too. You're the best doctor in the world!"

In February, four months before Jack died, he attended my all Chopin program at Benaroya Nordstrom Hall in downtown Seattle. He was already feeling the pain of the resurgent cancer. There was a large turnout for this concert, and many good friends were in the hall. But it was my visibly ill friend Jack, who appeared first backstage afterwards. "Fred, you triumphed!" he exclaimed, "It was a real event, a real event!" his eyes gleamed as he pronounced his positive verdict even as the unaccustomed pallor of his strong face manifested disease. His voice, too, failed to ring with its usual masculine tone.

It was the last time Jack made it to a concert of mine. He was soon hospitalized again. He vowed to win a release from Seattle's Swedish Hospital in early June to attend the Musical Experiences program of Haydn and Schubert trios. Such loyalty! Even with his well known antipathy to Haydn he was ready to drive his doctors and hospital staff to distress to make the concert. But he was too sick. Jack could no longer grace one of my performances with his love and support.

I saw him every other day over the last three weeks of his life. Sometimes we talked about music. Sometimes he speculated about what he would most like to do next, should he be given a new lease on life. Sometimes he vented his anger on Robin, his "sworn enemy." He flirted with the nurses and engaged in convivial conversation with all the doctors and staff that passed his bedside. The only thing that dulled his active, engaged mind was the medication, which was needed for the persistent, gnawing pain in his lower abdomen and pelvic area.

Occasionally he talked to me about death. "I think this might be it," he told me. "It might be time for me to exit, make room for someone else; let some new life take my spot."

It was a virulent staph infection that ultimately took hold of him and precipitated his death. The day before losing consciousness, Jack had a lovely and uplifting visit from his daughter Sarah. Later that day, he had a transformation of mind and spirit. He announced that he was overcome with an overwhelming gratitude; a gratitude for his life, a gratitude for all. "No anger," he was heard to say in his weak voice, "I'm not angry at anybody, not angry about anything—no more anger. I'm just so grateful, so grateful for everything."

Jack lost consciousness the next day and lasted five or six more days before passing away.

When I came to the hospital for the last time, I finally met Dr. Carkin. She was leaving Jack's room and she had tears in her eyes. I was instantly struck by what a lovely countenance she had, made even more beautiful by her tears. She smiled, shook hands, and managed a joke about being happy to finally meet "the best pianist in Seattle." I of course countered with expressing my pleasure in meeting "the best doctor in the world."

"I'm not crying for Jack," she told me, "I'm crying for myself, I will really miss him." Dr. Carkin told me that Jack had recently insisted that she listen to particular symphonies by Tchaikovsky and Sibelius. When she reported back to Jack that one of the assigned works hadn't really resonated with her, he had asked, "were you listening attentively?—not reading, or cooking—really listening carefully? You should really listen to it once more." We both laughed at this quintessential Hornung advice.

When I was left alone with Jack to say goodbye, I put my hand on his arm. He was unconscious; his eyes closed and his breaths long and uneven. "Jack," I said, "Dr. Carkin is beautiful, and guess what, she loves you." He uttered a sound as though he would have wished to speak. "Jack, I love you too, thank you for everything, for being a great friend." Jack moved his head and made a louder utterance. I knew he was aware of my presence and wanted to express himself. But Jack was through being verbal.

I still think about the last words he did speak; words that neither judged nor compared, neither advised nor proclaimed; just simple words of self awareness; "I have no more anger, only gratitude—I'm just grateful, so grateful". It was my friend Jack Hornung's final victory.

It was our mutual love of music that gave rise to our friendship. It has repeatedly been my great, good fortune to have bumped up against some wonderful souls, and music has almost always been a conduit in bringing us together.

He was unique, Jack Hornung; a true individual, some might say an eccentric, a character. I would call him an authentic man with an authentic heart. To me, he was a wonderful friend, a genuine friend. And my life was the richer for knowing him.

# THELMA AND FOUR THAT DIDN'T TAKE

Naturally, a piano teacher will encounter a number of students, who for one reason or the other, will not mesh with him, and no working relationship is ever established. I have had my share of such students. Some stand out in my memory. An example of one is a little boy named Ben.

I remember him well. He had just turned six, and had the unmistakable mannerisms of a certain type of Jewish New Yorker that is immediately recognizable to anyone who's ever lived there.

He was brought to me at the music school in Flushing by his mother. It was July, and the plan was to let Ben have six lessons before determining whether to continue or not. He never appeared the least bit timid or vulnerable in my presence, the way many young children do. On the contrary, there was a casual confident air about him. He showed no special talent, nor was he especially overwhelmed by these simple beginning classes. But he wasn't really engaged or excited. I never saw the look of wonderment cross his little face. He struck me as a child who had already learned to live more through his head than through his emotions.

After the sixth lesson, now in August, I asked him, "Well Ben, how do you like piano lessons so far? How do you like playing the piano?" The way that Ben dispatched of this question is what has made him so memorable to me. He looked at me directly, held his hand out bracingly at about a forty five degree angle from his elbow, and with a face that was both reassuring and determined, said "I don't hate it." He paused, so that these words, clearly intended to soften the blow that was to come, could take full effect. His face became more pliant and he continued, "But frankly," and here his voice undulated a bit and became almost lyrical, and as he slowly shook his six year old head, he said with impeccable timing "but frankly," and here a wonderful pregnant pause— " I'm not crazy about it." And with that, Ben had deftly negotiated an end to piano lessons. He had done it with self assurance, and with the tact, the gestures, the vocal inflections, and the general expressiveness which he had already imbibed from the particular ethnic New York City milieu of which he was a part.

A couple of hours later, I left the school and was walking through the busy Flushing neighborhood of shops and apartment buildings on my way to the subway to go home. Along the way I passed a play-ground. And voila! There was Ben! My now former student was swing-ing calmly on a swing set amidst the shouts and hubbub of children at play, and parents overseeing them. He displayed no vigor, no zest, no emotion. In fact he seemed lost in thought as he swung tranquilly on his swing. He didn't see me. I remembered his words, "I don't hate it, but frankly— I'm not crazy about it." I smiled, watching him a little longer, and then continued along to the subway station and the ride back to Manhattan.

That was the last time I saw him. And even though it's been twenty seven years now, and I hardly got to know him, I still remember Ben.


Sometimes, children will say something quite unexpected in their naïveté. Paula, a little Philippino girl of five and a half years, was a case in point. Like Ben, she came to me for six summer lessons. Her mother sat in on all of them. Both mother and daughter seemed reticent, and neither spoke much. It is not unusual for young children to be shy at first with their piano teacher, but Paula's mother, a petite, attractive, and demure young woman, seemed more timorous and quiet than most parents, a bit nervous as well.

At the fifth of our six lessons, she excused herself to use the restroom. She closed the door to the piano studio behind her and walked down the hall to the ladies room. Little Paula and I were left alone for the first time. Paula immediately looked up at me from her place on the piano bench and said, "Can I ask a question?" This is actually a moment I cherish with shy beginning students who had hitherto barely spoken a word to me. It means they're comfortable enough with me, trustful enough, to say something unbidden. I felt delighted upon hearing Paula's words, and answered, "Of course Paula, what is it?"

I didn't care whether her question concerned our piano lesson or not. Just the fact that she was taking the initiative in venturing to share a thought or ask a question, pleased me. I awaited her words with eagerness.

"Well, um…my mommy wants to know if you have hair on your chest." The question set me back. What the devil? What kind of question was that! I had been caught off balance. I remember one thought that did flash through my mind. "My chest? Who ever looks at one's chest? Do I have hair on my chest?" Well, of course I recovered myself and answered as honestly and succinctly as I could. "Yes, I have some hair on my chest," followed by, "let's return to Twinkle, Twinkle Little Star."

We did. A minute later Paula's mother returned to the studio, sat down and resumed watching the piano lesson. Paula remained tight-lipped for the duration of our session. The following week we met again for the sixth, and what proved to be our final lesson together. Nothing was mentioned by either Paula or her mother concerning the question of hair on my chest, or, for that matter, anything else touching on the subject of my anatomy.

One can only speculate as to what sort of conversations between mother and daughter may have prompted the asking of Paula's surprising question, or those which may have ensued afterwards.

I'll never know. Whatever one may infer from this slender story, it is representative of the many surprising, unpredictable moments that anyone teaching kids will encounter.

John appeared in my studio at the Brooklyn Branch of the conservatory in early December. It was his first piano lesson. He was a complete beginner. John was 85 years old. Somehow after putting it off for four score and five years, he thought it was finally the right time to get started on becoming a classical pianist. Within five minutes of meeting one another, John informed me his goal was to play the music of Rachmaninoff. By the time he told me this, I had already noticed that his hands shook.

John was a fairly tall, trim, pleasant-looking gentleman. He was witty and affable. I could not help but like him. However, as pleasant and likeable as I may have found him, I was determined to avoid the thankless task of attempting to teach him Rachmaninoff. Nor for that matter, Chopin, Liszt, or Bach. Like many adults who dream of playing the piano, John had no idea of the difficulties involved. Obviously, learning to play an instrument is something best begun at an early age. The later in life one gets started, the less likely it is that one can progress very far. John, at 85, and a total beginner, wasn't saying that he wanted to have a little distraction playing around on the piano. No, he was declaring his goal of playing Rachmaninoff, one of the most difficult composers of all. Only an advanced pianist, a virtuoso in fact, can truly play Rachmaninoff and do him justice.

"John, why of all composers do you want to play Rachmaninoff?" I asked. "Because Fred, when I was a young man I heard Rachmaninoff perform in Carnegie Hall, and it made one hell of an impression." A thrill ran through me, as it always does, when I hear a firsthand account of someone who has attended a Rachmaninoff recital. Most of the older pianists and musicians that I met in New York revered the great Russian master above all the other twentieth century's legendary pianistic figures. "So John has decided he wants to play Rachmaninoff," I sighed inwardly to myself. This was a pathway I had no desire to tread upon. I set about dissuading him by making him see the futility of such an endeavor, in hopes that he would quickly realize the folly of pursuing it. I didn't want to say bluntly, "No John, you're too old." I gave a step-by-step description of what a student must do to finally arrive at the possibility of approaching Rachmaninoff. I purposely made it as long a list as I could. "John, first of all, you don't know the names of the keys, you don't know how to read the notes, you don't know how to hold your hands at the keyboard." I didn't say anything about the obvious disadvantage of having hands that shook involuntarily. "You would have to learn how to count rhythm, play scales, arpeggios, chords and all manner of technical exercises. You would have to learn to play simple songs, and eventually work up to the easiest student pieces by Mozart, Bach and Haydn. Then it would be on to the easier sonatinas of Clementi…." I told John that all of that takes time, and afterwards, he would at best have attained the status of early intermediate level, still an enormous distance from the imposing summit of Rachmaninoff. I stopped talking, assuming that he had gotten the point, and would of his own accord revise his plans. He gazed at me with a slightly confused, disconcerted look, and responded, "Fred, your approach sounds more suited to a younger man. I don't have much time. I have to get to Rachmaninoff quickly!"

At this point, I abandoned discretion, and said, "John I'm sorry, but I don't see how you can, it takes years of hard work to learn to play well." He responded, "Couldn't I just somehow get the feel of it?" I finally told him I hadn't the means or the desire to attempt teaching him Rachmaninoff. I suggested that he try to find another teacher who felt more in accord with his wishes. He agreed amicably and I felt relieved.

We spent the remainder of our lesson time together chatting quite pleasantly. I remember having asked him what type of work he had done. He sighed, and told me he had been a salesman. When I asked him how he had liked it he answered by saying, "Philosophically, psychologically, and spiritually, it was an utter waste of time," then adding, "but a man has to make a living." Then he sighed more deeply and said, "Fred, I must have rung every door bell in Brooklyn." Those are sad words, but somehow John didn't look terribly sad. In fact, there was a poised, even debonair quality about him.

I'm glad I was able to avoid the task of teaching a beginner of John's advanced age. It is important for an individual music teacher to reserve the right of accepting or not accepting a particular student. I was able to arrange for John to take lessons with another teacher at the Brooklyn

Conservatory, a versatile pop and jazz musician named Roger, who had once worked with Frank Sinatra. Roger was an easy going sort, who was willing to have some fun trying to help John "get the feel of it." John took a few classes with Roger before giving it up.

I only saw him one more time. It was about a month after our only session together. I was walking along Seventh Avenue, the busy commercial hub of Brooklyn's Park Slope neighborhood, on route to the Conservatory, when I spotted him on the sidewalk. I called out to him and we greeted each other. It was just after the Christmas and New Year's vacation and I asked him if he had had a pleasant New Year's holiday. I remember his response. "Oh Fred, it appears that I celebrated a little too exuberantly this year." I asked, "Have you recovered?" This spry, engaging old Brooklyn gentleman replied, "oh dear, I'm afraid that I've probably recovered as much as I'm ever likely to recover." I laughed. I don't remember John so much as grinning. We wished each other well. That was the last time I saw him. He had never really been my student. He didn't play a single note of piano in my studio. And yet, John is not forgotten.

Two other individuals spring to mind who came calling as prospective piano students. The first lasted all of one session, the latter for maybe four or five.

One afternoon, I answered a knock on the door of my Brooklyn studio. There stood a young Hasidic Jewish man, in his mid twenties. Two intense dark eyes stared out from a face bordered by long black sideburns, a bushy black beard, and cropped black hair topped off by a black hat. He wore a white shirt, a black jacket, black pants, and black shoes. After we exchanged introductions, he informed me in a somewhat raspy voice that he wanted to learn to play the piano. He never smiled or relaxed his nervous, intense gaze. I can't remember this young man's name, and although this would be our first and last piano lesson together, I haven't forgotten him. He had never played a note of piano in his life, so I started by showing him the layout of white and black keys. He looked at me dubiously as I spoke to him. "This note here is middle C," I said, pressing down the key and letting the pitch sound. "Why?" he asked sharply. "Why is it called C?" I was taken aback. No one had ever asked me why middle C is called middle C before. I showed him the pitches of the scale and explained the letters that are used. "We use the first seven letters of the alphabet," I explained, playing them individually and singing out the pitches. "Why?" he was quick to ask. "Why use letters?" I said something about the fact that the letters are merely symbols for pitches. Other symbols, such as do, re, mi, fa, sol, la, ti may be used.

Then I thought to try a different tack, and so I showed him how to play a simple five finger exercise. "Now you try it," I said. "Start with your thumb." He sat down and began trying to play it. I felt we were making some progress, as he hadn't demanded to know why he should start with the thumb. "Okay good," I told him. "Now try to hold your wrist a little lower." "Why?" came the immediate response. "Why should I hold my wrist lower? It feels alright the way I have it." A few more minutes of fielding his inquiries, all of which started with the same defiant, sharply-spoken word, *why*, and I had had enough.

At a community music school like the Brooklyn Conservatory, the teachers were expected to be flexible about trying to take on all comers. But in contemplating the prospect of weekly lessons with this young man, I could only think to myself, "Why?" Let's just say that I judged it to be a totally meshuganah project to work with this querulous fellow who seemed to prefer questioning and debating every aspect of piano playing over simply trying it, and tasting the sweetness of musical experience. Another man of religion, the great Persian, Sufi poet Rumi once wrote, "The eye goes blind when it can only ask why."

I told my would-be piano student he would simply have to refrain from asking questions after everything I told him. I was not willing to stop and dissect every instruction I gave. He would just have to faithfully follow my instructions, period. I was relieved when he failed to show up the following week. My feeling then, as it still is today, is that

I am a piano teacher, not a Talmudic scholar delighting in debating every angle of the law.

The young Catholic priest who came to the Brooklyn studio for lessons a month or two later, was a very different sort. Another complete beginner, a man of perhaps 35, he appeared for his first lesson wearing the clerical collar, and a blue sweater. He smiled frequently and was extremely personable. There were no challenging interrogations of my instructions, no thorny discourses or disputations with this relaxed, friendly priest, who insisted I call him Dave and not Father. At our second lesson, Dave appeared without the collar, casually dressed in a sweater and jeans. He hadn't practiced as much as he'd hoped to, he informed me. Dave was an extremely sociable man. A smile of frivolity never seemed far from his face. At the end of the lesson, he remarked at how fast the time had flown, and wondered if I might like to join him some evening for a drink. "Fred, it would be nice to talk more with you. Why don't we meet over at Snooky's some time?" Snooky's was a tavern on Seventh Avenue just a few blocks from the Conservatory. I declined Dave's offer. The following week the young priest smiled more than ever, and seemed to fix his merry, dancing eyes on mine quite a bit. It seems he had again been unable to get in as much practicing as he had hoped for. Once again, this man of the cloth suggested we arrange to meet at Snooky's. "It's a great place to have a drink, talk, and relax," he assured me. He seemed keenly interested in getting to know me better.

Perhaps at this point I should briefly touch on the subject of sexual attraction in the piano studio. Firstly, it happens. Sometimes a student is smitten with the teacher. Sometimes the teacher is smitten with a student. And most interesting and complex of all, is when teacher and student fall madly for one another. In my 35 years of teaching private piano lessons, I can assure the reader that I've experienced all of the above. How I've dealt with the various situations that have presented themselves will not be a subject of this book. With my admiring student, the issue was naturally easy enough to resolve. When two people are not of the same sexual orientation there isn't much suspense of how

things will turn out. I don't remember exactly what I said to my amorous priest, but beyond the fourth or fifth lesson, at which he learned
precious little of piano playing, he stopped attending. The subject of
attraction that sometimes does occur in the piano studio is not an unin-
teresting one, and it is certainly one I've been confronted with before.

A student that I remember with fondness, and one that touched my
heart, was an older African-American woman, perhaps 25 years my senior, named Thelma Halstead. Thelma was another adult beginner. She
was a schoolteacher in a rough Brooklyn neighborhood, and thought if
she could just learn to play some of the easier Bach and Handel pieces
on the piano, it might bring a soothing and uplifting break from the
pressures of her job. Thelma was slow but steady in making progress.
She was extremely respectful towards me and refused to call me Fred
when I suggested that she do so. It would always be "Mr. Kronacher."

I remember her as a gentle, earnest person and she conducted herself
with a dignified air. She was a believer, and once told me, "Mr. Kronacher, who can hold the planets in place and make them rotate around
their own axis? Who has the power and intelligence to do this? God,
Almighty!" She said this only one time during the slightly less than two
years that we worked together, and she never proselytized. She told me
Bach and Handel must have been inspired by the Lord to have composed the music that they did. In fact, Bach would have wholly con-
curred with this view.

It was evident that Thelma Halstead had her hands full with a wild
and rowdy sixth grade class. She often arrived at her lesson looking
somewhat harried and shaken from her ordeals in the classroom. She
once related to me how unruly and disrespectful some of the kids were.
It angers and saddens me that our society does not demand greater
discipline of students. It's hard enough for under-privileged kids to get
ahead, but when they are not provided for with a properly-monitored
and controlled environment at school, it makes it even harder; harder for
a dedicated teacher like Thelma Halstead to really teach, and harder for

the children who are there to receive an education to learn. I sometimes wish that a marine would be stationed in each classroom to dissuade disrespectful and intimidating kids from disrupting the process of teaching and learning. Not to worry, I naturally advocate that it be a sensitive, well-trained marine; but one with enough muscle to quickly remove from class anyone who dares to threaten or humiliate a teacher or another student. I always felt for my student Thelma. How could this fine, kind-hearted, gentle-mannered lady deal with the explosive anger and violence that some of her twelve year old pupils brought to her classroom?

Thelma was my student for roughly a year and nine months, and she kept her eyes on the goal of playing a Bach minuet and a Handel gavotte. I enjoyed our weekly lessons. She would never be one of my star pupils, or become a proficient pianist, but she doggedly stuck to it, and lo and behold, the Bach G Major Minuet did, in fact, yield its sweet, gentle, flowing tones to the deserving Ms. Halstead.

"Thelma, you're really getting it now!" I encouraged her at one of our last lessons before I left New York to come out to Seattle. My decision to relocate is what terminated our congenial working relationship. "Mr. Kronacher," Thelma addressed me with a huge smile on her face. "You have taught me a Bach minuet. I've done it! I have played a beautiful piece of music composed by a great man, a man of God!" "Thelma," I said, "You played it well, without any hesitations or wrong rhythms."

The little minuet in G is an easy piano piece. Bach wrote it as a teaching piece for Anna Magdalena, his second wife and a novice musician. Many children play it when they are seven or eight years old. At the time that Thelma first succeeded in getting through this piece with some confidence and control, I don't believe I quite realized how much it meant to her. I get a thrill when a youthful pupil makes large strides and enters the stream that leads to higher achievement. When I hear a well-played Bach fugue fill my teaching studio, I am apt to rejoice more than when a beginner in her fifties succeeds with the little Bach Minuet in G. When sixteen year old Jackson Studzinski recently gave a fine, musical, and accomplished performance of a Mozart concerto here

in Seattle this past spring, I was delighted. Hearing worthy performances by my students in Beethoven sonatas, Chopin études, and other
more advanced pieces from the classical canon obviously satisfies me
most. But perhaps it is beyond my capacity to correctly judge which of
my students gains the most from having studied the piano. Obtaining
competence and excellence in a specific field doesn't guarantee appreciation and gratitude. How many fortunate people take their privileges for
granted? I've known my share of gifted, accomplished people who never
found sustained contentment. How many who can afford to eat a nice
meal out feel truly grateful when they enter a restaurant? How many
feel grateful when enjoying conveniences like hot and cold running water
or electricity, all of which were unknown to the overwhelming majority
of our ancestors? How many of us who are lucky enough to be able to
walk down the street with a reasonably healthy body feel gratitude? And
how many pianists who can play a beautiful but simple piece of Bach
are filled with wonder and joy? Thelma Halstead was thrilled by it. It
seems that simple pleasures shine most luminously to the lucky few who
retain the childlike heart. Thelma had such a heart.

Though I'd rather work with my current student Casey on his
Beethoven *Pastorale* Sonata," finding inspiration in perfecting its intricate
details and making this sonata breathe and come to life anew, I can't dis-
count the worth of being present and involved with less advanced pupils.

At our very last lesson, Thelma handed me an enclosed envelope
and made me promise that I wouldn't open it until my evening's lessons
were finished. When I finally unsealed it before leaving the Conservatory that night, I found a card with a short, lovely note, and $100 made
up of five twenty dollar bills. Thelma certainly was not wealthy, and her
gift touched me deeply. On the card, she wrote, "Dear Mr. Kronacher,
Thank you for being my teacher. You made it possible for me to achieve
one of my dreams. You helped me to play the music of Bach. I wish you
success and happiness in Seattle. I will miss you. Thelma Halstead."

I stopped off at the school office before walking to the subway, and
got hold of Thelma's home address. The following day I sent her a
bouquet of flowers.

As a piano teacher, one takes a great variety of persons into one's studio. Some learn to play beautifully. Some learn to play well, some not as well. With some, no accord is reached. But it is beyond the teacher to know how each of these various relationships will unfold, or how deep a note may be struck by one's best efforts.

# VIENNA

I was finally in Vienna, the city that has always roused my imagination and held such meaning for me. The city that had been home to my mother and her family; the city of Mozart and empire; the city of graceful elegance and enduring art; the city of coffeehouses, waltzes, Freud, and Hitler.

In the waning days of June 2003, at the age of 50, I finally set foot in this historic city in the heart of Europe. My mother never talked in great detail about Vienna, the city of her childhood. She didn't need to. She represented it in the music she loved, from Beethoven to Johann Strauss, and in the distinctly Viennese German she spoke whenever she was with her sister Litzi. Despite all she had been through there, she still retained a feeling of wistful love for the place where she grew up. "Ay Vienna, ach Freddy, how I would like to see Vienna again," she said to me more than once. Such words were always pronounced with a strange mixture of love and melancholy and made me too, long to see Vienna.

The idea of organizing a music lover's tour of Vienna under the auspices of Musical Experiences had occurred to me some time before, and with the invaluable help of my friend Karin McCullough, this idea was brought to fruition. So it was with 13 music-loving tourists on board, that we flew off to the Austrian capital. We would see the museums and palaces, attend concerts and opera at the Musikverein and the Staatsoper, visit Mozart's apartment near the Stefansplatz, and Beethoven's house in Heiligenstadt. Our tourists would soak up the city's charm, feast on wienerschnitzel and strudel, and attend my after-breakfast talks, focusing on that evening's musical performance.

For me, it was the opportunity to finally visit the city I had heard so much about, read about, dreamt about. My mother said Vienna was beautiful. Aunt Litzi exclaimed that it was, "so elegant, you can't believe how elegant," generally followed by a bitter outburst, "I would never go back there!" Uncle Ted would say, "They think they're so cultured, they were the worst barbarians." And Uncle George, the most even-tempered of the four Berger siblings, simply stated that, "Vienna is a beautiful city," and took his American wife there to show her his boyhood home and the "beautiful city."

I was up early my first morning in Vienna. After a quick breakfast of fruit, yogurt, a semmel, and coffee, I descended upon the streets of the old inner core of the town, the "Alt Stadt." My pension, the Neurmarkt, was just around the corner from Saint Stephen's Square, dominated by its great Gothic cathedral, with its resplendent colored tile roof. It was here that both Haydn and Schubert had sung as children. Walking up to the portal, I noticed a poster announcing an upcoming performance of the Mozart Requiem. It would be held in Saint Stephen's, just blocks from where Mozart feverishly worked on this score, trying desperately to complete it before his encroaching death could silence his genius. It would be left to his student Süssmayr to complete the unfinished requiem. Moving about the busy streets, I became absorbed in the architecture and ambience of the many shops, churches, cafes, and dwellings. I felt keenly cognizant of the fact that my mother's eyes had too fallen upon these windows, spires, gables, walls, and arches. She had trod these very streets as an impressionable schoolgirl, and later in adolescence, even whilst the menacing clouds of virulent racism swirled overhead. Yes, my mother, my aunt Litzi, uncles Ted and George, my grandparents who I would never meet, and so many of my musical heroes, with whom my kinship is not of blood, but of spirit; they had all of them been here. They had all seen the light pastel colors illuminated by the June sunshine, the dark grey nooks and crannies hidden within the mortar, the displays of torte in the café windows, the beckoning glitter of fashionable gowns through shop displays, the ruddy brown shutters, the monuments and fountains, the theater of passing pedestrians, the whole cityscape that I was now in the midst of for the first time.

Though I possessed a street map, I rarely consulted it, ambling about wide awake to the overall atmosphere of these old streets. I hadn't been walking for more than 20 minutes when I was given a special welcome by the city of music. Unaware of it at the time, I had found myself drifting past the Augustiner Church, next to the Hofburg, the old palace of the emperor. From within this building floated out the muffled strains of Mozart's Mass in C. I was stopped in my tracks by this ethereal music, wafting faintly about me, from an unknown source. "Where is this music coming from?" I wondered. A celestial cloud of sound enveloped me. Was this a dream? I had only been out walking less than half an hour, and Mozart was in the air! Was my imagination playing tricks on me? I followed my ears and soon came to realize that I was at the Augustiner Church, and upon entering it, was immediately dazzled by the light and space of this beautiful cathedral. Now the unfettered force of the orchestra, organ, and chorus poured forth. I learned that I had stumbled upon a rehearsal for that morning's 11am mass to be given an hour later. Hence I was alone in the pews, witnessing the remainder of the rehearsal, enclosed by this historic space, the morning light streaming through the stained glass windows, the elegant old chandeliers twinkling, as Mozart's splendor filled my receptive soul. Everything about this first experience of Vienna was sheer magic. It was true. This really is the city of Mozart! It was visceral.

I strained my ears trying to comprehend the conductor's German as he spoke to the musicians. I am not fluent in German, and had prepared for this trip by practicing with tapes. I had never studied the language properly. My parents had pointedly refrained from speaking German to my sister Erica and me. Such was my father's antipathy towards Germany. Still, the Viennese German that my mother and Litzi spoke to one another, was deeply lodged in my ear, and I recognized its cadence and inflections right away, in the speech of this German musician.

When I walked outside at the conclusion of the rehearsal, I felt as though some part of me had come home. Continuing to wander, I came across the lawn in front of the Hofburg itself. Now a public park, this verdant space was being enjoyed by strolling Viennese, some playing Frisbee, some picnicking or just relaxing on the grass. Across the lawn was the "Schmetterling Haus" or Butterfly House, built by Emperor Franz Josef, to display a great collection of butterflies from around the world. Just in front was a large, elegant outdoor café, where I took a seat and ordered a pastry and a coffee. There I sat, installed at a grand café, out of doors, in the lovely Austrian sunshine, gazing across at the Hofburg, a linzer torte now at my table, in the heart of historic Vienna.

Later that afternoon, our whole group assembled at the hotel and set off for a tram ride along the Ringstrasse (the elegant boulevard that encircles the Alt Staadt), and a walking tour of Alt Staadt, capped off with a stop at Café Demel for cake.

The following morning, I gave a short lecture presentation on *Carmen*, the opera we were to see that evening. I was in my element, enjoying myself, and our group seemed enthusiastic and very happy. After breakfast, Karin led most of our entourage on a tour of the Schönbrunn Palace, on the outskirts of town. This visit to the sumptuous Habsburg's Versailles held little interest for me, and so I excused myself from this particular outing. Here was my chance to go alone and seek out the apartment building where my mother had lived the first 18 years of her life.

With city map in hand, I began my pilgrimage at Saint Stephen's, and set out along the colorful Rotenturnstrasse, with its shops, restaurants, cafes, and bourgeois atmosphere. I had Litzi's voice ringing in my ears. "We lived in Leopoldstaadt, you'll see Freddy. You'll see how close it is to everything. Ja, Grossperlstrasse, in Leopoldstaadt." I arrived at the Danube canal, walked across the Tabor Strasse Bridge, and entered the old neighborhood known as Leopoldstaadt. Here it became necessary to scrutinize my map quite carefully, due to the tangled web of streets running in seemingly haphazard directions at various angles. I got a bit lost in this old residential district made up of mostly apartment buildings. Finally I located Grossperlstrasse and the address where Mom, Aunt Litzi, Uncle George, and Uncle Ted lived with their parents; my grandparents.

Not only had I never had a chance to meet my grandparents, I had never even seen a photo of them. The apartment building that stood at 13 Grossperlstrasse had been renovated in the 1950s; so explained a plaque near the main entrance. There could be no purpose therefore, in trying to locate the exact apartment. I stood in front of this building for quite some time. I can't say that I was immediately overpowered by emotion. For one thing, the building itself was not as it had been, and I found myself more interested in the surrounding older buildings which gave the street its general ambience. The neighborhood itself was quiet and somewhat drab. As in many older European cities, the preponderance of parked cars impeded on what remained of the old world atmosphere. Still, I stood in front of this building on Grossperlstrasse for quite some time; my mother's street. I imagined how she and her siblings might have appeared as lively young children, emerging from this building. And then pictured my mother and Litzi, in their mid teens, smartly dressed, heading out together to the old town across the canal, to be swept up by the enchanting, sophisticated and seductive swirl of this beautiful city. "Ach, Wien, Ach Vienna," my mother would sometimes sigh. "Ay, I would like to see Vienna again,"

Next I found the Augarten, the nearby park that Litzi had told me about. It is a quiet, green, peaceful place. Here were mothers with their young children and babies, much as no doubt my grandmother and her children once spent quiet hours, some 75 years earlier. This was a small glimpse into a tiny slice of my mother's childhood world.

Across the park on Augartenstrasse stood the public school where the four little Berger children had all attended primary school. Today it continues its function of serving the district as a primary school. I stood and looked upon this school. I stepped into the entrance where their little feet had once scampered all those years ago. An official of the school came forward to meet me with an inquiring look on his face. "Guten tag," I said. Speaking slowly in German, I told him that I was visiting from the United States, that my mother and her family had lived here in Leopoldstaadt once, and that my mother had been a student in this very school. He appeared pensive for a moment, then his eyes flickered nervously and an uneasy look spread over his face. "That must have been a long time ago." "Ja," I replied. An awareness dawned on me that this middle-aged gentleman perceived that I was Jewish, and that my mother had left Vienna long ago for the obvious and unspeakable reason deeply embedded in the recess of this city's psyche. He remained silent, an uncomfortable air having enveloped the moment. "Well," I broke the silence. "I just came to see where she went to school, good day, aufwiedersehen." I walked away feeling slightly put off by his coolness, but also aware of having in some way embarrassed him. This little incident seemed to touch a nerve and made for an awkward moment for this particular citizen of Vienna.

One of this city's native sons, Sigmund Freud, had devoted his life's work to studying the mysteries of the conscious and unconscious mind. One needn't be an ardent proponent of Freud's theories to perceive the divisions and complexities of the mind, here in the birthplace of modern psychology. Walking back to the hotel, I felt a strong desire to talk with my mother. She had passed away only six months earlier, at the age of 82, never having returned to the city. She would have wanted to know every detail about my adventure. It was sad that this conversation would never occur.

Instead, it was Litzi, her younger sister by one year, who I phoned from my hotel. "Hi Litzi, I'm in Vienna!" "Ja, Freddy, you're there, in Vienna. How is everything?" Litzi's voice crackled with excitement. I told her a bit about our group of music-loving tourists, and that we were all having a wonderful experience. "Today we saw the Ringstrasse." "Ay," she sighed. "Gott, the Ringstrasse is so beautiful, isn't it beautiful Freddy?" "Later," I continued, "our group went to Café Demel." "Gott, the Demel is still there?!" she exclaimed. "The Demel!" She sighed, her voice trailing off with distant longing. Then I told her I had been to Leopoldstaadt, to her apartment building, the primary school, and the Augarten Park. "You saw the Augarten? You saw how beautiful it is?"

Places that Litzi hadn't seen in 65 years were now vibrantly alive in her memory. She recalled it all with intimacy and great emotion. My aunt, who has since passed away, was a highly emotional, temperamental, high-strung woman. She was given to exaggeration and drama. But talking to her that afternoon, I heard none of the overblown hyperbole, nor any of the piercing bitterness that she so often expressed. Rather, I perceived a heart full of warmth and wonder, albeit a heart that had been betrayed and wounded. Litzi was deeply moved as the precious images of her youth, and of the old city she had once given herself to completely, rose up before her.

"Walking back to the pension, I visited the Stadt Park," I told her. "Your mother and I used to go for ice cream all the time in the Stadt Park." She went on, "Ach, the Stadt Park is so beautiful!" "And then Litzi, I visited the Kurzalon." The Kurzalon, at the end of the park, is the elegant old ballroom where Johann Strauss conducted his orchestra and Viennese society waltzed to his infectious music. "Ay, the Kurzalon, ja, the Kurzalon! So schönn, how we loved the Kurzalon." I told her we were going to the Stadtsoper that evening, the magnificent opera house built under Franz Josef in the 1870s. Litzi and Mom had been taken there as girls by their opera-loving father to see the great tenor Beniamino Gigli sing in a performance of "La Bohème." They were true daughters of Vienna, immersed in music from their earliest years.

Litzi fell silent as I rambled on, telling her all about our plans later in the week, to attend a production of Strauss's *Die Fledermaus* at the Volksoper. I knew that Litzi, like my mother, had been to the Volksoper, Vienna's smaller opera house, and that they both adored *Fledermaus*. But my enthusiasm was now met unresponsively. Perhaps all these youthful memories had overwhelmed my aunt. Perhaps Litzi was thinking of her mother, and that fateful day in Vienna, when she and my mother said goodbye to their mother Ethel, at Vienna's main train station.

It was a farewell I never heard my mother speak of, and only in my mid 30s did Litzi once relate to me the devastating details of these final moments spent in the presence of my grandmother.

On a November day in 1938, my grandmother Ethel, my mother Gretel, and my aunt Litzi set out for Vienna's main train station. The two girls, then 18 and 17 years of age respectively, would take the train to Genoa, from where they would sail to New York. They were fleeing the Nazis. My grandmother was sending her daughters away in order to save their lives. She, Ethel, would stay and hope to get news of her husband Josef, who had already been arrested.

From Litzi's account, my grandmother showed great courage in remaining upbeat and positive en route to the train terminal, telling them they would love their Aunt Rita and their Uncle Leo in Brooklyn, with whom they would live. That they would love New York and America; and they would all be together again when the Nazi nightmare passed over. She smiled, was encouraging, and acted cheerfully. After embraces and farewells, my mother and aunt boarded the train, and as it started to pull away, Litzi decided to turn around and look through the window for one last gaze at her mother. She caught sight of her on the platform, now down on her knees, her head in her hands, sobbing uncontrollably. "My children—oh God, my children." The train pulled away leaving Ethel, my grandmother, weeping on the platform. My mother and aunt would never see her again. They would have to live the remainder of their lives with this painful image seared into their memories.

It wasn't until after the war had ended, that they learned with certainty, through the Red Cross, that their mother had perished at Auschwitz.

"Litzi, are you still there?" I waited for a reply, holding the telephone receiver in my left hand. "Ja, I'm here," she replied in a low, flat voice. All her excitement had ebbed away. She remained mute. I understood that it was now time to end our conversation. "Litzi, I will call you again in a few days." My aunt was left in her Queens apartment, alone with her now freshly aroused memories of youth. Alone to recall all the beauty and all the pain of childhood and coming of age, amidst the unique city and the shattering turn of events that had left its powerful imprint, and its lasting scars.

What did I know of the details concerning my family's ordeals during these horrible years? Very little. My parents, like so many that had survived, spoke seldom if at all with precision about what they'd been through. I never learned any of the facts surrounding my uncles Ted and George, and their escape to England. I only knew that they had somehow been smuggled out of Austria. My aunt was the only one in my family who offered me occasional firsthand accounts and personal memories. And even the dramatic, theatrical Litzi was generally silent on what she had witnessed and born. The few times she spoke about these events to me, she was sparing. I dared not pry. Yet the little snippets that would sometimes drip from her lips gripped my attention like nothing else could.

Once at her apartment in New York, she spoke about listening to the radio in Vienna the day that Hitler triumphantly rode into the city after the *anschluss*. His speech from the Heldenplatz in central Vienna had been broadcast and my aunt listened to the hypnotic voice bristle through the wireless in her home on Grossperlgasse. " I couldn't believe what I was hearing" she had told me." It was clear that he was a raving, hateful  madman, and still I felt this strange charisma. His voice was magnetic! I can never forget when he said—'the Jew is a dog, and must be destroyed'" Litzi,s voice became hollow and quiet as she continued" and this was followed by cheers. Thousands cheered this man's words" Litzi, like my mother had always loved Vienna. They were proud of their city. Now their world was lost. They were suddenly faced with doom. None of this would my mother ever talk about.

For the members of our group, enjoying the city was a much sim-pler proposition.  Everyone seemed thrilled by the impressive sights, the musical performances, and the city's undeniable charm.  The tour proved a success.  In fact, things proceeded so well, that I chose to lead a second tour of the Austrian capital three years later.  And once again, I felt deeply drawn to Vienna's beauty, its gracious pace of life, and its complex history.  A history that touches me personally, from Beethoven's music to my family's tragedy.

So much of my limited time there moved me.  Many visions visit me regularly.  The magnificence of the Stadtsoper provided a highlight for our entire group.  We heard Bizet's *Carmen* and Mozart's *Magic Flute*.  The performance of *Die Fledermaus*, my mother's favorite, at the Volksoper was simply splendid. The gaiety, sophistication, and buoyancy of Strauss's operetta was captured perfectly by the conductor, singers, and excellent orchestra. After this performance, a bunch of us went out to the Museum Café for a drink. I had read about the Museum Café in the memoirs of Elias Canetti, in which he describes his days spent in Vienna during the 1920s. We were all in a festive mood and a few friends egged me on to play the piano, which stood quietly at one end of the café. After hedging some, I gave in to my gathering desire to play something Viennese in this very Viennese setting. I walked over to the piano and played a few of the waltzes from *Fledermaus*; music I had lived with since I was an infant. It was music deep in my blood, passed to me through lineage. The patrons and waiters of the Museum Café produced a burst of applause when I finished. Walking back to our crowded table, I thought of my mother, and of Litzi, feeling very much a son of Vienna.

A visit to Schubert's boyhood house made an indelible impression. There is the simplicity and modesty of the dwelling on Nussdorfer-strasse, the rather drab appearance of the rooms, and then the original manuscripts of *Gretchen Am Spinnrade*, the *Wanderer Fantasy*, and other masterworks, framed and displayed on the walls. Here too sits the composer's piano.

But the artifact that shot straight to my heart was his eyeglasses, sitting unheralded in a small display box. In every drawing or painting of Schubert, one sees him bespectacled, and here I was in his old house, gazing at his personal spectacles. Yes, the composer of the *Unfinished* Symphony, and the *Death and the Maiden* string quartet wore eyeglasses. He handled them every day, put them aside, cleaned them, and peered through them. They sat on the bridge of his nose when he played through his piano sonatas and chamber works at the musical soirees known as *Schubertiades* in the 1820s. He wore them in joy and in grief. This small, intimate object dwarfed the piano in its importance. These tiny lenses reflected intimations of his hopes and dreams. These were the eyeglasses that aided him day after day as he jotted down his musical ideas, perfected his scores, and made his supremely lyrical art decipherable to posterity. Those eyeglasses, sitting unadorned in serene stillness, how they spoke to me!

I am a devoted Schubertian. He was the most Viennese of the truly great composers that lived there. For me, his music distills something of the cosmopolitan flavor of the Habsburg's capital in *Mittel Europa*. It is music that draws from both East and West. It captures some of the melancholy of the empire's Eastern peoples, and something of Hungarian spice and dash. It also captures the *Gemütlichkeit*, that special cozy Austrian charm. It sings with lyrical beauty and poignant, romantic wistfulness. It moves to a Viennese lilt, but also slows down to capture the dark hues of loneliness, despair, and tragedy. How this little, plump, pock-marked, bespectacled, poor man, who lived for a mere 31 years, almost all of it in Vienna, achieved this accomplishment is of course a wonder.

Near the end of my second visit to this city, six or seven of us attended a concert at the Musikverein, the famed concert hall which serves as the home to the Vienna Philharmonic. It was a concert designed to please tourists; not a so-called "serious program." Nonetheless, the group of musicians that comprised the ensemble that evening was first-rate. I went because I wanted to see the hall itself, and in the end was deeply impressed by the quality of the performance. A lesser known Mozart symphony was played with real love and care, and something more. That thought came back to me, "This really is the city of Mozart." When the symphony was finished, I looked at my friend and tour member Kimiko, sitting to my left. We exchanged knowing glances of approval. Then she said, "They have Mozart in the blood here." I had never heard a Mozart symphony phrased with such a natural feeling, inflection, and beauty in a live orchestral performance. At evening's end, the *Blue Danube Waltz* was played. It is one of the anthems of Vienna and it simply thrilled me. I have heard some belittle the music of Johann Strauss. And I have heard some describe Vienna as a city of artifice. I don't know the city well enough to analyze this opinion. Naturally most Viennese would rather speak with pride about Beethoven having made his home there than Hitler having done so. Many are surely uncomfortable recalling the hero's welcome the Führer received when he entered Vienna, after having annexed Austria in 1938; the act that sealed my grandparents' fate, and sent my mother and aunt to America, a fate which has led to my very existence. I am sure that Vienna has its share of haughty hypocrites, who point with vanity to the gracious cultivation of their city, with its unique artistic legacy, while willfully shielding their eyes from the sordid collapse of human decency that once befell their community. But does not hypocrisy exist in all societies? Hypocrisy is found everywhere and is always easy to point out.

In my own country there is an impressive Holocaust museum in Washington D.C. This is a good and fine thing. No one should forget, or be able to deny. But where is the expensive, shiny, gleaming museum dedicated to the genocidal decimation of Native Americans? I mean a museum analogous to the holocaust museum, focused exclusively on the tragedy that was visited on native peoples. Not an uplifting celebration of their now vanished world. Why is it not standing proudly and conspicuously among the great monuments and museums of our nation's capitol? After all, the holocaust was not perpetuated by America. But the destruction brought down upon the ancient tribes and nations of this land was: right here on American soil. Where are the exhibits that shine the spotlight on the cruel and rapacious policies of our government? Or the compassionate illumination of the terrible sufferings that millions of proud people were forced to bear? Where is the heartfelt admission of guilt and remorse for the countless atrocities? And oh yes, where on the national mall is the Slavery Museum?

As children we all learned the phrase "justice and liberty for all". Right from the beginning, this land proudly proclaimed "all men are created equal". Sure, hypocrisy exists everywhere, but I still believe in the promise of this country, and appreciate its virtues. It is not so easy to render judgment. A black man won a national election and now resides in the White House. And less than two decades after the Second World War, a Jew was elected president of Austria.

Vienna may cling to its grand and at times artificial façade, but it has its substance too. Yes—much like the United States of America, it has its substance and it has its greatness. That Mozart performance at the Musikverein was not artifice. It was no glitzy Las Vegas floorshow, no sugary Austrian whipped confection either. It was real art, played with a depth of understanding that seems to dwell naturally in this enigmatic city.

As for the Danube River, it isn't blue but rather more a shade of brown. None the less, the waltz with the misleading name has sent hearts soaring for over 140 years now. And not just those in Vienna, but hearts all over the world, from New York and London to Tokyo and Buenos Aires. Pseudo-intellectuals may dismiss Strauss, but no serious classical musician that I have ever known and respected has. Brahms and Mahler loved Johann Strauss. So have millions of others, from educated connoisseurs to regular music-loving citizens. I floated out of the Musikverin into the warm, lovely evening air riding the lift of this waltz.

If I could only see my mother now, I would say to her, "Mom, talk to me about Vienna. Tell me more about growing up there. You know, I've been to Vienna twice now, I have a lot to tell you." How I wish that talk could take place.

To me, Vienna is not just a beautiful European city. Not just a cultural jewel. Something of the grand sweep of its saga has laid claim on my soul. Vienna is a complex aggregate of light and dark. It stands as a symbol of humankind's wide potential of behavior. Like Schubert's music, it holds much grace and beauty. And too, as with Schubert, it holds a deep dark sadness. It is a city that has a hold on my heart and psyche as no other. As my mother Gretel used to say with such longing, "Ay Vienna, ach Wien, how I would like to see Vienna again." And always with love and melancholy in her voice.

# Reflections, May 2009

May has arrived and we are being graced with a lovely, idyllic day in Seattle. The indescribably beautiful Pacific Northwest spring is upon us. Blossoms are bursting forth all over this green city, and the air is fragrant with the sweet, rich, aroma unique to my lush, adopted hometown.

I find myself enjoying a coffee at a favorite neighborhood café, Peet's Coffee Shop on Green Lake, not far from my house. Moreover, I find myself in a state of reflection. Two days earlier, I played a piano recital of sonatas by Schubert and Beethoven. I was grateful for the wonderful nineteen twenty four rebuilt Steinway grand provided for this concert. It had that distinctive singing, focused, *old-world* tone that I so cherish in a special piano. I feel I played well. My concentration was good, and I played with all my heart.

The Beethoven was Opus 53 in C Major, the *Waldstein* sonata. How I love this sonata now! It's funny, but I resisted learning and playing this work for many years. It never quite captured my fancy until recently. I must thank Karin McCullough, my dear friend, piano student, and a fine pianist and teacher herself, for inspiring me to search more deeply into this much played masterpiece. Karin began studying this sonata with me about a year and a half ago. She threw herself into it with great fervor and I found all my prior reservations slowly melt away.

Only a few passages still struck me as unconvincing; one in particular, in the final movement, where the beautiful, lyrical main theme is heard above a trill and a very rapid ascending scale in the left hand. These bars continued to irk me. However, with deeper study and practice, this passage too became alive and meaningful to me.

The first movement had formerly sounded to me a bit like an étude. I'd heard performances of this movement with plenty of speed, fast fingerwork and rhythmic drive, but I failed to recognize the true voice of Beethoven. The fast fingerwork didn't move me, and was rarely played with real crispness. The secondary theme, comprising a series of simple steps with a chordal accompaniment, first stepping downward, and then back up again, never touched me. Now I have grown to love this simple theme, and the lovely way Beethoven embellishes it a few measures later. I now perceive the warmth in these notes; these very notes which once struck me as dry and uninspired.

The entire first movement is elegantly laid out and organized by a musical architect of the greatest intellect. And now that I have awakened from my slumber, I am alert to the powerful spirit that suffuses this grand cathedral.

But it is especially the long final movement that really takes my breath. It starts with a slow, serious, introspective introduction which builds to a sharp, intense, stabbing emotional state, before subsiding and giving way to the lyrical and noble main theme of the Rondo. This rondo is one of Beethoven's greatest. Its primary theme recurs several times in various guises; in different keys, in altered rhythms, in different registers, and with varying and ingenious accompaniments. Add to this the master architect's design of interspersing several contrasting musical episodes full of fire, drive, merriment, and tenderness. This is Beethoven the great improviser, the electrifying virtuoso who stunned his contemporaries with long piano improvisations, replete with wild mood swings and sublime, creative beauty. This rondo is much more than a perfectly erected edifice. It is the passionate, rhapsodic Beethoven set loose. Here, the great organizing intellect, and the unfettered rhapsodic soul of one of human history's greatest artists are united.

How could it have taken me so long to get the message? What changed?

Something in my perceptions must have changed. My eyes and ears were opened and I became receptive to the beauty and power of the *Waldstein* sonata. So my mind is mutable. Perceptions change. Tastes alter.

All life is flux, said Heraclitis, more than two thousand five hundred years ago. And each one of us is evolving always, right along with everyone and everything else in this perpetual dance of shifting rhythms and colors.

It's very satisfying to have this quiet respite at Peet's, on this fair, mild, late morning. The long relationship with Beethoven had translated into a successful performance in front of a receptive audience. Basking in the warm afterglow of this project, I find myself reflecting further on the nature of transience. I cannot help but muse on how I've changed as a teacher; how I enjoy it more fully now than ever before.

So much of one's pleasure in teaching, as in so many other activities, seems to be a matter of staying focused in the present moment. Being focused on the task at hand, being in the moment, unbesieged by distracting thoughts can  at times be difficult. Yet it is an invaluable asset to all of us, certainly to a piano teacher. I find that the more present I am, the more attentive, alert, and sympathetic to the human being present in my piano studio, the more helpful I can be, and the more pleasure I derive. The trick, it seems, is to remain patient and present. With this attitude and approach, I find that if a student makes a minimal good faith effort in practicing, has at least a smattering of ability, and brings a touch of enthusiasm, teaching the piano can be immensely satisfying, rewarding, and not least of all, great fun! Why shouldn't it be?

Being  attentive and respectful towards another person, to gain the trust of another person, to relate and often bond with another person, and to share one's love of music and of life itself with another person— this brings immeasurable joy.

While it has always been easy to enjoy the most talented and congenial students,  my ability to now appreciate a wider spectrum has broadened. Of the thirty or so pupils that I see each week, really only one is difficult to enjoy, due to a complete lack of motivation, and is probably not suitable for continuing much longer. With all the others, persons varying in age from five and a half years, to sixty years, and varying in musical aptitude, I can truly appreciate them all and gain satisfaction from our time shared together.

As with Beethoven's great C Major Sonata, it appears that a change in perception and attitude brought me to a greater appreciation of what already lay before me. The key to it all seems to be the ability to stay absorbed in the present moment.

Though this sounds easy enough, it is not so easily accomplished. Much can get in the way, such as one's own self-created expectations; "Why can't this child memorize more easily" one might wonder. Or one's own imagining of what should or should not be, such as the thought "he should practice more diligently", or "she should have mastered this rhythm by now, how exasperating that she can't play this passage correctly!"

The teacher may wish for things to be different than they are, or accept and work creatively and mindfully with things as they really are. One must perceive the difference between fantasy and reality. This in no way precludes a teacher from attempting to further inspire a student, insist on greater discipline, or if need be, dismiss a student altogether. Some students progress slower than others. Some are more talented, others less talented. But with patience and persistence, I have found myself repeatedly surprised by students who will suddenly find inspiration, become more mature and disciplined in their practicing, and make huge strides as pianists and musicians.

My student Matthew springs to mind. Matt, now twenty, has been my student since he was seven years old. For a long time, he made but minimal progress. He just didn't seem to take to the piano. Somehow, I failed to spot the musical aptitude that he in fact had, hidden away somewhere within him. He lacked discipline, but that is of course a common issue with children. I still remain somewhat stupefied that I couldn't better notice the basic musicality inherent in Matthew. Fortunately, Matt persevered. I didn't give up on him, and how glad I am today. His interest in music and piano playing has increased steadily, and by the time he turned seventeen he was becoming a real pianist. Suddenly, there was zeal where formerly there had been apathy. The Brahms g Minor Rhapsody was brought to life by Matthew's evolving technique. Matt was now learning challenging pieces with gusto. His facility on the keyboard became impressive.

Today, Matthew is twenty and continues to be my piano student. He works a job unrelated to music, but his love for music runs deep. He can't get enough of listening to great music, and he recently acquired a decent Yamaha grand piano for himself. Presently, he is doing a fine job with Bach's difficult c Minor Partita, no small accomplishment. He gravitates towards music that is a bit over his head, such as Prokofiev's Second Sonata, and the aforementioned partita. Though his Bach has some rough edges, he is getting close to a quite respectable performance. Matthew has amazed me. His overall development as a person seems to have mirrored his progress as a musician. He has grown into a wonderful young person. Playing the piano has surely been a great benefit.

Peet's is busy today. Looking up, I spot a friendly face. Nancy, like me, a frequent patron of this café, is coming towards me wearing a wide smile. Nancy is a sharp, engaging woman, perhaps fifteen years my senior. She attends many of my concerts. We exchange greetings and chat for a few minutes. She asks me how my writing is going. After some friendly banter I resume my reveries.

With insight, compassion comes of itself. And when the student senses that his teacher likes him, and has really taken a genuine interest in him, he will naturally respond better to the inevitable corrections and criticisms that rain down upon all those who have ever studied the piano.

One of every good teacher's main tasks is to motivate. We cannot just point out mistakes, complain about insufficient practice, and show displeasure. We must try to really reach the student, and connect with her. Sometimes with certain kindred spirits, this happens naturally and effortlessly. But in all cases, being present and focused will bring about greater insight and, in turn, greater empathy. Once the student feels acknowledged and respected, that makes everything easier. She will then be available to receive the balm of uplifting praise, as well as the sting of honest criticism. The teacher must have the freedom to be direct, and not feign approval over shoddy, lackluster playing. Praise rings hollow when not given sincerely. Children seem to know this more acutely than adults. You can't fool them.

It seems that much is possible with patience. *Ah* – how easily said. Patience is a virtue I have not always possessed in adequate supply. And patience is an indispensable ingredient that goes into the making of any good teacher. Impatience, conversely, is the pesky foe of mindful presence and equanimity. Alas, I have frequently been bedeviled by this nettlesome visitor. How often has my mind been invaded by turbulent impatience, and subsequently carried out to a sea of restlessness and distraction. How often has this particular piano teacher entertained thoughts such as "when will this lesson end? I want to get to my own practicing." or "when these lessons finish today, I have delightful plans for dinner with good friends. I can't wait." And other such variations.

But this is the theft of the present moment, a lost opportunity of being fully engaged and alive through teaching. With presence and patience, the natural proclivity for love and enjoyment emerges of itself. Then creativity is not merely probable, it is inevitable.

It isn't very hard for a teacher to slough through a lesson if he wants to. Suppose, sitting opposite nine-year old Will, due for his lesson later this afternoon, I ask him to play the d minor scale. Then as he begins playing, let's say I suddenly find my mind rebelling, refusing to focus on Will's scale. No longer fully present, the mind takes to wandering. Perhaps a disagreement I had with a friend may occupy my thinking. Perhaps I try to remember if I've paid a particular bill, or take to dreaming about the pretty woman with the long golden, blond hair and inviting smile who exchanged pleasant words with me right here at Peet's a few days ago. Maybe I just find myself wishing to be transported somewhere else; strolling along the Seine in Paris, examining the bouqinistes, or freely roaming the high, flower-strewn meadows of the Swiss Alps.

That is not what Will would want. It is assuredly not what his parents want. They aren't paying me for a stream of meandering reveries. Furthermore, this little scenario does not benefit me either. Being present at Will's piano lesson rewards us both. There really is nowhere else to be and no one else to be with. It really doesn't get much better than living presently, right here and now, performing my job with full alertness. The Swiss Alps can wait. Certainly dreaming about them can wait!

The remembrance that Lucas is on my schedule this evening brightens my mood. Lucas, a ten-year old, is a wonderful boy, a fine piano student, and happens to be enamored with baseball, much as his teacher was at a similar age.

On nice days, and when time permits, we play catch out in front of my house. He loves it, and optimistically brings along his baseball glove to most of our lessons. I'm impressed with his athletic prowess. He really whips that ball to me with quickness and force. He deftly fields ground balls and high flys with agility. I wonder how I might have stacked up to him back in the day when I was a ten-year old ball player. I wonder, was I as good as Lucas? Our occasional lively games of catch have helped Lucas to bond with me. I think it's helped to keep him moving forward as a pianist. It really is a fine thing to love both baseball and Beethoven.

I sometimes wonder what people mean when they speak of "my time". What does it mean when someone says "I worked hard at my job all day, now it's time for *me*, it's *my* time now?"

When I am in the midst of showing a nine year-old how to count a rhythm properly, or writing in a fingering of a Mozart sonata, or quizzing a six year-old on the notes, is that "my time?" or speaking French with my student Selene, or asking six year-old Sana how many teeth she's lost since last week, and sharing a smile over her eagerness to show me her newest loose tooth. Is that my time? Is zealously attacking a Chopin polonaise, or pulling weeds in the garden "my time"?– or is washing the dishes my time? Or conversing, debating, and laughing with friends? Or being swept up in a love affair?

Is helping a child with homework "my time", or looking after an infirm relative or friend? Or is it swimming, skiing, or watching a film, or perhaps reading a book? Could it be throwing the ball around with

Lucas? Is noticing the sound of the wind as it rustles through the leaves what people mean by "my time"? Or just maybe, is sitting and contemplating this question at Peet's coffee shop on this lovely, spring morning a good example of "my time."

I stop and take a sip of my coffee, and gaze out the window at the lake. The surrounding verdant park presents a scene of people out walking, friends talking, mothers with babies in strollers, lovers hand in hand, joggers, cyclists, rollerbladers, volleyball games in progress, and a few kayaks, canoes, and paddle boats out on the lake. It makes for a picturesque tableau.

A final sip of coffee and it's time to go home. There are lessons to give. Elle, Philip, Will, Vivika, Iona, Julien, William, and Lucas are coming, and they will want their teacher to be present for them today.

Aya Griswald

Henry Chen

Iona Hillman

nina hillman

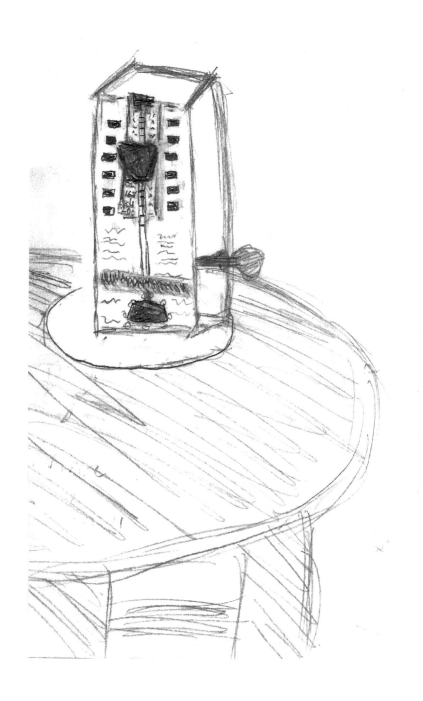

Sana Mills

Yurina Tamura

Zhemin Shao

# Mozart on the Lower East Side

During the last few years that I lived in New York, I joined with a few good friends in playing concerts around town for people who would otherwise not have a chance to hear live classical music. We were a youthful, and I suppose you could say idealistic bunch, and we performed in hospitals, nursing homes, retirement homes, senior centers, churches, and schools. I played solo programs as well as collaborative ones, and was fortunate to have worked with some remarkable colleagues.

Among them was a very fine mezzo-soprano by the name of Mercedes Alicea. Mercedes was about ten years older than me, had grown up in Puerto Rico, studied voice as a young woman in Europe, and had performed there, both in opera and in recital. She had settled in New York, and we met at the Brooklyn Conservatory of Music, where we were both members of the faculty.

Mercedes was a strong, stout, solidly built woman. She had light brown skin, short dark hair, and a face that often wore a stern, serious look, but could break into the sunniest of smiles at any moment, revealing a warm heart. Mercedes was a religious woman, a devout Catholic, and a spiritual seeker who kept an open mind to different paths and traditions. The two of us shared searching conversations on the questions of finding purpose, joy, and peace.

She was particularly drawn to the mystery of St. Francis of Assisi, and introduced me to the book "The Little Flowers of St. Francis" which chronicles stories of the saint. I was also drawn to St. Francis, known as he is as the patron saint of animals, and for his inclusive view of the sun, the moon, and all of nature, in his experience of the infinite.

Mercedes believed in the path of service to others and the idea of giving concerts in nursing homes and hospitals was right up her alley. And she was good at it. Besides being a wonderful singer, she exuded warmth when greeting and mixing with people in the audience.

Musically, my most memorable occasion with her was a performance of Schumann's song cycle *Frauenliebe und Leben* that we gave together at the conservatory in Brooklyn. She sang the eight Schumann songs with focused intensity and beautiful vocal control, and I felt in total harmony with her at the keyboard, from the opening motif set in the piano, to the touching coda, again in the piano, recalling the cycle's opening notes.

Overall, however, the most memorable of our performances together came one autumn morning at a small nursing home in Manhattan's Lower East side. We met there to give a short Mozart program for the residents. Upon arriving, I quickly noticed that most of the people were not only elderly and disabled, but a great many seemed to be severely senile or in various stages of dementia. I wondered if our concert would be of any worth to anyone there. We had prepared a program of three or four Mozart songs, two arias from opera, and I was to play the Rondo in D Major, and one of his piano sonatas. There was an audience of maybe 30 residents, most of them in wheelchairs. They appeared an unlikely group to show alert receptivity to Mozart.

Mercedes said to me, "We will make music with our hearts Fred, and Mozart's spirit will penetrate the hearts of some of these people." She smiled her genuine, almost childlike smile. Then she closed her eyes, and very softly prayed to herself in Spanish. I was impressed with her serious commitment to a concert of this kind. She honored and respected this small captive audience, some of whom appeared to be barely conscious. And she took her responsibility as a singer and performer seriously. I felt happy to be there with her that morning.

We mounted the small stage and I took my seat at the console piano which fortunately happened to be quite respectable, and had been recently tuned. I looked out at our little audience as Mercedes made some introductory remarks. I still remember how old, how ancient, even ghostly they appeared. An eerie stillness seemed to pervade the room.

We began with one of Mozart's little known songs *Ridente la Calma*, very light and accessible music. Mercedes sang beautifully and the music rolled out like a gentle tide towards our listeners. Something inside me felt right. There were no distracting sounds emanating from the audience; no coughs, no candy wrappers being unfolded, no talking, no fidgeting. At worst our audience was impassively listless, simply in a dull stupor, unaware of the music. At best they were really attentive, engaged in the flow of notes coming from the stage. I sensed the latter. It's hard to explain, but a performer can usually sense when an audience is with him. It's a magical feeling, because it means the goal of communicating something beautiful, as is the case with great music, is succeeding. Sharing music, whether as a performer or as a listener, is a form of communion. I began to feel this magical communion was starting to happen this particular autumn morning in this small, barely noticed nursing home, tucked away in the jumble of concrete, bricks, and pavement, of lower Manhattan

After completing the second song, we performed Cherubino's aria *Voi che sapete* from the *Marriage of Figaro*. This aria has a pure, lovely tune. It is at once charming and sublime, the type of melody that only Mozart seemed to be capable of tossing effortlessly out of his sleeve. It has a simple guitar-like accompaniment which the pianist plays in the orchestral transcription. As I knew this piece so well, I didn't need to read the music on the music stand. Hence, I could steal a leisurely glance at our audience. The image of what I beheld has remained in my memory like a snapshot.

Old wrinkled faces were looking up at us wearing attentive expressions full of wonder. Toes, encased in sturdy black orthopedics, were gently tapping in time to the music. There were heads slightly swaying along to Cherubino's song. And the eyes! Those aged eyes, which had looked upon so much of life, appeared so round and large to me. They seemed to glow with some mysterious, inscrutable intensity as they fixed upon Mercedes and me. I had never seen such eyes as I saw that morning.

These people may have been mentally incoherent and confused, but they weren't dead. They were alive! In fact the whole room seemed to be filled with a kind of mystical, living, breathing energy; an energy that felt quaint, and antique, as if from another time. Indeed, many if not most of these elderly men and women, had been born in the final years of the 19th century. It is hard to explain this palpable atmosphere of a time lost that hovered over us.

Whatever was happening, I knew that the music was being heard and absorbed. Mozart was winning the day! The remainder of the concert is a blur to me. I know I played the rondo with joy and certainty that people were with me, along for the ride. The piano sonata and the final songs and arias with Mercedes sailed by merrily. All along I felt transported by the unique experience of this singular concert; this singular audience, this particular time and place, this peculiarly lovely extended moment– all unnoticed, ignored, and of no importance to the busy, bustling world outside.

After the concert, Mercedes and I visited and chatted with the residents of the nursing home. Mercedes beamed effusively and hugged several people, appropriately careful not to crush the feeblest of them. I too enjoyed making the rounds, greeting people.

Several people smiled at me, but a good many were non-verbal. What stands out most in my memory is being approached by two ladies. They seemed to be very close, perhaps best friends. One woman did all the talking, the other said not a word, but appeared totally involved and supportive of what her companion had to say. "Listen," began the loquacious one. "We've been talking, my friend and I." At this her friend nodded in agreement. "We've been talking and we think you play the piano so well. But listen, we think you have to keep on practicing." The silent one nodded again, with a look of complete agreement and total absorption on her old face. "We want you to keep practicing the piano, and don't let anything stand in your way," the speaker continued. "Just you keep right on practicing and playing piano and we're sure, my friend and I," and here the two elderly friends exchanged knowing glances, "we're sure you will persevere. We both just know that you can do it! That you can succeed!" Now her friend nodded her head more vigorously. "We are certain that if you keep on practicing, no matter what happens, that if you just keep on practicing," and now with even greater urgency in her voice, she built a crescendo that drove towards its climax. "We just know you can do it! And you will do it! We just know you can, and we feel sure that you will— so long as you just keep on practicing, the two of us know, we are absolutely certain, that you can—and you will—become president of the United States!" The two ladies looked at each other triumphantly, and then both looked at me beaming with confidence.

That was the first time in my life that I had been encouraged to run for president. It has thus far been the only time. I did take their advice though; I continued to keep on practicing.

It had turned out to be a special morning. I had had the privilege of making music with Mercedes, of sharing Mozart with old souls, and of brushing against an aura tinged with old world charm; of breathing the perfumed air of a now-vanished era.

Mercedes had been right. The music that we performed with our hearts did indeed penetrate at least some members of our audience. Though befuddled in mind, people's hearts were not confused. Mozart's arrow had struck its mark.


I played the piano in many a New York City neighborhood. New York is probably the most ethnically-diverse city in the world. It contains extreme variety in its neighborhoods, and its people represent every economic class, lifestyle, and range of values. I learned from these forays into the many districts how complex a city it really is. I learned for example, that there's no such thing as the "Jewish community" or the "Black community."

When I hear the term Jewish community, I wonder which Jewish community is being referred to. There's the group of old immigrants from Eastern Europe, mostly Poland, which I once played Chopin for on the Lower East Side. There's the community of Hasidic Orthodox Jews in Brooklyn's Williamsburg district, and other such pockets throughout the city. There are the middle-class, well-educated Jews on the Upper West Side, often tending to intellectual pursuits, and valuing the arts.

Traditionally, many of these lean politically to the left, and have been staunch supporters of the civil rights movement. Often they are outspoken critics of American foreign policy, and some are even stridently opposed to Israeli foreign policy.

Then too, there are those like my Uncle Ted in Queens' Forest Hills neighborhood. Ted, an industrious businessman is fiercely loyal to Israel and has little patience for those he refers to as 'peaceniks.' "Freddy, trust me, it's naïve to think that letting down your guard will bring peace," he's told me. He enthusiastically backed Reagan's military buildup. He's always seemed hawkish to me.

Ted had been brought face to face with unimaginable cruelty by the age of fourteen. He escaped from Nazi Austria by the skin of his teeth, getting safely to England, but losing both his parents and many of his boyhood friends. My uncle is a hard working, fair minded, good guy. I really like him. He sees certain political issues differently than I do. He has more than earned a right to his views.

There are Jews like my parents and my aunt Litzi, who having survived the Holocaust, show empathy and solidarity to other victims of oppression and racism. For others, like my uncle, the lesson learned from his traumatic ordeal seems to be, "Why do they hate us?" "We must be strong," and "Never again;" an us-against-the-world mentality.

Now the father of a Jewish friend at college was something else; a virulent racist. A profusion of racial invectives poured from his lips. I had never heard anything like it growing up. I never could feel comfortable around Sam.

The suburbs in New Jersey where I grew up had no single Jewish community. There were secular Jews who were politically progressive, secular Jews who were politically conservative, religious Orthodox Jews, Jews who study Buddhism and practice meditation. There were the crass, pushy, brazen businessmen. There were honest, upstanding, ethical businessmen. There were scientists, stockbrokers, doctors, teachers, shopkeepers, lawyers, scholars, business-owners, rabbis, and more. And these were just the Jews in the New York metropolitan area! The term "Jewish community" is meaningless to me.

Playing piano in several African-American neighborhoods in New York showed me that the term "black community" is similarly simplistic and misleading. I have some memorable experiences from my visits to both Harlem and Bedford-Stuyvesant. I will relate a few of them here.

Setting out for Harlem the first time, I admit to having felt some trepidation. People had told me it wasn't safe. So it was with a mixture of caution and an optimistic sense of adventure that I boarded the uptown bus in my neighborhood on Manhattan's Upper West Side. It was winter, and all of us on the bus were clad in an array of winter coats, down jackets, wool caps, scarves, and gloves. As the bus proceeded uptown, winding its way through the bustling city streets, the white faces on board dwindled away, and the brown and black faces increased steadily. When the bus rolled through Lennox Avenue in the heart of Harlem, and as I buzzed the driver for my stop, I couldn't fail to notice that I was the only white person in the bus. "Don't go to Harlem, it's dangerous for a white guy." The words I had heard spoken so often, almost always by white folks, who had never actually visited Harlem, rang in my inner ear. Harlem didn't feel at all ominous when I stepped onto its sidewalks. This was the first time that I had presented the only white face amidst a sea of darker-hued ones. This new circumstance was one that I adapted to quickly. These dark-skinned New Yorkers produced a most familiar sight; the sight of people going about their business in a large, dense city. Moreover, I felt a vibrant, positive and welcoming energy emanating up from the street.

It happened to be a beautiful winter day, cold but with bright sunshine and clear blue skies. There was a general cheeriness in the atmosphere, or so was my perception. I walked briskly in the crisp, winter air towards the senior citizen community center where I was expected to play the piano. "Wow here I am, right in the heart of Harlem," was the thought that filled my mind. New York's famous "black" neighborhood presented me with two distinct images. One was the comfortable, homey milieu of well-maintained apartment buildings, shops, businesses, and that convivial big city buzz of people out and about. But amidst the reassuring, impressive buildings and shops stood the abandoned, desolate, often gutted buildings. Sometimes a quite impressive, fine-looking old apartment building, stood next to a wreck of a building that looked as though it had been torn apart by an air raid.

Arriving at the community center where I was expected, I was given an extremely warm greeting by the director of activities, a rather large woman with a lovely countenance. "Mr. Kronacher, we're so happy to have you here this afternoon. We've had the piano tuned just yesterday. Let me show it to you." She smiled and proudly led me into a large room where sat a nice grand piano. I felt so welcome and full of positive energy as I ran my fingers over the beautifully-tuned keys. It was just then that I made the distressing discovery that this piano lacked a damper pedal. It was simply missing. It wasn't there at all!

As anyone who plays the piano knows, the damper pedal is a necessity to a pianist in almost every type of music. My hostess looked mortified when I said, "But there's no pedal." I hated to have to explain to this gracious woman that the pedal is extremely important. "Well, anyhow, it's not your fault," I told her. "I'll find a way to play something; we'll make the best of it." Then I added, "The piano is certainly in tune."

Alas, what a dilemma! I decided to change the program and play as much Bach and Mozart as was in my memory. These composers, especially Bach, require less pedal than others. In the case of Bach, the pieces can be executed without any pedaling. So it was out with Schumann, Brahms, and Debussy, and in with Bach. One thing that I did try to play however, and I still wonder at what in the world I was thinking, is the Beethoven *Pathetique* Sonata. Somehow, with some spur of the moment fingering changes, I actually meandered through the beautiful adagio second movement. I guess the challenge of trying to make it as legato as possible without the use of the pedal appealed to me.

An audience of 40 to 50 people from the neighborhood gave me a lovely welcome and warm support. To this day, I still don't know how I made it through that second movement. I have played quite an assortment of pianos over the years, from the sublime to the wretched, and all levels in between. But this was the only time I tried to perform a program on a piano without a *sostenuto* pedal. It was an experience and makes for a story, but I still wish I could have played for those nice folks on a piano with a proper pedal.

On the walk back to the subway, I ran into some unpleasantness. A group of five or six older teenage boys noticed my presence and began yelling out threats. "Hey honkey, what cha doin' here? You lost whitey? Don't be walkin' on my street!" I decided to abandon my route, which would have taken me directly into their midst on the sidewalk. I found an alternate street to the subway stop. That was the only unfortunate incident of its kind that I encountered on my several visits to New York's African-American neighborhoods.

Perhaps a month later, my friends Robert, Hae-Kyoung, and I were back in Harlem, to play the B-flat Major Trio by Schubert, this time at a different community center.

Robert Tennen and Hae-Kyoung Kim were friends and marvelous musicians; Robert a cellist, Hae-Kyoung a violinist. Both were graduates of Juilliard and extremely gifted musicians. I always felt honored to play with them. We journeyed to Harlem together to perform as volunteer musicians.

The audience we played for that fine afternoon was unlike any other audience we had ever played for before. They were demonstrative and ebullient to the extreme. We hadn't gotten more than several measures into Schubert's B-flat Major Trio, when a woman shouted, quite *fortissimo*, "Praise the Lord!" Another strong voice shortly followed in exaltation with, "Oh Lord, this is sweet!" Then another, "Praise the Lord!" rang out in jubilation. These people may not have been schooled in classical concert etiquette, but they were clearly receptive to Schubert! The three of us were somewhat taken aback by the "Praise the Lord," "Oh Lordy", or "Play that music honey," and other similar cries, all filled with real emotion, that intermittently pierced the air, joining the melodies, harmonies, and rhythms of Schubert's trio. We played the entire four-movement work, over 40 minutes of music, urged on by a most-supportive and full-throated group of music lovers. Hae-Kyoung and Robert didn't miss a beat, and the three of us felt appreciative of this unique interaction, with these vibrant, loving, musical men and women.

I suppose in one sense, this audience could be considered musically "unsophisticated." They hadn't been taught to withhold applause until the end of a piece of classical music. Yet, in a very deep sense, they were as sophisticated as can be; keenly present, riding the music's waves, sensitive to the melodic sweetness, rhythmic drive, and harmonic momentum of beautiful music.

Schubert composed this trio for piano, violin, and cello in Vienna, at the age of 31, in 1828, his last year of life. It sure seemed to strike sparks up in Harlem, New York City, 1983.

After the music, we had the pleasure of mixing with some members of our spirited audience. One appreciative woman was blind, and her friend lamented, "Gladys, oh how I wish you could have seen it." "I heard it honey, I heard it, and Lord it was sweet!" "I know you heard it, but I still wish you could have seen it," she continued. "Good Lord," she pointed at me. "Can this man *rip* apart a piano!" She put special emphasis on the word *rip*. Although ripping apart a piano and the music of Franz Schubert seem incongruous to me, I decided to take her statement as a compliment. Hae-Kyoung and Robert were regaled with similar exuberance.

Not more than a few weeks later, I met up with my friend Mercedes, and we took the subway to Brooklyn's Bedford-Stuyvesant, another black neighborhood. This time, our concert was to be held in the evening, and it was dark when we got off the subway in Brooklyn. The cheeriness of Harlem by daylight that I had experienced a few weeks back was noticeably absent. The streets were deserted. We were clearly in a financially-distressed neighborhood. A number of the buildings appeared uncared for. The overall atmosphere was grim, even ominous. We walked purposefully towards the Seventh Day Adventist church where our concert had been scheduled.

When we arrived, and stepped inside the church, the whole world seemed to change. The place was aglow with light and energy. The main sanctuary was packed with over 300 immaculately-dressed residents of the neighborhood. All the women wore lovely dresses and all the men wore suits. The children too were arrayed in their Sunday best. One could feel the anticipation and excitement in the air. So many people were smiling, exchanging greetings and embraces with each other, and radiating a joyful glow. What a striking juxtaposition it was, after walking the dark, depressing, surrounding blocks from the subway. How strange it seemed that here in the depths of depressing urban blight, I should find myself engulfed by so many beautiful happy faces!

I spotted one of my piano students from the Brooklyn Conservatory, Jelaine Bailey, a wonderful girl of 13 years, with her family. "Hi Mr. Kronacher," she called to me. "Look Jelaine, your teacher is here," added Mrs. Bailey smiling broadly. I waved and smiled, noticing how well-dressed they were, and how happy and vibrant they appeared. I can't remember ever having been surrounded by such a joyous, radiant energy in the more affluent, orderly suburbs of New Jersey, where I had spent my childhood.

The program itself combined songs and operatic arias with solo piano pieces. I don't recall all the exact works, but I'm sure my solos included some Scarlatti and some Chopin. Our elegantly-clad auditors interrupted not a single phrase of music, nor did they ever make the faux pas of applauding between movements. Their applause was effusive when it came, though it lacked a single voice raised in exaltation proclaiming, "Praise the Lord." We received our share of compliments and gracious words of appreciation. But no one suggested that I had ripped apart a piano.

After the concert, I tried my best to explain to one graying, distinguished older gentleman, why I didn't choose to end the Scarlatti f Minor Sonata on a major chord, when he assured me it would have been a permissible and satisfying choice. I later came to learn that this church had a strong respect for classical music, and that all the parishioners were instructed in the rudimentary knowledge of music. I wish I could have played all the time for such an inspiring group of people. This "community" of people, if it can be called such, exuded pride, joy, and dignity. Mercedes and I made the walk through the bleak, empty streets back to the subway with fresh optimism in our hearts. Being with this group of black Brooklyn citizens had been no less than elevating. But it had also been rewarding to play for the good folks in Harlem, whose musical education had been less formal.

Later that same winter, I made a couple of trips to play on the Lower East Side for audiences comprising primarily Eastern European, Jewish, senior citizens. Most of them had grown up with classical music, and many of them had a good measure of respect, and in some cases genuine passion for the classical canon.

One evening, I gave a program of Chopin for a very attentive group of ladies and gentlemen, who whispered encouraging comments in Yiddish between selections. "Er spielt gut," "Ja, ich liebe Chopin," and other such phrases caught my ear. Although I did not speak Yiddish at all, and my German at that time was also quite limited, these simple phrases I could recognize from having heard my mother and Litzi exchange similar pronouncements.

After the recital, these old Jewish New Yorkers, many of whom had been born in the old country, asked me if I would accompany two of the ladies who wished to perform a Yiddish song or two. I accepted, took my seat at the piano, and then bore witness to a comical drama which unfolded presently. A microphone was placed in front of the piano. A woman abruptly rose and strode quickly towards the piano. She must have easily been 80 years old. Grabbing the microphone resolutely, and turning imperiously to face the assembly, she proclaimed boldly, "I'll sing first!"

"Oh no you won't! Not this time! You always go first!" came a sharp retort from another stentorian voiced woman of similar vintage, rising from her chair. "My wife is right, Mrs. Leschetitzky always goes first," the husband of the second contestant to declare an intention to sing had now joined the fray. "Mrs. Charinsky, sit down and stop kvetching, you'll get your turn. I'm ready to sing now," declared Mrs. Leschetitzky defiantly.

She then nodded to me to indicate the music should commence. I
held off from playing the introductory chords, as I could see
Mrs. Charinsky charging forward at full bore. She grabbed at the microphone and screamed, "Give me that microphone; I'm not letting you
sing first tonight! You have some chutzpah! Who do you think you are,
the Queen of Sheba?"

Mrs. Leschetitzky had an impressive grip on the microphone,
and she held on tightly, defending her spot in the bend of the piano,
with the strength of a lion. "How dare you attack me like this! You
meshuga, get back!" I continued to watch with amazement as the fracas
was quickly joined by the two vocalists' husbands. Insults were hurled
about with vitriol, and the grappling over the much prized microphone
continued amidst a swelling chorus of complaints from the general
assembly. I had the feeling that most of those present had become
accustomed to such histrionics. One old gentleman was heard to grouse,
"For God's sake, why do they always have to fight like this?"

To the best of my recollection, no serious punches were landed, no
blood was spilled, and no injuries incurred. Some of the spectators
expressed their displeasure with calls for peace. "Enough already!" A
few others took sides, voicing their judgments over who was more entitled to sing first.

In the end, peace was finally restored, and Mrs. Leschetitzky's tenac-
ity proved insurmountable. She sang first. And how she sang! With
voluminous, poignant tones, she delivered a piercingly beautiful performance of Yiddish song. Anguish, as well as fervent hope, resonated
in her powerful old voice. Everyone was moved, including the young
piano accompanist.

A still smarting, grim-faced Mrs. Charinsky followed her rival to
the stage. She was not about to be outdone. Another achingly beautiful
Yiddish song was sung with vocal skill and unabashed ardor. These two
cantankerous octogenarians sang with great soul! A rapt audience of old
Jews listened and understood. They understood the sense of tragedy,
of loss, and of prayerful hope reflected in these songs, and in these two
very personal heartfelt renditions.

In the early spring of 1984, Mercedes told me that she had a friend named Francesca, a very fine soprano, who wondered if I'd accompany her in a program of Italian operatic arias for a community center, located in an Italian community somewhere in Brooklyn. I agreed, imagining a musical group of opera-loving Italians as our auditors. After all, Italians love music generally, and even those who don't go for Bach or Brahms surely embrace Rossini, Verdi, and Puccini. Or so at least, I faithfully assumed.

I thought fondly of performances I had attended at the Metropolitan Opera House of Italian works like *Rigoletto* and *Tosca*, which drew loyal support from the large Italian community in New York and its environs. And it wasn't just the intelligentsia; the scholar who could quote Dante in Italian, or recite Virgil in Latin, that would erupt in bravos after Pavarotti finished the aria, *E lucevan le stelle* in the Tosca I once heard. It was the Italian-American police officer, or Macy's salesclerk, or cab driver as well, raining bravos down on the celebrated tenor.

At intermission one could listen to beautifully-spoken Italian as well as a rich variety of dialect, from Venetian to Sicilian. And of course, English New York-style, be it Brooklyn-ese or Bronx-ese. And yes, there were those of us present who weren't even Italian. As for myself, I felt a great kinship with these musical, passionate people. All of us in the opera house were brought together in love for this dramatic, melodic art. We all reveled in the glories of soaring melodies, emanating from the well-trained voices of the virtuosi of the stage. Everyone was invited into the rich operatic pageantry. If it was Joan Sutherland or Roberta Peters singing Violetta from Verdi's *Traviata*, instead of an Italian diva like Renata Scotto, it was okay. The art of Italian opera held room for all. We could all be Italian. This art form had shown itself to be universal.

Francesca and I rendezvous-ed in her Brooklyn neighborhood. I felt sanguine walking to our appointed hour of Italian songs and arias. Passing by an inviting old world pasticceria with cannolis, éclairs, and cookies beckoning through the glass only furthered my optimism.

Attaining our destination, we were shown into a rather drab, color-less room, in which sat a smattering of maybe 30 people. Most were clustered around five or six card tables. Some card games were in progress. A few were just sitting quietly with a cup of coffee or a soft drink set in front of them.

A piano was wheeled into a central position in front of this listless-looking entourage. The vital Italian "la vita e bella" atmosphere I had so looked forward to basking in, was nowhere to be found. "They'll put away their cards and come to life when they hear Francesca sing Verdi," I assured myself.

We started with a lovely Italian art song by a Baroque composer. It failed to make a dent in the general torpor that hung heavy in the air. Next an aria by Rossini managed to cause a few people to at least put down their cards and pay a little bit of attention, but no inspiration manifested itself. Where was that sunny *"vivace con brio"* enthusiasm I had been so drawn to at the opera? Clearly not at this gathering of tough, languid, Italian New Yorkers. When Verdi's aria *Sempre Libera* from *La Traviata* only barely stirred them, I was ready to leave. Francesca leaned over towards me and said, "Fred, forget the arias, it's no use. We'll do *O Sole Mio* and *Santa Lucia*. That, they'll like. Trust me, I know this crowd."

Francesca then announced, "Next, I will sing "O Sole Mio." Applause followed. Cards were set aside and people's faces began to brighten. Well, *O Sole Mio* was a big hit with these folks. "I told you," Francesca said with a resigned look. Next came *Santa Lucia*; more applause, more approval. So we got some life out of our audience after all. But I felt disappointed. I love Italian folksongs like *O Sole Mio*, but my expectations of presenting Rossini, Verdi, and Puccini to a receptive Italian audience had not been met.

I had an old friend in New York named Frank Caldiero. He was 62 and I was 22 when we became friends at the Manhattan School of Music, where I was a piano student, and he was a professor of humanities. We used to meet once a week at the Chock-Full-O'-Nuts coffee shop across from Columbia University at 116th Street and Broadway. We would talk about life, music, literature, politics, sports, women, philosophy, religion; everything. He had emigrated from Sicily when he was seven years old. He once conveyed to me the sentiment that "there are

Italians, and then there are Italians." Frank Caldiero, in certain respects, was a tough, crusty, jaded New Yorker, and his exact quote was, "Fred, there are Italians and there are wops." I remember my uneasiness at hearing the use of the derogatory ethnic slur, and I responded, "Caldi," he let me call him by his nickname, "Caldi, what about you, are you a wop or an Italian?" He put down his cup of coffee, looked at me steadily and said, "I'm an Italian."

I find such classifications simplistic and distasteful. People are more complex than that. Playing music for people of various backgrounds, temperaments, and tastes, has taught me to look more deeply.

One time, Hae-Kyoung, Robert, and I visited the New York University Hospital for patients recovering from disabling injuries. Many were recovering from serious car accidents, and a majority were in wheelchairs. We were poised to begin playing Beethoven's Trio, Opus 11, in B-Flat, when a grizzled, disheveled, leathery-faced fellow shouted from his wheelchair in an angry rasp, "Can't anybody here play some goddamned Irish music?!" "I can," I shot back. I looked at Hae-Kyoung and Robert and asked their permission. "Let me play a song for this guy. It will only take a minute." Then I played *When Irish Eyes Are Smiling*. I played it as tenderly and as lovingly as I could. I remember distinctly having played it in the key of G-flat.

This gruff, surly, hard-bitten man broke down and wept. "Thank you, thank you, you're a good lad," he muttered through his sniffles, while wiping the tears away. "God bless you," he added gently. The three of us then got down to business and Beethoven's trio was rendered.

Music is a communicative art. It can touch people, sometimes profoundly. I hope our sincere offering of Beethoven touched people in an uplifting, positive manner that afternoon at the NYU clinic. To what extent we may have succeeded, I'll never know for sure. But *ah*—that Irish song, played spur of the moment, in G-flat Major, *that*, I'm certain, touched deep inside, at least one human heart.

# ZHEMIN

Zhemin is a quiet boy. He doesn't say a lot during piano lessons. Zhemin says a lot through his music though. This 10-year old student is becoming an excellent pianist. Today, I tell him that I'm writing a book, and would like to include him in it. "May I interview you?" I ask. Zhemin smiles and softly responds, "Okay." Zhemin's father Bohai, who brings his son to my home each Saturday morning, looks up attentively.

Zhemin has been my student for three years. Rie, the mother of my students Nina and Iona, had recommended me to Bohai. She also recommended Zhemin to me, telling me, "Zhemin is very smart, very very bright. I think he might be the smartest one in Iona's class. You should teach him!"

"Zhemin, where were you born?" I ask. "China," he answers. "How old were you when you came to Seattle?" He hesitates, unsure of the precise answer and casts a glance towards his dad. "Two and a half," comes the answer from Bohai. Zhemin wears a bemused little smile on his face, and assumes an air of lively alertness. He seems to be flattered by the interest I'm showing in him. "Tell me some of the things you really like." His smile remains in place, but no answer is readily brought forth. Finally he speaks, "Piano." A good answer! His father chuckles and assures me, "Zhemin really has a strong interest in the piano; it's one of the things he most enjoys."

"What else, Zhemin?" He looks at me directly, still with a smile, but no words come to him. "Do you have a favorite subject at school?" "Math," he answers with no hesitation. Zhemin doesn't pad his responses with unnecessary verbiage. He favors one-word answers. "Zhemin is very good at math," adds Bohai, the more voluminous speaker of the two. Rie has told me that Zhemin is a math genius. "I bet math comes easily to you." Zhemin says nothing but Bohai jumps in and tells me, "The math at school is much too easy for my son. My wife and I help him to learn more advanced math when he asks us questions." I don't feel Bohai is bragging, nor do I sense that he is an overly pushy parent. He is just filling in the gaps that his laconic son withholds from the interview. Bohai is a bio- chemist and his wife is a computer scientist. They both received their education in China and have been living in the United States for eight years now.

"What else, Zhemin?" I continue my interrogation, "What else do you like?" No response—"Do you have a favorite sport?" I venture. "Soccer," is his succinct and efficient response. "Soccer is a good game, isn't it?" I muse. "How about baseball, do you like baseball?" "No," is his unequivocal answer. Oh well, I won't hold that against him. "He's never really tried baseball," offers Bohai.

Though Zhemin hasn't spoken a full sentence yet during our little interview, he is not showing the least bit sign of boredom. His eyes beam brightly, his demeanor happy, his mind focused. "What else, Zhemin?" –His gaze remains fixed on me, but no answer is forthcoming. "What about chess?" I know full well that Zhemin excels in chess. He's won just about every tournament he's ever been entered in. "You like chess, don't you?" "Yeah," he answers modestly. "What else do you like Zhemin?" I persist. "He likes to read," it is Bohai's voice now bringing me this information. "You do?" I keep my focus on my piano student. "What type of books do you like to read?" He thinks for a few seconds then responds, "Fantasy." His smile becomes a bit wider after telling me this.

"Not just reading," Bohai jumps back in, "but my son has just written a book." "Really!" I exclaim. Zhemin's smile becomes even wider. "You've written a book?" "Yeah," my interlocutor quietly replies. "What's it about?" –No response. "What type of book is it?" "Fantasy," he tells me, coming close now to a real laugh. "He is going to have it published," Bohai's voice again asserts itself. So, it seems Zhemin is a young man of letters, even if not of flowery, lavish oratory.

I turn to Bohai and gently say, "Bohai, I'm not interviewing you. I'm interviewing Zhemin." Bohai chuckles. Soon I glean the knowledge that Zhemin's book will be self-published and comprises exactly 188 pages.

"Zhemin, what do you want to do when you grow up? What work do you think you'd like to do?" Zhemin does not hesitate at all in answering this question. "Lawyer." He says the word lawyer forcefully and appears the most surefooted he has in the entire interview. "Lawyer?" I exclaim incredulously. Bohai is laughing now and says to me, "I don't think Zhemin will be a lawyer," he adds, "he doesn't want to be a biochemist or a computer scientist because that's what we do." I look at Zhemin who continues to appear amused and content, and say, "Really? A lawyer? Why?" His eyes stay focused on mine, but he says nothing. I tell him that a lawyer needs to be good at speaking in public. "And Zhemin is quiet, he's shy," enjoins his father. I finally quiz him on which type of law he thinks he'd like to practice. I prod him, "Immigration law? Corporate law? Environmental law? Public defender? Prosecutor?" -- "Prosecutor," he almost shouts it.

I'm surprised by this, but Zhemin is just 10 years old, so his musings do not necessarily portend a future in jurisprudence. A few days later, finding myself in a piano lesson with Zhemin's friend Henry, my most loquacious student, I tell him about Zhemin's declared intentions of one day pursuing a legal career. "He seems awfully quiet for a prosecutor," I wonder aloud. "Henry, you on the other hand, I could imagine you being a lawyer." Henry cheerfully concurs, announcing, "I could definitely be a good lawyer! But, can I tell you something? I don't think I will be a lawyer. But you know something? I'm good at debating. Everyone says I'm good at debating. You must admit that I'm a very good debater." I agree with him, and after he fidgets a moment with his glasses, he resumes, "Can I tell you something else? —I probably could be a lawyer. But you know something? I'm too young to decide. I have time, I'm 10 years old. —I don't have to decide yet." My wise and garrulous student pauses, waiting for me to select the new piece from Schuman's *Kinderscenen* he had earlier implored me to assign.

When my interview with Zhemin concludes, we turn our attention to the piano. Suddenly my taciturn 10-year old student becomes communicative and assertive, not verbally, but with notes and rhythm. He can really play the piano. Zhemin is a gifted child. He has that wonderful capacity of focusing the mind like a laser. He soaks up whatever is put before him. This quiet, unassuming math whiz and chess champion is also musical and plays the piano with real understanding. He does need to be coached and nudged along some, to develop greater expressivity in his playing. But he is clearly musical and his style is anything but robotic. I sense he has it in him to delve more deeply into the core of this ethereal art, and attain a more refined, musical sensitivity.

His Beethoven Opus 2, f Minor Sonata has strength and rhythmic snap. Zhemin courses through the score of the first movement with musical savvy and palpable pleasure. He handles this work's quick grace notes deftly, and bounces out the staccatos with élan. He attacks this work's *forte* chords with athletic vigor and relish. This boy of few words pours out a profusion of well-struck, well-placed notes. Beethoven's music proudly asserts its forceful genius through Zhemin's body, mind, and soul.

Like the prosecutor he professes to aspire to, he makes Beethoven's case with lucid understanding. He lays out the sonata's exposition with clear logic for all to hear. The development section is then navigated with persuasive alacrity and intelligence. Chess master that he is, every step, every section, every phrase of this piece is mapped out with mindful attention. He stops halfway through the sonata's recapitulation, which is not yet learned. Thus, the closing argument of this piece is not yet ready for presentation. "Good progress Zhemin," I tell him. "Thank you," he replies.

Later we work together on Schubert's Impromptu Opus 90, nr. 2 in A-Flat. The main section's cascading sixteenth notes dance and glitter under his nimble fingers. The lyrical middle section, however, is lacking in nuance. Playing poetic melodies with subtle shading and coloring still eludes him. We must keep searching for the essence of this music.

And we will. Zhemin will improve those *cantabile* passages and bring greater *emotional* intelligence to them.

Our lesson concludes with one of Bartok's Roumanian Dances. Zhemin is working on the first dance from this colorful set. He plays it well; its sharp rhythms bite with insistent precision. As advertised, this Roumanian Folkdance kicks and stamps with earthy bravado.

One senses how much he enjoys playing the piano. His posture is good, his back upright, perfectly straight. And with a minimum of motion, his body comes alive and moves subtly with the music. I'm glad Zhemin loves the piano. Music clearly nourishes his spirit.

Quiet people can be confounding to some. They sometimes appear to be veiled in a shroud of mystery, unlike the majority of us who can converse fluidly and superficially about things, skating carefully on the surface of complex personas. At a small dinner gathering I recently attended, I heard a lot of talk over plans to buy the perfect house in the most esthetically pleasing setting, judgments as to the merits of a regional German wine, political pontification and venting, and a chorus of self-righteous laughter over a joke aimed at a public figure caught in an embarrassing scandal. Then came gossip about some people not present, and a complaint was lodged against an old boyfriend. This fellow, not around to defend himself, was referred to as a "real jerk."

Well, no real harm intended—no real harm done. I guess we all need some "downtime" to laugh and relax. But were we relaxing? Was this what people mean by "quality time?" How natural, joyful, and at ease were we? How alive? How real? I left that evening feeling disappointed at the lack of any real kinship or communication.

There was a time that I could more comfortably participate in such interactions. More and more now, I tend to avoid them. Growing up seems to be taking me a long time. There appears to be no end to it. But why live a long life if not to keep growing. Why stay stuck in a stagnant pool when life's flowing river carries us ever forward? Transience is a law that can be resisted for only so long. Relinquishing stale habits and limiting conveniences brings freedom. When it's time to let go and move on, it's simply best to do so.

Zhemin, though verbally spare, is far less of a mystery to me than most adults. He is less the sphinx than the sophisticated, sardonic, well-traveled man of the world. He is less adept at hiding himself behind a plethora of words. He stands more in the light, out in the open, simply himself.

When he returns next Saturday, I'll be curious to hear that Schubert middle section. Let's see how he bends and shapes that lovely melody. Let's see how much warmth and feeling; how much *love* he brings to these pages of Schubert. Let's see how receptive this wonderful boy can be to the tender beauty of this music, which first bloomed 185 years ago in the mind and heart of a poor, dying Viennese composer. Yes, I will be very curious. I really want to hear what he'll have to say.

# PLAYING IN THE SCHOOLS

I felt apprehensive walking into the Meridian Park School that first morning. Playing music and talking about it to second graders seemed like a great idea when I conceived of it. But as I strode into the red brick school building, I wondered how good an idea it really was. My mind was accosted by doubts. Would these kids show any interest in what I had to offer? Would I be irrelevant? Would anything really meaningful or worthwhile transpire here?

A little over an hour later, I left the Meridian Park School in a very different state of mind. It had come off very well; in fact my expectations had been exceeded.

Everything had been arranged through the mother of one of my piano students. I had been put in touch with the school's music teacher, Shari Anderson. She had invited me to address two of her music classes; one a group of 30 second graders, another, a group of 30 fourth graders. Arriving at the school office on the morning of my "debut," I was told to sign in and wear a sticker badge with my name on the breast of my shirt. I'm not sure why, but this made me feel silly. I hadn't been in an elementary school in years. Meeting Ms. Anderson, now my friend Shari, and a "Ms." to me no longer, was a pleasure.

I explained that I wanted the children sitting as close to the piano as possible. Shari readily agreed, and arranged for the kids to sit in three rows of 10, right up to the battered but recently tuned studio piano.

The subject I chose for that first morning was Mozart. "How many of you have heard of Mozart?" I asked. About 20 hands were raised. A few of the children smiled broadly. "How many of you play a musical instrument?" Maybe 12 hands were raised. I started talking about

Mozart's childhood. The stories of the little five year old pestering his father to let him play the violin and then the clavier seemed to interest this group of seven year olds. I recounted how the little wunderkind was taken to great cities like Vienna and Paris to play concerts. The kids seemed fully alert and engaged, their eyes riveted on me. So far, so good.

Then I played the rondo that concludes the A Major Piano Sonata, known as the Turkish March. When I finished, they applauded and smiled. They showed no signs at all of boredom. Many hands shot up, and comments and questions came forth. "Why do you close your eyes when you play?" "Hey, my grandma plays that song!" "How fast can you play?"

I told them Mozart moved to a big city, Vienna, that had a lot of ethnic diversity. "Seattle has a lot of people from all over the world too, don't you think?" "Yeah, but it's not really that big of a city," came one rejoinder. "But it's not really small," added another. The kids decided that Seattle was pretty big, but not *that* big.

I explained that Mozart had heard Turkish music living in Vienna. "Just by chance, is anyone here Turkish?" I queried. A little brown-skinned girl with dark hair and dark eyes raised her hand. "I'm not from Turkey," she spoke excitedly, "I'm from Pakistan, but my best friend, she's from Turkey." I noticed how proud she was to be able to share this piece of information. I played two more short pieces on the piano and the class seemed alive and engaged. My doubts were swept aside. I must confess to having been pleasantly surprised. My auditors weren't the least bit distant or preoccupied. They were wide awake!

I told them that Mozart was a great pianist, and that among other things, he could play very fast if he chose to. "How fast can you play?" was again asked. "Yeah, let's see how fast you can play!" "Very fast," I boasted, "I can play incredibly fast". "Let's see!" "Yeah, let's see!" they shouted, becoming quite animated. I felt emboldened to try a silly gag, as I was having so much fun, and feeling so relaxed and at home.

"Are you ready? Watch closely." They leaned forward. It became very quiet. "Watching?" I readied my hands at the keyboard. It was silent. Quickly I lowered my hands touching the keys without depressing them, removed my hands and turned to face this lively group of seven year olds. "Did you catch it?" I asked. "Did you see? Did you hear it?" For a few seconds no one responded. "Hey, you didn't play anything," a plump little boy in the first row complained. A series of wary smiles formed on the young faces looking at me. Then followed guffaws and accusations of trickery.

We were having fun when I looked at my watch and noticed there were five minutes left before we needed to stop. "I've had a great time visiting your class today," I told them. "We can stop now, or if you'd like I can play one more piece by Mozart." To my amazement and delight, this group of American second graders clamored for more. "One more, one more piece!" "Yeah, play one more!" The verdict had been delivered. "I'll play one more, and no joke, this really is a fast one!" Out of the corner of my eye I caught a glance of two little boys sitting just in front. One elbowed the other in the arm and muttered, "This is going to be *really* good." I then launched into the sparkling last movement of the F Major Sonata, playing through the exposition of this work. After their generous applause, I told them that I'd be back in a month, and we'd learn about another composer. "Next time Beethoven," I thought to myself.

"When I come back next time, we'll learn about another really great composer," I said. "He is the great musician who moved to Vienna the very year after Mozart died there. Does anyone know who I'm talking about?" Quickly a red-haired boy threw his hand into the air. "Louis Armstrong?" His strong voice rang out clearly. I chuckled, and noticed Shari Anderson, still very much a *Ms.* Anderson to me, wearing a huge smile and looking at me with mirthful pleasure. "No, it wasn't Louis Armstrong," I responded, although, Louis Armstrong was a great musician. Louis Armstrong lived in America, much later, in the 20th century."

"Was it Beethoven?" shyly asked a soft-voiced little Asian girl. "Yes, very good, Ludwig van Beethoven arrived in Vienna right after Mozart died. Next month we'll learn about Beethoven." This instilled a handful of whoops of approval and one or more pronouncements of "Cool, Beethoven!" from my youthful group.

An awareness arose within me that this was jolly good fun, and of course something even more. We were entertaining ourselves by sharing something; sharing time together exploring human expression through the wonder of music. I knew I had found a new "calling," and that I certainly would be back to the Meridian Park School in a month's time.

Since that first session with Shari Anderson's second grade class, I've made the acquaintance of many more second, third, fourth, and fifth grade students in the greater Seattle area. Probably the biggest surprise for me has been how eager, open, and attentive these kids have been. Their reactions to the music and to my story-telling have been unpredictable; sometimes amusing, sometimes touching.

Beethoven always stirs them. After playing the first movement of his powerful *Pathetique* Sonata, I asked, "What does this music make you feel?" Almost all the students raised their hands, eager to relate their reactions to the *Pathetique*. Powerful, moody, angry, stormy, were a few of the adjectives used. When I asked, "How does Beethoven sound to you compared to the Mozart we heard last month?" one confident brown-haired boy responded, "Beethoven's better!" He proclaimed his verdict, shaking his head with complete certainty. Then I called on a light-haired girl wearing glasses, who followed up in a questioning, philosophical voice, "I don't know—Mozart makes me feel more in harmony." We talked about the different feelings that music can evoke. I'm still impressed that a little seven year old girl felt Mozart's capacity to bring the soul to a state of harmony. Of course, the pro-Beethoven declarations; "Beethoven's way cool!" "Beethoven rocks!" were satisfying to hear as well.

I had a wonderful time teaching classes on Haydn to Shari's second and third graders. We learned the famous story of the *Surprise* Symphony; how Haydn, annoyed with an elderly gentleman who would inevitably fall asleep and snore loudly during the slow movements, decided to give him a "surprise" with his now much-celebrated Symphony No. 94.

I told the kids that the musicians loved Haydn, and even nicknamed him "Papa." Then, after explaining Papa Haydn's ploy of lulling his elderly victim to sleep with the opening bars of the slow second movement, began playing it for them on the piano. As the familiar, well-loved tune sounded through the classroom, the children smiled, fidgeted with anticipation, and even giggled in expectation of the big *fortissimo* chord I had promised them was coming. I played the big G major chord a little extra *fortissimo*, and the class erupted in gleeful howls of delight. Papa Haydn's rascally, playful humor still seems to work with 21st century seven and eight year olds. These children need only to be introduced to great music to get it.

Well, after I explained that this movement was a theme and variations, and played through some of it on the piano, they were full of questions and comments.

"How old was Papa Haydn? Was he very old?" I had to think a bit before answering. "Well, he was about 60 years old when he composed the Surprise Symphony. Remember, that was pretty old back in those days." Then a most earnest looking boy with curly brown hair wanted to know, "How old was the old man that always snored?" I had no idea. "I'm not sure, maybe 70." "Do you think that old man expected to be famous, and people would still know about him and talk about him way after he died?" Here I recall hearing Shari's laughter.

Well, after all, I had told the class that Haydn's music was still loved and appreciated all over the world in many countries, even 200 years after he had composed it. Maybe this nameless gentleman, the butt of music's most renowned joke, might have had an inkling he would be remembered too. "That old man, he's not still alive? He died right?" asked another boy in the last row. "Remember, this story comes from 1792, about 220 years ago. I'd say that he died. Imagine how old he would be today if he were still living!"

The kids were fascinated with Papa Haydn and the "old man." "Maybe one of you could figure out how old he'd be if he were still alive," I said. Then a little girl up front raised her hand and volunteered a question. "How old are you?" Shari laughed again. "I'm 56," I told her. We were just getting back to Haydn and a look at one of his lively piano sonatas when a tall, thin boy with an angular face raised his hand

and ventured, "I think I figured out how old that old man would be if he's still alive today—97!"

I expect this boy's math skills will improve in the coming years. The class eventually arrived at the conclusion that Haydn's "old man" would be more than 270 years old in the highly unlikely event that he is still alive today.

Will some of these children remember Papa Haydn and his wonderful symphony years in the future? I'm betting that some of them will, and that some of them will be moved to examine great music more closely. My job is as a foot soldier of music; to be a link in a chain that keeps this music alive. I believe in the worth of the music that I teach, and that makes the job pure and clean. By sharing music, we are really sharing a profound slice of our common humanity. We are sharing something precious that is beyond words to name. The children are open and impressionable, ready to taste a sip of this unique elixir. They are not yet jaded; not yet worn down by the commercial coarseness of our modern society. They are still open to wonder, and at the optimal time to be exposed to a Mozart or a Tchaikovsky.

They have accorded me their full attention, and their youthful, curious spirits. They're still young enough to speak their thoughts candidly, unburdened by self-conscious proprieties that they will learn soon enough. Their fresh candor and bright eagerness make for many surprising moments. Once, after playing a tango for them, I asked if anyone knew which country in the world was famous for the tango. A chubby, little red-haired girl ventured a response. "Minnesota?" Her strong clear voice rang out full of hope and optimism.

During a class featuring Brahms and Schumann, a little Chinese boy with a slightly crooked half smile volunteered the following information: "I happen to know that Brahms was born in the city of Hamburg. He played with toy soldiers well into his adult years, and he was a close friend of Clara Schumann". He spoke rapidly in a sort of monotone, barely pausing between sentences. "He always sent Clara Schumann his music to get her opinion. Sometimes she told him it needed improvement." I broke in, which wasn't easy to do, as this youthful scholar seemed to be just getting warmed up. "Wow" I said. "You certainly know a lot about Brahms." The boy sitting just to this student's right, who happened to also be Chinese, spoke next, and with a sardonic role of his eyes declared, "He knows a lot about *everything*". This elicited a groan or two and a few tepid laughs.

Undeterred by the subtle critique of his classmate, the class pedant began reciting more facts about the lives of both Brahms and Clara. This fount of knowledge poured forth a stream of historical material, obviously gleaned from his voracious reading. I seized on a small opening in his near breathless, runaway recitation of facts, and managed to shift the class back to the actual music of Brahms. I feared our orator was about to reveal information concerning Brahms' troubled youth playing the piano in the brothels of Hamburg, and of having developed relationships with several prostitutes. That particular aspect of Brahms' biography was not on my agenda for this group of ten-year olds.

In a class devoted to Bach, I asked the kids to all pronounce the great composer's name. "Now don't say Bock," I told them. "His name is pronounced Ba*ch*," I pronounced it with special emphasis on the guttural German 'ch' at the end. "Okay, now let's all say Bach together," I implored them, and the whole class pronounced Bach with plenty of gusto, really enjoying the guttural finale. Afterwards, a little dark-haired boy asked somewhat timidly, "Is that a Hebrew name?"

Sharing great music with schoolchildren has been very rewarding. I love it, and plan to continue this activity in the months and years ahead. It's turned out to be the "right thing" for me. Although I hadn't been so certain when I arrived at the Meridian Park School that first morning, I was quite convinced of the rightness of this work by the time the second class had finished.

I was putting my coat on, getting ready to leave, already feeling buoyant when a little light-haired, slightly freckled girl, probably nine years old, appeared by herself in front of me. All her classmates had shuffled out, and so the two of us remained alone.

"Um, well— I want to thank you for coming to our class today. Well—I want to tell you something. See, when I was little, well—I used to sometimes get scared at night, and then I couldn't fall asleep. Well– my dad once visited Vienna, and guess what he brought me home for a present? A music box, and, well—um, when you open it, it plays a song by Mozart!" "How nice," I responded, genuinely charmed by this little girl and her story. "Well, anyhow," she continued, "Even though I'm pretty big now, well,– sometimes I still can't sleep at night, but now, if I'm feeling kind of scared, well—I open my music box and I listen to the Mozart. And well, it makes me happy, and then I feel better – and I can sleep." She looked at me smiling shyly, a twinkle in her eyes. "That's wonderful," I said. "What a wonderful music box." After a short silence, her smiling little face still fixed on mine, she concluded by saying, "Well, I just wanted to tell you about my music box that plays Mozart." With that, she skipped off to catch up to her classmates, having given me a wonderful gift.

I walked out of the schoolhouse with this girl's voice in my ear and her gentle face in my mind's eye. I didn't even know her name. And so it was with a well-rounded joy that I departed the Meridian Park School that first morning; a well-rounded joy that seemed to reside at the very center of my being.

# MR. GOLDSAND

I studied the piano with Robert Goldsand at the Manhattan School of Music. Meeting him for the first time in his studio, I was struck by his civility, his cordial persona, and his old world European manner. I also sensed a slight, underlying edginess in this esteemed musician and fine gentleman.

"Kronacher, it is a pleasure to meet you." He shook my hand, and then asked for my phone number. I told him, noticing that he wasn't bothering to write it down. This was when I became aware that Mr. Goldsand had a photographic memory. He bid me repeat the number a second time, then looking at me, pronounced "Ja, now I've got it."

Goldsand was a remarkable pianist from the old school. Born in Vienna in 1911, the year that Mahler died there, he had been a child prodigy and had studied the piano with Moritz Rosenthal. Rosenthal had been a student of the great Liszt, and was a major pianist with a big career. Goldsand played the piano with a somewhat stiffer than normal wrist, which he held lower than normal as well. He wanted to impart his rather unique technique to all his students. This created a conflict for me, as it ran contrary to the type of technique I had hitherto developed.

Mr. Goldsand was not given to histrionics, but he made his desires clear with straightforward language. He was a persistent stickler in obtaining the results he was looking for. A kind of compromise was struck. I adhered enough to his ideas about piano technique and musical interpretation to win his approval, without abandoning all of my own.

Whenever I was his last student of the evening, he would invite me to stroll along Broadway, and insist on treating me to a cup of tea, or try to buy me a loaf of bread at one of his favorite bakeries. "Kronacher, they have such good bread here," he would declare when we would come upon such a place. "It has a good, solid crust. I only like bread with good, solid crust. And as you know by now, I only like piano playing with a good, solid tone."

Goldsand demanded a tone that rang with a full, resonant focus. He derided what he would sometimes refer to as "soggy, mushy, pale-toned" pianists.

One evening he took me to the Metropolitan Opera where we saw Alban Berg's *Lulu*. I had been overwhelmed with Berg's more celebrated opera *Wozzeck* when I saw it at the Met, perhaps a year earlier. It was a special treat, being my teacher's guest and companion at the opera, but *Lulu* didn't captivate me much as a piece. At intermission, Goldsand asked me how I liked Berg's opera. I answered somewhat cautiously, "Well, I don't think I quite understand this music." A crafty smile formed on Goldsand's face, and he remarked, "There's not much there to understand, it really isn't very good." The old romantic from the Vienna studio of Moritz Rosenthal wasn't having any of this atonal, modern music. He then told me, "My wife and I were friends with Alban Berg in Vienna, but I still can't pretend to see much beauty in this music." His back seemed to slightly stiffen when he told me this. When I dared to tell him how much I loved Puccini's *La Bohème* he smiled and said, "Ach, ja! Of course Kronacher, that is one of my favorites too." So my teacher, the respected old world romantic pianist, who could play pretty much the entire known piano repertoire by memory, and photographic memory at that, had affirmed my penchant for Puccini. "You know, Kronacher, that opening to Act III is a favorite of mine," he told me. He then began whistling the opening motif of *La Bohème's* third act, in which snow is seen falling on the outskirts of mid-19th century Paris. There would be no thorny, turgid analysis of Berg's atonality, or his use of tone rows this evening at the Met.

Goldsand had been a *wunderkind* in Vienna. He gave his first public concert there at the age of 10. When he was 16, in 1927, he crossed the Atlantic for the first time and gave his New York City debut in Town Hall. In 1977, 50 years later, he appeared in Carnegie Hall to present a grand jubilee piano recital. The concert he played that evening was one of four that I attended by my eminent professor.

He certainly had his own distinctive style. From his wrist position to his way with phrasing, pedaling, choice of tempi and overall interpretation, he was unique in every way, an especial individual. Even if I wasn't always in agreement with everything he did, I always felt pulled in by his originality. He didn't mimic anyone. He was proudly himself.

This was during the modern era of conformity, when piano students listened reverently to Vladimir Ashkenazy, admittedly a magnificent pianist, and whether consciously or not, aspired to play just like him. Goldsand was from the *ancienne époque* when an artist was encouraged to be unique, to find his own path. He had heard all about Liszt's ideas, piano technique, and musical tendencies from Rosenthal, growing up in Vienna. Liszt himself had once played for Beethoven as an 11 year old boy. Goldsand was proudly cognizant of this lineage. One can't find a concert pianist like Robert Goldsand today. For the romantic pianist, individuality was expected. They didn't grow up with recordings. They didn't fall over themselves to imitate some idol, or prep themselves to win a competition by attaining some ideal of generic perfection. They were, rather, encouraged to cultivate their individuality. Goldsand was one of the last of this breed.

I recall his performance of Beethoven's *Appassionata* as being a bit too stylized and quirky for me, but having beautiful moments, and played with love and commitment. The group of Chopin etudes was fascinating. Every etude revealed an evocative world of color and character. Goldsand's inimitable technique coupled with his unique, inspired imagination produced the most intimate and engaging performance of Chopin etudes that I've ever heard.

Mr. Goldsand's personality would never give one the slightest hint of this inner rebel; this free thinking musician, this pianistic minority of one. I think of Rubinstein's comment, "A musician must be himself. He can only be different. He cannot be a second Paderewski or Rachmaninoff." Robert Goldsand was to outward appearances a courtly, mild, conservative, bourgeois gentleman. He bore some traces of an aristocratic, European stamp. But he was not one to stand out from the crowd. I noticed some shyness and some underlying discomfort lurking within the psyche of my kind professor. Like my mother, he had been forced to flee Vienna, the historic music capital he had loved so much. He only mentioned the ordeal of living through this eruption of hatred and violence one time to me. "Having gone through the horror of those years, let us all hope we don't ever see a figure like Hitler appear again," he once said to me. Goldsand arrived in America in 1940. Like everyone who's world had been shaken by the rumblings of Europe's ghastly convulsions, his life could never be the same.

Goldsand gave a piano literature course to all the graduate students at the Manhattan School. He was opinionated, and I couldn't share in all of his pronouncements. He had no use for Bartok, and referred to Liszt as a "cheaper" Chopin. But he proved to be quite open and eclectic in his tastes. The old romantic from Rosenthal's studio championed Bach and played him on concert programs regularly. This was at a time when Bach was seldom programmed by other pianists of his vintage and background. And he championed Prokofiev. "He is cut from solid stone, like Beethoven," he once told our class. His repertoire was expansive, from Bach on through to Gershwin, Prokofiev, even a little Schoenberg. Aided by his phenomenal memory, he could play just about everything. On more than one occasion, he performed the full cycle of Beethoven's 32 sonatas in a series of recitals. One time he played the last movement of the Opus 26 A-flat Sonata for me. It is a rushing, contrapuntal propulsion of forward-driving energy. He played it dynamically, and when he finished, he looked at me and said, "Ja, I still remember, I can still do it. You know, I vowed to myself I'd never forget this sonata." My 65 year old professor didn't want to take his unfailing memory for granted. He knew that nothing lasts forever.

I once had a powerful dream in which Mr. Goldsand played a part. I have occasionally had music arise in dreams. This is not particularly uncommon for musicians. The dream I will now describe occurred when I was just finishing my time studying with Goldsand. It was such a vivid dream that I remember it yet.

I dreamt that I was opening the door and entering Mr. Goldsand's studio. I stepped in as usual, having come for a lesson, and saw him sitting in his accustomed armchair with the window behind him; the gray city air serving as a backdrop. I began playing the Mozart Sonata in A Major. The first movement is a Theme and Variations, and I recall playing quite a bit of it. At some point, I stopped playing and turned towards my teacher, but Mr. Goldsand was not any longer sitting in his armchair. He had been replaced by another gentleman. I looked closely, and recognized that no less a personage than Mr. Johannes Brahms, the great composer, was now ensconced in the armchair! Brahms would be my teacher for the remainder of this piano lesson!

I quickly ascertained that Brahms, who was reputed to have died in 1897, was in fact still very much alive. He looked remarkably good for a man of 144 years of age; not so heavy set as in the photos I had seen. His beard was neatly trimmed and he wore a conservative suit, contemporary of the 1970s. He appeared to me to be no older than 80.

At all events, it was definitely Brahms that sat across the way. He spoke to me in English, with a gravelly voice and a strong German accent. "Kronacher, do you know ze seventh variation?" I was startled by the question. The Mozart sonata in question has only six variations. "No sir," I replied. "Doesn't the first movement end with the sixth variation?" "Ach Kronacher, I vill show you ze seventh variation."

At this point I stood and stepped aside as Herr Brahms settled himself at the piano. I then watched and listened in delight as a most Brahms-ian variation took flight. Though I cannot reproduce the notes today, I recall it being all in the key of A-flat major. Brahms' fingers were hitting all the keys corresponding to the music that filled me rapturously in this nocturnal improvisation. It happens that I am a pretty good improviser in my waking conscious state, and I can do a decent improv "a la Brahms," but this surpassed anything I was capable of. I clearly recall Brahms crossing his left hand over the right and playing some rich *legato* thirds in the treble. What a dream!

It doesn't end there. After finishing, the famous composer said, "Zere, zat's variation seven. Most people don't know it. Now, Kronacher, vill you come viz me for a coffee?" I naturally accepted, and the two of us walked over to the Manhattan School's cafeteria. I couldn't have felt more proud, Johannes Brahms and I entering the busy school cafeteria together. All eyes were on us. "Look, Brahms and Kronacher, talking like comrades." I sensed the inner thoughts of the envious students. That was when I awoke from the dream.

Leaving off exploring any analysis of this dream, I can declare that it filled me with beautiful music. Where did it come from? Did I improvise it in some hidden corner of my brain? Did it flow through time and space from Brahms himself? Or, as some readers may dubiously wonder, was it really meritorious of praise at all, or just an illusory mirage of a dreamy sojourner. Who knows for sure, but unlike the vast majority of dreams, it remains strikingly fresh in my memory.

After the period of lessons with Mr. Goldsand ended, I continued to practice steadily. I lived in New York for another seven years, but saw him only on a couple of occasions. One time, perhaps five years after having been his student, I came across him in my neighborhood. We were both out walking on upper Broadway and hailed each other with friendly good cheer. "Kronacher, so good to see you. How are you?" he smiled greeting me. "Will you let me buy you a coffee?" We were soon installed at a small coffee shop. I asked him how his wife was, what upcoming performances he had planned, and about the Manhattan School. He was curious to hear that I was doing a lot of teaching, about the repertoire I was playing, and that I was giving a few recitals. I remember telling him that I was working on Chopin's great Third Sonata in b minor. "That piece is almost inhuman," was his comment. It is of great difficulty, and Mr. Goldsand humbly acknowledged its formidable challenges.

At one point in our conversation, he talked a little bit about his boyhood teacher, Rosenthal. "He had a fairly major career," he told me. "A bigger career than I've had." I sensed some feelings of disappointment embedded in that statement. "Fritz Kreisler, the violinist, he had the biggest career of anyone in Vienna when I lived there." Goldsand was keenly cognizant of which musicians had won the largest followings and the most plaudits. As a performer, one needs to perform for an audience. It won't do to play superlatively just for oneself and the four walls of your room. A performing artist desires to share his art with other human beings. He needs a public. It is understandable that a brilliant pianist like Robert Goldsand, one who had been before the public since the age of 10, would have a sensitive ego, and would muse about the level of success he had attained.

Once as a student at the Manhattan School, I was deep in practice in one of the school's practice rooms. I looked up and noticed one of New York's many ubiquitous pigeons perched on the sill just outside the window. I was weary of practicing alone, and decided I would perform for the pigeon. I played with as much feeling as I could, spinning out a Chopin nocturne in an attempt to touch my visitor, and keep her riveted to the spot. At occasional intervals, I'd glance up at the window, and would be buoyed by the continuing presence of my fine, feathered auditor. I kept this performance up until the pigeon finally flew off. I don't know if this gray, winged resident of New York was a Chopin lover or not, but I needed to play the piano for *someone*.

Robert Goldsand had performed since he was a little boy. He had grown up hearing adults praise him for his talents. This massages the ego. Later, as a mature concert artist, he would be subjected to the vicissitudes of both high praise and needling criticism from music critics. Few can remain immune being judged in this manner. Any performing artist must wrestle with the relationship he has with his ego. It is a relationship that cannot be dismissed. One must come to an accommodation of the ego's demands, as well as the genuine, selfless love of music itself, both of which reside in the performing musician. I perceived this tension at play in my proud, sensitive, gentle teacher.

Near the end of our visit, Goldsand asked me, "Tell me Kronacher, are you still at the same phone number?" Before I could answer in the affirmative, he rattled it off correctly. The phone number that I had given him some seven years earlier, was still safely tucked away in that stellar memory of his. It was one of the millions of pieces of information he had stored away.

I was living in Seattle when my father called one day, and informed me that Robert Goldsand had passed away. He had clipped out the obituary from the New York Times and mailed it to me. I soon learned that Goldsand had been stricken with diabetes, and the first stages of Alzheimer's. Being diagnosed with Alzheimer's must have been quite a blow. That superb memory began slipping away. The finely tuned computer began falling into disarray; coming undone. All those notes, all those phone numbers, all the personal memories of people and places, all beginning to crumble and disintegrate.

In Oliver Sacks' book _Musicophalia_, the noted neurologist states that music is often one of the last things to go in patients afflicted with dementia. I wonder which musical excerpts my teacher retained in his inner ear, as he faced his impending death. As life's capricious, swirling gale of change blew through him, poking holes in his once perfect mind, and chipping away slabs of memory and pieces of ego, I want to believe music still brought him some comfort. I can't but hope that even as he relinquished his identity as a pianist and teacher, and as so many personal ties slid away and he settled into pure, essential being, that the naïve and genuine love for the art to which he had devoted his 80 year long life still touched him. Perhaps a favorite melody of Schubert, or a passage of his beloved Beethoven Opus 26, or maybe just a simple, lovely folk song, first heard as a baby, still flowed coherently through his faltering mind, resonating deep in his heart.

Robert Goldsand was a fine gentleman. He was always fair, honest, respectful and diligent. He carried both pride and humility within his gentle soul. I remember him with affection.

# GETTING BY IN THE BIG CITY

Emerging from the cocoon of student life was difficult. I graduated from the Manhattan School of Music in the spring of 1977. I now held a Master's degree in piano performance from a major conservatory, to go with a Bachelor's degree in applied piano from Ithaca College. It was expected that I now go forth and begin a career. I had been guided only by a desire to become a good musician, and I honestly had not devoted much thought to the nasty reality of earning a livelihood. I loved the student life. I had worked hard for six years, and had blithely assumed that somehow everything would just work out.

Having the rent-controlled apartment on Riverside Drive proved to be a lifesaver. It would not be necessary to make much money to keep my head above water, and continue to practice four to five hours every day. I had no intention whatsoever of halting my work at the piano. I preferred to live the life of the struggling young artist, much like a character from Puccini's *La Bohème*. The first two years after graduating from conservatory were the hardest. New York had thousands of competent pianists competing for relatively low-paying jobs. I found work at a few ballet studios in the city. It wasn't work that I much liked, but it was tolerable and not difficult for me.

My first summer out of school, I earned some money as a street musician. I had taught myself a little guitar in high school which turned out to be quite useful, as I teamed with my friend and fellow conservatory student Jeff Ellenberger, a fine violinist. We played in Greenwich Village five nights a week that summer. Our favorite location was the corner of Jones and Fourth Street, just in front of a Greek restaurant. We would generally set up shop there with the blessings of the restaurant's owner. I arranged all kinds of pieces for violin and guitar, easy arrangements where Jeff's fiddle could carry the melodies aloft, above the strumming of the harmonies on my guitar. Our repertoire included a little of everything; operatic arias, tunes from the Broadway stage, Beatles' songs, Strauss waltzes, famous melodies from Mozart, Schubert, Brahms, and well-known folk melodies. That summer in Greenwich Village was a colorful one indeed. We were approached by a great variety of people and wound up being invited to play for pay at parties, weddings, and bar-mitzvahs in the city and its suburbs.

Our typical working hours in The Village ran from 9pm up until anywhere from midnight to 1am. After knocking off for the evening, we'd often find a café to enjoy a cold drink, count out our earnings for the night, and just unwind, talk, and share some laughs together. Jeff was, and still is, a good-hearted, honest, fine fellow. People who know me today are incredulous when I tell them that I didn't get to bed until two in the morning most nights that summer. It was quite an aberration from my normal daily rhythm.

One evening, as Jeff and I commenced playing Brahms's best-known Hungarian Dance, a vivacious, petite female mime, perhaps 20 years of age, appeared out of the group of persons watching and listening to us. She tipped her black top hat towards us, smiled, and began dancing a quite skillful, improvised ballet to the music. She was a graceful little thing, wearing a black leotard, black tights, and black ballet slippers. Her face was painted white, but her brown eyes sparkled and her painted red lips smiled with a girlish sweetness without a trace of coquetry. She was adorable.

Jeff and I were now impelled to play with greater fervor. The crowd on Fourth Street swelled, and the beautiful dancer twirled, swayed, and leapt to our impassioned rendering of the Brahms Dance. When the music stopped, cries of approval filled the hot, humid air, and dollar bills and coins came raining down on the open violin case left at our feet. We told the young mime to take her share, but she refused. We asked her her name. She told us, "Petite," in a muted voice. We introduced ourselves and then asked again. "What is your real name?" She smiled sweetly and repeated, again *sotto voce*, "Petite." "Will you dance some more?" She nodded. We played. Jeff and I were entranced. The crowd around us swelled even more and 'Petite' charmed this Greenwich Village street audience of New Yorkers and tourists.

After an enchanting half hour of music and dance, the crowd had grown large enough to disrupt the flow of traffic on Fourth Street. Two policemen turned up to insist on the street being kept clear. Petite, after continuing to refuse our appeals to take her share of the gathering bounty from the now quite full violin case, finally removed her black chapeau, turned it over, held it smugly to her chest, and daintily made the rounds amongst the delighted street audience. After making her collection, she gave Jeff and me a lovely little glance, a tip of her hat, and then flew off into the city night. Just like that she was gone. Like a fairy, she simply vanished into the crooked jumble of old Greenwich Village streets; into a hot summer's eve, into the fabric of an immense city, and into the aroused imaginations of two young street musicians. We spoke about Petite many times after that evening, but neither of us ever caught sight of her again.

Some nights we were invited into Village restaurants to play for tips and dinner. We appreciated the opportunity of being able to sample the menus at the various ethnic restaurants that we'd normally find unaffordable. I recall dining on Greek, Mexican, and Spanish cuisine, all on the house that particular summer. We were also hired to play parties. These paid *gigs* took us into some quite posh surroundings. Many of these luxurious spaces had pianos, and I was consequently able to greatly increase and improve our repertoire. Now I could put down the guitar, improve my accompaniments, and throw in a Chopin waltz or a Gershwin prelude as part of our act.

Playing music at social events is something I've done periodically over the years. Unlike the concerts given gratis at senior centers, schools, or hospitals, these gigs were strictly for pay. In these circumstances, the musician is usually there to provide background music. People are milling about and talking at such events, and few are listening attentively to the music. The musicians are hired help. They play for pay and provide the ambience that their employer has hired them for. Today, I no longer play these jobs, as my financial situation no longer necessitates it.

Of course it was interesting to gain entrée to diverse sets of people. One time Jeff and I were hired for a Christmas party out on Long Island. I no longer remember the name of the town where it was held, but we took the train to the appropriate station where we were told the host and hostess's son would pick us up and drive us to their house. An expensively-clad young college student swooped by in his new red Jaguar, and called out for us to jump in. We then zoomed off to his family's home. Within a matter of five minutes, we were motoring through an isolated, tree-covered hillside with no houses in sight. Shortly, a veritable chateau rose up before us. We were then shown into the front entrance of this stony, palatial mansion. The main entrance gave way to a large, tiled, open room with a high vaulted ceiling. A huge glistening Christmas tree stood at the center of the room. We were told to feel at home, help ourselves to the sumptuous buffet, and then shown to the corner of the room where stood the piano.

Now typically, musicians play a set of 40 minutes or so, followed by a 15 or 20 minute break. But on this particular occasion, my friend Jeff put down his fiddle after one or two short pieces and announced, "Come on Fred, let's eat!" "We just got here!" I replied, somewhat annoyed. "Let's at least play a few more selections first." Jeff did not feel the slightest embarrassment about proceeding to the buffet table so soon. But I considered it to be inappropriate. We played another five minutes or so, but that was enough for my colleague. Jeff sauntered off to help himself to generous portions of the delectable spread of foods laid out before him. I wasn't happy about it, but fortunately no recriminating words were spoken by our busy hosts. I still wince and smile simultaneously recalling the scene. I don't know how our hosts acquired their wealth, but whether old money or new, this was the grandest and most impressive residence I had ever set foot in. I can't say that I entered into any scintillating conversations with any of the guests. Though this wasn't my world, everyone was friendly, we played our music, ate well, and received good pay for our efforts.

Another paid gig landed my friend Robert, his faithful cello, and me, in the immaculate Central Park West apartment of Pia Lindstrom. Perhaps the name Pia Lindstrom may be recognizable to New Yorkers, as she hosted a popular television program in the city during those years. Her fame also rests on being the first daughter of Ingrid Bergman.

When Robert and I stepped out from the elevator on the top floor of the prestigious Central Park West apartment building, we were immediately greeted by both a butler and a chamber maid. The elevator had opened directly into this large private apartment residence. Ms. Lindstrom welcomed us personally with warmth and unaffected cheer. We were shown into the large main salon that contained immense windows, revealing a sweeping view of the park below. It was winter, and the lights twinkled magically off the snow on the trees and lawn spread out before us. A good Steinway was put at my disposal, and although people talked, ate, and drank whilst our *background music* wafted through this large, elegantly furnished chamber, many guests applauded after each piece. Some of Ms. Lindstrom's guests asked us insightful questions about music as well. This party was frequented by a mix of intellectuals and people from show business.

At such gatherings, I would invariably be approached by someone who had studied the piano earnestly. There seemed to always be a middle-aged person that would introduce himself and then remark, "Ah, the Chopin f-minor etude, I played that once." Or, "Ah, the Brahms g-minor Rhapsody. Say, do you also play the b-minor rhapsody?" I generally enjoyed conversing with such people. Often I would invite a trained pianist to take over for a few minutes and play something. Invariably, my interlocutor would decline the offer telling me, "Oh no, I haven't played seriously for years. I work as a computer programmer now. I'm way out of practice. I hardly touch the piano nowadays. But when I was at Juilliard 20 years ago, I was quite accomplished."

These type of exchanges always got me thinking. How, I wondered, could someone with talent who had worked so hard to attain a high level of excellence, just completely let go of playing music. Today I think I can better understand. After one has known the experience of plumbing the depths of great music, equipped with a hard-earned and well-greased technique, it just won't do to give a casual, half-baked going-over of a score one had formerly mastered. It would only tease the mind and prick the heart; a little like receiving a warm, but platonic kiss on the cheek from your first and truest love, now married to another and lost to you forever.

I would always come away from these sorts of encounters with a slight sadness. "I don't want that to happen to me," was a recurring thought of mine. Somehow, I remained resolved to never let it happen to me. I knew I didn't want to work with computers. Nor did I want to be a stockbroker, real estate agent, or even work in an office at all. I remember harboring the thought that a profession which might suit me if music couldn't work, was that of a postal letter carrier. At least then I could be out of doors and walking every day. But I was determined to stay a musician. The love I have for this art seems to be steadfast. Today, I am glad not to be counted amongst the club of one-time pianists, too rusty or jaded to play an etude or a rhapsody with conviction and accuracy.

Pia Lindstrom was a charming hostess that evening, and she thanked us graciously for the music. My only regret was that her illustrious mother was not present. It was probably the closest I've come to brushing up against real Hollywood royalty.

Occasionally I was hired to play solo at an event. Each of these occasions provided me with a window into yet another slice of society. It was through the father of my college girlfriend Teri, that I was employed to play Chopin at the Polish Consulate in New York. Teri and I had been sweethearts at Ithaca College, and had kept our romance alive for another two years or so after leaving Ithaca. I had come to New York to study at the Manhattan School of Music. Teri had gone out to Tucson, to study anthropology at the University of Arizona. We visited one another a couple of times and spoke on the phone. After our relationship as lovers had dissolved, we managed to hold onto a friendship.

In fact, Teri, who lives not far from me today in Eugene, Oregon with her husband Jan, and their two children, remains a cherished friend. Her father Morty was always well-disposed towards me, and helpful whenever possible. In the seventies, Morty was living in New York where he was a vice president of Schefflin and Company, a firm which imports wines and spirits into the United States.

One fine day, Morty called me to ask whether I'd be willing to play some Chopin at the Polish Consulate. Alas, it would not be a 'concert.' My playing would provide a musical backdrop to a party being held in honor of the president of a particular Polish vodka company doing business with Schefflin and Company. The money was good and I gratefully accepted the job.

On the evening of this little fête, Morty and I *rendez-vous*-ed at his Midtown apartment, and then shared a cab to the embassy. It was raining steadily that evening, and when we stepped out of the cab in front of the embassy, both of us attired in tuxedos, a doorman ran forward to cover us with a large umbrella and shield us from the downpour. I recall the unpleasant feeling this caused me. It was something I wasn't used to. This employee of the consulate was getting soaked, but Morty and I were walked to the building entrance under cover. Other guests arriving by taxi were given similar coddling. Most of them appeared accustomed to this and seemed to take their privileged status for granted. Once inside, another employee began taking my coat off for me. "It's okay," I protested to him. "I can take my coat off." Morty muttered something to me about how it was this man's job to take the guests' coats off for them, and that I ought to let him do it. Morty, a regular down to earth sort of guy, was just trying to smooth out some hard edges. Again, I noticed how comfortable the other guests appeared at receiving this sort of pampered treatment. Somehow it rubbed me wrong.

We entered a large elegant room, brilliantly-lit with crystal chandeliers. I soon found my way to the grand piano and commenced playing the music of Frederic Chopin. This capacious space , replete with aristocratic opulence was now filled by executives and sales representatives, schmoozing and drinking. Few cared a wit about Chopin. Many may have been ignorant that he was Poland's greatest composer, and a revered figure in his country. Some were surely unaware that the music emanating from the piano was Chopin. This was a crowd of business people, experts in sales, marketing, and cutting deals. The alcohol flowed freely. A good deal of vodka was swilled, and as you may have surmised, it wasn't just any old vodka, but the particular brand being imported by Schefflin and Company.

I played mazurka after nocturne after waltz after impromptu, as well-dressed people drank, ate, talked business, and for the most part ignored the music of Chopin. But as is always the case, a select few did notice. Not everyone was impervious to the music. Four or five people gravitated over to the piano and stood their ground. They listened and watched as I played one piece after the other. They smiled at me. They touched their hearts with their hands. They were drawn to the music.

That night, after I got home, I called Teri in Arizona. It was two hours earlier there with the time change so she was still up. "Teri, I played piano at the Polish Consulate at your dad's event." "How was it?" she wanted to know. "Did you have fun?" We talked for awhile and had some laughs.

Teri and I first met at a little party in a college dorm room some 38 years ago. A lively game of charades was in progress. She used her body language to entice someone to say the word 'wolf.' From there, it was a quick and easy leap for me to guess Wolfgang Amadeus Mozart. That was the beginning of our relationship. I introduced Teri to lots of music in my bid to court her. Quite a lot of it was Chopin, which she readily took to heart.

When I graduated from college and the two of us prepared our individual plans to move on in our lives, Teri asked me, "Fred, if we were living 20 or 30 years ago, do you suppose we'd get married at this point?" Her question insightfully raised the issue of times having changed, of shifting expectations and social norms. Neither of us was ready to get married at that point. We both had other dreams to chase. We cared for each other and both of us felt real emotion in moving nearly 3,000 miles apart. Letting go can be poignant, but letting go is the way of life. How glad I am that Teri is still my friend.

As for Morty, a more satisfying, unadulterated pleasure spent with him occurred in October of 1977 when he invited me to be his companion at a World Series game between the Yankees and the Dodgers at Yankee Stadium. It proved to be no ordinary ball game. Morty and I bore witness to the deciding game of the series, in which the Yankees clinched their first world championship in 13 years. Moreover, it was on this cool October evening that Yankee slugger Reggie Jackson cracked three homeruns. Remarkably, the colorful, controversial Jackson had only deigned to swing at three offerings during the entire game. Each time he chose to swipe at a pitched ball, his well timed stroke sent it soaring over the outfield fence and into the stands. The third blast was the most prodigious, landing in the distant center field bleachers. I remember elbowing Morty in amazement when Reggie connected on that third home run. Morty had looked away momentarily and I didn't want him to miss this piece of baseball history. "Morty!" I cried as I jabbed him into full attention. "He's hit another one!" Yankee Stadium, the house that Ruth built, was in a frenzy, and Morty and I shared in the celebration.

By 1979, I had been hired to teach the piano at the Brooklyn Conservatory of Music. I taught at both branches, the one in Flushing and the one in Park Slope. Later I taught one day a week at the Bloomingdale House of Music on the Upper West Side. I was now finished accompanying ballet classes, and playing guitar in Greenwich Village receded into mere memory. They are memories I'm glad to still possess.

In time, due to being underpaid at the schools which employed me, I decided to search out greener pastures, beyond the hard edges of New York's rough and tumble, where it would be easier to establish a more sustainable living. The Brooklyn Conservatory of Music paid its teachers roughly half the amount of tuition it took in. Obviously, as a private teacher, one could charge just about the same tuition fee as the school, but keep it all for oneself. It became apparent that teaching was the most rewarding and enjoyable manner for me to earn my living and still stay the course as a musician. Today, my love of teaching music stands up equally to my love of playing music.

People always ask me how I chose Seattle. There is no clear, easy answer. Once I determined not to fight it out any longer in New York, I began looking around for a suitable town to set up shop. I did some research and much deliberating, and Seattle simply won out. It was not prohibitively expensive back in 1986 when I first arrived here, as it has since become. It is a green, civilized city. It has an ethnically diverse, open, tolerant, and well-educated population. Lake Washington, the Puget Sound, snow-capped mountains, and rich emerald forests surround my town. I have met wonderful people from all corners of life and every part of the world. Seattle has welcomed me with generosity. Coming here has been the right thing.

The old days of scraping by those first years out of school in New York still supply me with rich memories. I remember with special fondness a few occasions when my sister Erica came down to the Village to cheer Jeff and me on out on 4th and Jones. Erica enjoys music, although her soul was never seized by the harmonious art in the way that mine was. She has always been supportive, attending most of my piano recitals in New York and New Jersey, as well as a few of the musicales in my Riverside Drive flat. I especially remember her with a few of her friends, happy and smiling affectionately, watching us entertain the rich melange of Greenwich Village pedestrians along the sidewalk. Erica lives in New Jersey today with her husband and children. She's always been a good sister.

Jeff and I met such a wide assortment of characters on the street. There seemed to be a never-ending parade of humanity promenading past us, those hot summer nights. We often tailored our repertoire to help some of the after dinner crowd separate a bit more quickly from some of their spare change. "Jeff," I'd say after spotting a few couples speaking Italian heading our way. "Quick, let's play *Traviata* or *Santa Lucia!*" When we noticed heads topped off with yarmulkes, we'd break into our *Fiddler on the Roof* Medley. A funny episode occurred once when a young couple came strolling by. They seemed reticent and tentative with each other. One sensed this may have been a first date. The young lady stopped and expressed a desire to listen to the street music. "Oh, I really want to hear this, I just love music," she said to her companion. Her young man wore a cocky grin and quickly assumed a knowledgeable air. It happens we were playing Gershwin's bluesy song *Summertime* from *Porgy and Bess*. The confident, gallant young fellow chose to show off a little for his date, and impress her with his erudition. Just after we finished the song and after the young lady had gasped, "God how I love this!" he spoke to us. "Wonderful, just wonderful" he declared, assuming a learned air. "I'm a big fan of classical music," he continued. "Now don't tell me—let me think, don't tell me—okay, I think I've got it, was that Bach or Strauss?"

Of course Bach and Strauss, whether it be Johann Jr., Johann Sr., or Richard, are near impossible to confuse. I suspect he had the waltz king Johann Jr. in mind. Confusing Bach and Johann Strauss is a bit like confusing a glass of wine with a mug of hot chocolate. And then Gershwin is quite distinct from either. But we refrained from embarrassing him, and I do believe he scored a few points with his girl.

Perhaps the highlight of my short career as a street musician was when NBC filmed Jeff and me playing in the Village, and broadcast it a couple of weeks later on national television. They were doing a segment on New York's eclectic coterie of street musicians. We were the last act of this segment, closing out the Today Show that particular day. Jeff and I watched the broadcast together. There we were, on our favorite corner of 4th and Jones playing my arrangement of Strauss's *Emperor Waltz*; coast to shining coast. My mother saw it in her Queens apartment. Teri tuned us in in Tucson. All our friends and relatives from all over the country watched. After all the hours spent practicing the piano, it was only as a guitar-strumming street musician that I've ever made it onto national television. Today I no longer own a guitar, but I do possess some wonderful memories. And though I've never hit 'the big time', I'm still at it, playing and teaching the piano: Still a musician after all these years.

# A FEW ADVANCED STUDENTS

Sally looked vexed when I asked her to repeat the first phrase. She had barely begun playing the slow Chopin b minor Prelude, and already her teacher had stopped her. "Try to play the first 'b' in the bass quieter. You need to have room to make a crescendo," I told her. I recognized the rueful look that showed on her face. She played it again and succeeded making a nice crescendo. "That's it!" I called to her, "All of those phrases now, start them all more *piano*." She played on, balancing the voices very well, and shaping the left hand melodic line with subtle nuance.

Sally has been my student for ten years or so. We are good friends, as well as having had a long established working relationship at the piano. Her prelude moved along beautifully until I felt impelled to grumble about some over-pedaling. "Don't pedal those sixteenth notes," I suggested. This piece of advice was met with another look of rueful impatience. Sally stopped, played the passage in question, and improved it. Finally I badgered her about bringing the low 'b' in the bass out in slight relief from the soft b minor chord that accompanies it in the right hand. It is the most affective cadence in this prelude; a special Chopinesque moment. This time Sally was with me all the way. She sensed right away my meaning. Then she played through the piece again with feeling and refinement. The low b minor in the aforementioned cadence couldn't have been better.

Teaching competent, serious pianists is a challenge. How far can you push them? How much technical perfection can one aspire to? How much artistic finish? How encouraging or demanding should the teacher be? Naturally this depends on how hard a student wants to work, how much innate ability she possesses, and how strong or fragile an ego she has. Those are a few of the factors to be considered. All in all, each individual student brings a unique mix to the lessons.

Sally has grown enormously as a pianist. She has now played a wide repertoire with real feeling and refinement. On this particular day, she wasn't in the best frame of mind. She started the second movement of Ravel's Sonatine a little too briskly, with a bit too jaunty a feel. I let her play it through before daring to level any criticism. Then I pointed out the legato phrasing that Ravel had marked in for the upper melodic line of the opening bars. "Legato Sally—legato, not disjointed, and not too jaunty. Legato like an oboe solo. I bet Ravel would have given this to the oboe if he'd orchestrated it." Sally looked carefully at those slur marks in the score; those slight little curving arcs that musicians cannot ignore. She knew she'd have to try to honor Ravel's wishes and make those notes more legato.

This presented a problem for Sally. Her hands are small for an adult and she struggles with certain stretches. She tried it and quickly became frustrated, abruptly closing the book and irritably announcing, "It's no use, it's impossible for my hand. I might as well give up on this piece." This was something I had seen before with Sally.

I suggested she omit one note of the chord if need be. Then as we explored the passage carefully together, we hit upon the idea of using the left hand to take the note that the right hand couldn't quite reach. An alternative way of executing the phrase and fully honoring Ravel's intentions came into view. "Hmm, maybe this will work," Sally conceded, a grin reluctantly taking form on her face. Sally can be both tense and intense, fussy and determined. Being intense is not a hindrance. Nor is being determined. Being fussy is necessary to reaching a high level of musical achievement. Tension, however, can be a hindrance. Musicians must learn to relax and control their nerves. This is one of Sally's challenges. That she demands a lot of herself is why she has become such a fine pianist. Now…if she could just relax a bit more.

With 18-year old Sasha, it's a very different dynamic. Sasha has been my student since she was eight years old. I've watched her grow up. She's always had the talent, and now she has developed the zeal to go with it. Although she dreams of a future career in medicine, not in music, she loves the piano, and has become focused on mastering great works from the piano literature.

At a recent lesson, she exuded joy, laughed easily, took my critical comments as well as my encouraging ones with an easy, even calmness. Her Chopin *Aeolian Harp* Etude in A-flat Major really impressed me. "Sasha, you're really making this music come alive. It's really singing!" I told her. "You just need to practice a few spots slowly and you know very well where those spots are." "Yeah, I know," she replied. Sasha doesn't practice enough to reach her fullest potential. That's okay. She still plays well and by God she has something! Her etude really impressed me. When she tore into the third movement of Beethoven's *Moonlight* Sonata, I could only smile and hop aboard for the ride. She's not note perfect, but she really takes command of this music. She really feels it, and she doesn't tense up or shrink away from its difficulties. Yet I must still push her. "Sasha," I say. "You know the spots that need to be cleaner. Let me hear them now, much slower." She smiles, knows just which measures to play, and dutifully plays them through under tempo.

Sasha's mother is Russian, born in St. Petersburg. Her father is American. Sometimes I appeal to her Russian heritage. "You know the coda needs to be more dramatic. You play it too straight. Show me that Russian drama and power! And make the last trill really bright, and don't cut it so short!" I've been exhorting her this way over the coda for several weeks. "And, after a long fermata on that last *pianissimo* g-sharp, just tear apart the piano on those final measures! And don't wimp out on the last two chords!"

She tries it, but the last two chords are strangely out of rhythm. "Forte, strong, bold chords," I call to her. "But right in tempo—in strict tempo." The next time she tries it, she bungles the penultimate chord completely; a chaotic jangle of dissonant notes spills out. We both break up laughing. Sasha doesn't need it to be perfect. She'd like it to be perfect, but she doesn't *need* it to be perfect. I'm glad that she loves music and intends to continue to study the piano at college. I'm impressed with how comfortable she seems to be in her own skin at such a young age. Finally, another attempt at the coda is made. It's better, but still not perfect.

Jackson, aged 16, has been the most dedicated of my students these last few years. He has declared his intention of pursuing music as a career. Jackson has improved tremendously over the eight years we've been working together. At a recent lesson, we worked on preparing a recital. The first movement of Bach's B-flat Partita, was first up.

"Jackson, you must find the right flow and tempo from the first chord," I remind him. "The ornament should be easily and gracefully in tempo." He starts it again and is more relaxed. The music flows more naturally. "Great balance," I encourage him, as the melody emerges beautifully in the left hand. This piece totally befuddled Jackson when he first began playing it many months ago. I wondered why the opening rhythm, with its lovely mordent, gave him such fits. Now, he's playing it with serene control. Jackson is not a prodigy, but he's keenly intelligent, musical, and an irrepressible, self-motivated, highly-disciplined student. His stolid, taciturn persona belies an inner fire that pushes him towards excellence.

Next comes the Toccata by Poulenc. Jackson attacks this difficult, animated, witty work with a clear and deft touch. We've worked hard on that touch. "Don't let it become heavy or harsh," I've reminded him many times. He has the speed and facility needed to do this piece justice. "Jackson, show me the French wit, the color in those seventh chords, the beauty! The grace! It's a big waste if it's just loud and fast."

Jackson doesn't say a whole lot at our lessons. But he registers everything, and when he asks a question or offers an opinion, it is not idle talk.

I met Jackson when he was nine years old. His father, Leo, who I have grown to like a great deal, brought him over to the house for a lesson/interview. Jackson was big for his age, a stout, robust, large, red-haired nine year old bruiser. Leo informed me that Jackson played football in an organized league. I asked him to come to the piano and show me what he's been learning. He lumbered over to the instrument with the gait of an implacable defensive lineman. "This boy doesn't have the look of a pianist," was a thought that I cannot deny passed through my mind. At first his playing was without refinement. His touch heavy and clumsy. But there was hope.

Jackson improved slowly and steadily for the first two years of lessons. Then he really caught the bug, fell in love with the classics, and took off! He devotedly listens to a great deal of music, familiarizing himself with the works of many composers. He practices two hours daily in addition to pulling in top grades in high school. By age 13, he was laying out plans to leave home and attend high school at Interlochen Academy of the Arts. Interlochen is an excellent music and art prep school located in Michigan. His parents were naturally surprised by their 13-year old son's declarations. So was I. At 13, I had nowhere near the maturity or the focus, to think about leaving home and setting out solo. Jackson was quite certain that this was what he wanted. He has not wavered in pursuing this path. He has impressed his parents, Leo and Nancy, with his hard work and his seriousness. He has even turned them into lovers of great music. It is always immensely pleasing to me when parents are brought to great music through their child's enthusiasm.

Now at 16, Jackson will be leaving Seattle this fall, and proceeding on to Michigan to attend Interlochen for his final two years of high school.

"Jackson, you need to play this with more boldness and more fire!" I'm never wholly pleased with his Chopin c-sharp minor Polonaise. I sit down and play the opening page for him. "It doesn't have to be louder," I tell him, "It has to be clearly articulated and in exact rhythm. The rhythm has to bite." Jackson's Polonaise misses some of the romantic ardor and gallantry of Chopin. Both his parents come from Polish stock, which I remind him. He has assured me of his love for Chopin. "Where is your Polish soul?" I challenge him. "Don't be afraid of being fully expressive. This is romanticism!" He's improved the piece, but I feel the romantics come less naturally to him than some other music does.

Jackson's program includes the first movement of Beethoven's Sonata in E-flat, Opus 31 No. 3, and Gershwin's First Prelude. Nothing is perfect. Nothing is spectacular. Everything's quite good, but what's more significant is that everything just keeps improving. Jackson hasn't come close to hitting his ceiling. He just gets better all the time and all his pieces inexorably gel, albeit *poco a poco*. It's been one steady ascent with no backsliding.

Unlike Sasha, Jackson is stalking musical excellence with a deadly one-mindedness. Beneath his outward reticence and mild manners, lurks a steely resolve which tracks his prey with steady focus.

We often talk about music. He listens to everything. He shares his feelings, "Ravel doesn't appeal to me," he tells me. "Really?" I'm surprised. "I don't know what it is, but I don't like Ravel," he holds. "What about Debussy," I ask. Jackson smiles, "I like Debussy." "How about Mahler?" "I like some of Mahler," he wavers, "But his symphonies are too long in my opinion." He goes on to tell me, "I've come to the decision that Mozart is probably the greatest composer." He says he would like to study conducting. We talk about great conductors. "Have you heard any recordings of Wilhelm Furtwangler?" I ask. Jackson has not heard of the great German maestro. But he will. Undoubtedly by the time these lines are written, he will have listened to Furtwangler's recordings of Beethoven, Brahms, and Wagner.

He's been to Europe at least twice on family vacations. His parents love traveling there. "Jackson, I've never been to London, have you?" I inquire. "Oh yes, London is a fabulous city! I love London!" he asserts. "Did you perhaps catch an opera at Covent Garden? Or attend a concert at Wigmore Hall?" He smiles shyly, then answers, "Well, it was a few years ago, when I was about 10, and—well, I guess I hadn't really started my career yet."

I understood his meaning. Music had not yet become the focal point of his young life. He chuckled, embarrassed by the clumsiness of his words, seeing how cute they must have sounded to his teacher.

As a pianist and student, Jackson's strength is his diligent approach, his fine mind, a good memory, steady nerves and composure. What he needs is a more impulsive, rhapsodic dose of brio; to be freer, to soar more mercurially on his musical flights. It cannot be predicted where his journey may take him.

When Shigeko arrives every Wednesday morning at 10:30, it always cheers me. This attractive woman in her thirties always wears an elemental, genuine smile on her lovely face. Her four year old daughter, Karin, who comes along with her mom often wears a most irresistible smile on her cute little face as well.

Shigeko is a real pianist. She holds a degree from a music conservatory in Osaka, her native city. She and her husband moved here eight years ago, and now are raising their young children in this country. Shigeko is busy with her family, but manages to keep her playing at a respectable level. Her goals seem to be well-suited to her life situation. She doesn't need to make a musical career, but music is her love, and she studies it seriously with incision and with joy. She seems liberated from the egotistical need to excel. She doesn't bring any heavy, nervous insecurities to our lessons. One doesn't feel that she puts any unnecessary pressure on herself. She simply loves to play the piano, and tries to play it as well as she can.

"What will you play first today?" I'll ask her. "Bach," she frequently answers, with a smile. She plays the first movement of the c minor French Suite. We've worked together on delineating the two-voice duet that Bach clearly wrote in the right hand part of this score. She plays with clarity and grace. "You can make those inner staccatos more piano Shigeko." "Ah," she says, her face taking on a concentrated appearance, and she plays it very well.

Next we work on Grieg's lovely lyric piece *To Spring*. "Shigeko, you can shape the left hand melody more." I play it for her, then exhort her to be freer in suffusing it with color. Her English is not perfect, and sometimes I have to repeat myself. She laughs whenever I try one of my Japanese phrases. *"Omgaku wa uzugushi,"* I say, "Music is beautiful." "Yes," she nods and laughs.

Karin her daughter, has been coloring in her little picture book, but now she's come over to the grand piano to demand some attention.

Shigeko lifts her in her arms and kisses her. Karin smiles happily. Suddenly I remember I have a little raspberry cake in the oven. "Karin, Shigeko, come with me in the kitchen for a moment. Let's check my cake. I think it's done!"

We troop into the kitchen and I pull out my cake. I've long loved to cook, but I've never before been a baker. This summer for the first time in my life, I've been smitten with baking. My students are offered slices of cakes, tarts, and muffins on a regular basis these days. That is part of a general strategy to keep myself from getting fat on my homemade pastries. "We'll let it cool a little, okay?" I tell Karin. Her face shines with curiosity as I insert, then remove a fork from my creation. "See Karin, it's done." Shigeko laughs and assures me, "Ah it smells very good."

As the pastry cools, we return to the piano in the living room. Debussy's first prelude *Les Danseuses de Delphes* is next on this day. Shigeko eases her hands gently into the rich, gentle chords which begin this piece. She is a fairly finished, refined pianist. I praise her tone. "That's right! That's a Debussy tone!" I become inspired and wax enthusiastically on the subject of pianistic color. Bach, Mozart, Chopin, Brahms, Debussy, Prokofiev, jazz, boogie-woogie—so many types of sound can be elicited from the instrument. "You must use your ear and find the right sound for each piece of music," I tell her. In fact, this is something Shigeko intuitively does well. It takes a sensitive ear, an incisive understanding of the music, taste, and technique. I push her to bring some of the middle voices out more *forte* later in the prelude. "Make me hear those octaves with fullness." I play it for her. She is absorbed, her concentration is steady. There are no distracting nervous mannerisms. She doesn't waste time with incidental, superfluous talk, or wisecracks meant to cover for insecurity. She is efficacious in applying her concentration to the task at hand. That alone is a telling trait; part of what makes her a fine musician.

Our only distraction at lessons is the periodic appearance of Karin at the piano. "I think we can try the cake now. Should we?" I look at Karin. She speaks Japanese at home, and is only now starting to learn a little English. "Come on," I say. "Let's go in the kitchen and cut the cake." Karin smiles, Shigeko laughs, and we all retreat to the kitchen to sample my newest masterpiece.

I cut out pieces of my pastry. Its ingredients include all-purpose flour, buckwheat, almond extract, eggs, sugar, milk, and raspberries. I await their judgment with some apprehension. Just a few days ago, Lewis, a high school student of mine had tried a sampling of my attempt at chocolate cake." Do you like cake to be so dry as this?" he had asked.

Shigeko bites into her slice of pastry and tells me it's good. "Ah, very good." She is polite and wouldn't be likely to tell me differently. "Karin," she turns to her daughter and speaks to her in Japanese. "Oichi," is the only word I can identify. It means delicious. Karin is more circumspect about trying a bite. Her little face has a cautious, indecisive appearance. Shigeko bends down, offers a small piece to her daughter, and eventually places it into a receptive, wide-open mouth. Karin approves, "Oichi," she says. I am relieved to have had my efforts in the kitchen receive a word of approval from this candid, demanding little food critic.

Our lesson concludes with Shigeko playing the Debussy through one more time. She takes my advice and plays it slightly slower. It has a more austere, solemn air to it; more beautiful. What a pleasure to work on refining such music with a cultivated, sensitive musician like Shigeko.

This afternoon there will be an array of younger children and teenagers. The repertoire we shall explore together will range from simple student works to a Beethoven sonata, a Chopin waltz, a Gershwin prelude, and an Albeniz piece. I should be able to get most of my raspberry torte distributed. I'll set aside a small piece for my own dessert. Shigeko and Karin bid me goodbye. "Goodbye," Karin pronounces with a proud smile. It is one of the few English phrases she knows. "Have a nice day, thank you very much," adds Shigeko with a sunny smile and a slight bow. I exchange a staccato-like high-five with Karin on the front porch. I will look forward to their visit again next Wednesday.

# GREAT PERFORMANCES

Over the years I have heard some great performances. Among the many noted pianists I have heard are Rudolf Serkin, Arthur Rubinstein, Vladimir Horowitz, Rosalyn Tureck, Alicia de La Rocha, Claudio Arrau, Murray Perahia, Annie Fischer, Gina Bachauer, Robert Goldsand, Artur Balsam, Andre Watts, Emil Gilels, Alfred Brendel, Andres Schiff, and others. It's a long list. Additionally, I have appreciated hearing other less-known pianists; professionals, professors, and students who played exceptionally well also.

Some of the many excellent musicians who most indelibly imprinted souvenirs in my memory were internationally celebrated, but some were not.

An especially memorable evening occurred during my student years in New York, some 34 years ago. My friend Rob, a piano student at Juilliard, had somehow procured three tickets for a rare New York appearance by the great pianist, Emil Gilels. This was back in 1977, and if memory serves, it was late in the winter season.

Rob, my friend Mark, and I, all three of us conservatory students, were off to Carnegie Hall to see and hear this much-admired Russian virtuoso. Seats were hard to come by, and I felt almost giddy descending upon this venerable concert hall that cool, clear evening, with the much-prized ticket tucked away in my pocket.

An aura of exciting anticipation enveloped the sidewalk in front of the hall. A stream of cabs pulled up, depositing an array of New York's musical and social elite. Bejeweled and fur-clad ladies, well-attired businessmen and politicians, musical stars like Isaac Stern, celebrities from the Broadway stage, noted intellectuals as well as the passionate, proud

Russians, eager to hear their compatriot, and the musically hungry young pianists like my friends and me, were among those who swelled the gathering crowd.

One sensed how special an occasion it was. Gilels and Richter were hailed as the two greatest Soviet pianists, and their appearances in America were quite rare; true events! All around one heard the chatter of genuinely excited people. "Which three Beethoven sonatas would he play?" "Has anyone noticed if Horowitz is attending tonight?" "I adore Gilels' Rachmaninoff, don't you?" "I'm glad he's playing the Brahms Opus 10 Ballades; one doesn't hear them enough." "Would Richter be back to play here again?" Such comments were intermingled with those of the many people speaking Russian, and a smattering of other languages as well, the calls of recognition at the arrival of *un célèbre,* and the festive greetings exchanged by friends. An electric buzz hovered in the air.

Entering Carnegie Hall amid this bubbling mélange of humanity was an invigorating experience. I felt privileged handing my ticket over to the usher, and passing into the country's most hallowed concert hall. My seat was in the balcony, near the front railing, on the right side. I always appreciated the true music lovers that one could count on finding in the balcony at Carnegie Hall. The real devotees often sat up there. That evening the balcony was packed, mostly with older Russians, many of whom wore the look of those with meager means. Purchasing a ticket to this concert meant a real dent in the budget for some of these homesick lovers of music. But this Gilels concert was not to be missed. The rest of the seats in the balcony were taken up by zealous young musicians like my friends and me, and an assortment of New York's fascinating coterie of music lovers, encapsulating everyone from salesclerks and cab drivers, to social workers and schoolteachers. For those of us in the balcony, Carnegie Hall was a temple, and the master musician a holy sage who could transmit the lofty beauties of Music's great poets and prophets.

Meanwhile in the boxes and in the orchestra seats below, the jewels of *les dames elegantes* gleamed in the warm glow of the chandeliers; and the luminaries, the dignitaries, and the well-connected took their places amidst the less glamorous but sincere and dedicated music lovers in their midst.

Carnegie Hall was vibrating with life. A palpable excitement swept through the assembly. I checked my program and felt pleased to see the three Beethoven sonatas chosen for the recital's first half. The G Major of Opus 79, on the lighter side with a simple but beautiful second movement; the E Flat of Opus 81 A., known as *Les Adieux*; and the e minor of Opus 90, with its repetitive, lyrical, almost Schubertian finale.

A quick glance at my watch revealed it was precisely eight o'clock and the recital was due to begin at any moment. Then something lovely happened that I shall never forget. People all about began to applaud and slowly rise to their feet. Shouts of "Rubinstein! It's Rubinstein!" were heard. The great maestro, then 89 years old, had been spotted in his box. I remember the sound which welled-up from the depths of the hall, and the heartfelt ovation which filled this music-drenched chamber. And there he was! Arthur Rubinstein, standing and graciously acknowledging this outpouring of admiration and love. Slowly the applause died down, the house lights dimmed, and all eyes were turned to the lit stage, with the lone black Steinway waiting impassively for the esteemed Emil Gilels to appear and bring it to life.

Mr. Gilels strode out of the wings to an ardent welcome from the full house. He seated himself at the piano, and with a minimum of fuss launched into the Beethoven G Major Sonata. He commenced playing this music with a straightforward, direct, no-nonsense approach. I felt surprised by just how straightforward it was. It struck me as colorless. Phrase after phrase rolled by with little distinction or tonal shading. To my ears, this sonata was played, dare I say it, with brusqueness, even stridency. Phrases were dispatched with minimal tonal nuance, and seemed to be hustled along by a less than inspired pianist. Was this really the acclaimed Gilels? Could he be having an off night? Was he perhaps nervous? Or not feeling well? I waited patiently for the musical and pianistic magic to emerge. The second sonata, the *Les Adieux*, was somewhat better. Then came the e minor, where the beautiful finale was better yet, and for me the most captivating movement of the recital's first half. But magic? Greatness? I perceived neither. The whole Beethoven set struck me as a bit rough, brusque, and delivered with little of the poetry, charm, and expressiveness I had been expecting.

He left the stage to receptive applause. I kept my impressions to myself at the intermission and enjoyed soaking up the still-festive energy. But I must confess to having been underwhelmed by Gilels' performance thus far. I distinctly recall reading Harold Schonberg's review the very next day in the New York Times. Schonberg, the longtime music critic at the Times, and an excellent writer, had written, "Emil Gilels ran rough shod over three Beethoven sonatas." I frequently agreed with Schoenberg's reviews, and did so this time.

But then came the second half of the recital, and things began to turn. The four Brahms Ballades of Opus 10 are infrequently performed. Gilels found the right poetic touch, the right layering of voices, and the right introspective mood for this music. He appeared to be settling in, making himself comfortable, calmly and lucidly alert to the probing melodies and shifting harmonies of these Brahms works. I felt myself warming to his artistry, unfolding before the large rapt audience.

Then came music of Liszt, and with it a supreme pianism that one rarely hears. The great virtuoso and the great artist were rolled into one, as Mr. Gilels justified his lofty reputation. His final piece was Liszt's much-played Hungarian Rhapsody No. 2 in c sharp minor. His performance of it was truly unforgettable, and not merely for the technical prowess, which other modern pianists possess too. Rather, it was playing that I would call transcendental. He swarmed the piano with power, clarity, warmth, charm, and glee. Glee above all. I was reminded of the many descriptions I had read of Liszt's own concert playing. Those in attendance that night were transported to the golden age of heroic romanticism. It was a throwback to the era of the romantic virtuoso. The instrument poured out voluptuous, warm, ringing tones. It thundered, it sparkled, it sighed. And it danced an irresistible dance of seductive beauty, pulling the disparate members of this New York audience into a focused, indivisible one. We were all together now. In heightened alertness, we danced to the well-known sequence of notes, vibrating through Carnegie Hall. Liszt's living spirit, vibrating through time and space, had pulled us into the timeless essence of music.

Emil Gilels had been the necessary conduit through which all this energy had flowed. To say that he triumphed is an understatement. It was an elated crowd that spilled out into the cool air on West 57th Street that evening.

Upon reflection, I can't help but compare the splendid Gilels recordings of various Beethoven sonatas with the less satisfying Beethoven performances that night, those many years ago. Perhaps this shouldn't be so surprising, when one stops to consider that even the greatest pianists are, after all, human beings. Mere mortals, they are not robotically consistent. Their interpretations evolve and change over time. Their levels of concentration fluctuate. Their moods shift, and affect their concentration, and ultimately a pianist may be really "on" or slightly "off" in any given performance. It is this that partly makes a live performance so special.

Those of us who flocked to Carnegie Hall that evening weren't there to see the unveiling of a statue, or to view a well-made film. We were there to see a *performing art*. We were there to see a man play the piano. A talented, disciplined artist, but nonetheless a man, who would attempt to honor the music and touch the audience. It mattered not how well he may have played in the past, nor how sterling a reputation he owned. *Now* is the only moment that matters in a performing art. Yesterday's rehearsal run-through doesn't count. He would have to walk out onto the Carnegie Hall stage, before an expectant, sophisticated New York audience and deliver. Note by note, phrase by phrase, he would yet again have to execute the composer's intricate instructions, interpret his intentions, attempt to feel the muse, and hope to enter into the stream of the music's essence. And this would be witnessed by more than 2,000 souls; note by note, moment by moment.

And so it is with the performing arts, the creative process must occur anew each time. Thus, is it always necessarily unique and irrevocable. There are no second chances.

I count myself fortunate to have heard Emil Gilels play that evening. I realize I was given a singular glimpse into this brilliant musician's work. His Carnegie Hall performance was a deeply enriching experience. One I can never forget.

I was fortunate enough to attend two recitals given by Vladimir Horowitz. One at Carnegie Hall in 1975, and another in Avery Fisher Hall, at Lincoln Center in 1978. Horowitz was of course revered as a legend. He was in his seventies when I heard him. I was a student at the Manhattan School of Music back in '75, an had chosen to stand in line for several hours out on 57th Street, in front of Carnegie Hall, to be able to purchase tickets. I felt I just *had* to see the great Horowitz.

The first recital was very fine, excellent. Schumann's Sonata in f sharp minor dominated the first half of the program. I recall Liszt, Rachmaninoff, and Chopin being played after the intermission. The hype that surrounded this pianist was extreme. Horowitz was a great virtuoso, but no one could live up to some of the expectations that the public heaped upon him. He himself, in an interview, once related a story of how after pouring everything he had into a performance of Mussorgsky's *Pictures at an Exhibition*, overheard a lady sitting close to the piano in stage seats remark to her husband, "You haven't heard anything yet; he's just getting warmed up." Horowitz said that he felt deflated upon hearing this woman's comment. He went on to tell the interviewer that he had played the piece about as well as he possibly could.

I may have fallen prey to the unrealistic expectations I had been filled with by the talk amongst the piano students I chummed around with, and the reams of worshipful reviews found in print. I judged that first concert in Carnegie Hall to be merely excellent. The second time I heard Horowitz I came eager to hear this maestro, but without such fantastical expectations. This time, at the Avery Fisher Hall, the old Russian pianist transcended excellence. The magic appeared, and I had a true firsthand encounter with the legend of Vladimir Horowitz.

His Rachmaninoff had movement, clarity, color, and a certain style and nervous edge that made it different from anything I had ever heard before. The Liszt *Mephisto Waltz* was played with a different level of virtuosity than anything I'd ever witnessed as well. Unimaginable colors bounced out of his Steinway, flying out into the hall, holding his auditors spellbound. Speed combined with utter lucidity and amazing tonal control brought the big audience to a breathless unity. I felt the hall breathe as one, concentrate as one, partake as one, as rapid pianissimo arpeggios etched their jewel-like tones into our minds. This wasn't the fortissimo thumping of a typical fire-eating virtuoso. This was the most refined, delicate, and yet thrilling virtuosity I had ever experienced. Even for Horowitz to have conceived of these sounds and colors, together with this svelte, feline rhythmic movement, let alone executing it digitally, showed a type of genius. But he hadn't only conceived of it in his imagination, he played it on the piano. He played it with two hands and ten fingers.

So there, now I've gone and done it; added to the long list of ecstatic words sung in praise of this pianistic wizard.

As an encore, he played Chopin's famous *Heroic* Polonaise in A Flat. Now came the full fortissimos and the blazing octaves. The tone was big, grand, but not harsh. Sitting at the Lincoln Center subway station after the concert, I remember feeling still somewhat dazed by the performance I had just taken in. I had the vision before me of Horowitz making the piano jump in the air on some of the emphatic downbeats of the Polonaise. It seemed the instrument verily leapt from the stage on some of those dynamic attacks, although I'm pretty sure that the heavy concert grand remained firmly grounded throughout When the uptown number one Broadway local screeched piercingly to a halt in the station, I barely seemed to hear the noisy shrillness of its arrival. I was still bathing in A Flat Major, still in a Chopinesque, Horowitzian trance.


I saw Rubinstein play once. I was just 17 and had not yet quite begun my musical renaissance; still feeling my way tentatively in the dark, but edging closer to fully embracing my life's first love. I had recently received my driver's license, and I drove alone from my house in Livingston to the old Mosque Theater in downtown Newark. The lobby of this grand old theater was humming with anticipation. People seemed happy, as if they knew how lucky they were to be attending a Rubinstein concert. The great maestro walked out onstage to begin an all Chopin program, and was received with adoration.

There are two impressions that stand out in my memory about this piano recital. One was the palpable love and enjoyment that this vibrant, then 83 year old man then emanated. His presence was youthful, charismatic, and unaffected. His playing was similarly natural, unforced, and beautiful. Everything seemed natural, and yet the music had all the passion, temperament, tenderness, and power that anyone could ask for. The pearly runs, the golden singing tones, and the virtuosic brio were all brought forth by a seemingly joyous, emotionally clear soul.

The second impression is the response accorded to this legendary artist by the audience. It was pure love. There was a love that seemed to flow between performer and public that I've never experienced before or since. With Horowitz, the public's love was held back by the awe and even slight fear of his nervous, complex persona. People expected unrealistic perfection from Horowitz. Instead of relaxing and flowing happily in the stream of music, they sat in heightened expectation of freakish perfection and pianistic miracles. They loved him, but they also stood back from him with some reserve. They sensed he was somehow different, remote, not an ordinary guy. Rubinstein, they revered as a brilliant master of the piano, but also as a real down to earth man. They came to his concerts not to judge him, but to love him, and love the piano works he played with such clarity and ardor. They never came asking for perfection. They came to love.

The aged, magnetic, white-haired pianist was clearly in love too. He had come to play the piano and share his love of music and life with the large crowd. He gave six encores, and never appeared the least bit fatigued. The encores felt completely spontaneous, not planned out at all. The audience roared and stamped, begging for more, and out he'd come, taking his seat at the piano, thinking for a few seconds, and then selecting another piece out of his immense repertoire. He would then begin touching his listeners anew with his unique artistry.

Alicia de La Rocha was a marvelous pianist. I heard her four or five times. I especially remember her Mozart. I recall the crystalline sound, the quasi-Spanish snap of her rhythm, and the wonderful crispness of her staccatos. She brought a distinctive, fresh approach to the great Austrian composer. I especially enjoyed her performances of the D Major Sonata K. 576, and the F Major Concerto, both of which I heard at Avery Fisher Hall.

I recall her fine performance of Schubert's great final Sonata in B-flat. This is a very special, precious work for me, and one that I've performed myself. I have never heard any pianist completely win me over with their interpretation. Nonetheless, I greatly appreciated de La Rocha's personal approach and her deep commitment to this music. I distinctly recall that the Schubert sonata was the finale of a particular New York recital, and was followed by a spate of encores of Isaac Albeniz. I couldn't get enough of her Albeniz! This short, little, small-handed woman simply dazzled her audience with her great compatriot's extremely difficult, virtuosic music. Her Albeniz had luminous color, rhythmic excitement, clarity, and that extra passionate Spanish dueño. It was simply irresistible. I have Alicia de La Rocha to thank for my love of this composer.

I made it to three recitals of the great Chilean-born pianist Claudio Arrau. Arrau was an amazing pianist who could play anything. I remember hearing him in a fascinating radio interview with David Dubal, the noted pianist, scholar, commentator, and someone I also greatly admire. Arrau told Dubal that he realized as a very young boy that he had a feeling of great responsibility towards the piano. He talked about his teacher in Germany, Martin Krause, himself a former pupil of Franz Liszt, and about many aspects of his long life and career. He was asked, "Have you ever studied a piece that you found to be extremely difficult?" I'll never forget the matter of fact manner in which he brushed off this question. "No, not really," was his simple response. He mentioned one Liszt etude as being just a trifle difficult at first, but quickly overcome with some good practice. "Did you ever get a little bit lazy in your practicing?" his interlocutor inquired. "No, never. I always worked hard," came the straightforward response.

I came away from this interview impressed by Arrau, but also finding his personality a bit cool and colorless. It's funny, but each time I heard him play, I felt, here is a formidable serious pianist of the first rank, yet I wasn't thrilled or totally won-over by his playing. The phrasing, nuance, *rubatos*, et cetera, struck me as too staid, too plain. All the notes were there, played with apparent ease and certainty. This happened with Beethoven's *Appassionata*, Schumann's *Etude s Symphoniques*, and the Liszt Sonata. But something else happened too. When each piece was over, and he stood to bow and accept the applause of the audience, I suddenly sensed that I had heard a fine performance. Days after each Arrau concert I had attended, his performance stayed with me. I think it was his overview of the architectural structure of the larger scale works that made his playing unique. He saw the composition as a whole, not merely as a series of phrases. Although he never excited an audience the way a Horowitz or a Rubinstein did, he brought both immense technique and this ability to see the whole green forest, not just the individual trees, to his interpretations.

I want to contrast Arrau with another excellent, well-known pianist still before the public today, who I shall not name. Whenever I heard this pianist, I invariably would have almost the complete opposite reaction. From the first phrase of this musician's playing, I felt myself in agreement. "Beautiful touch! Lovely phrasing! Silky smooth legato, delicate pianissimo filigree." These were the types of impressions that I'd have. But the day after each recital I'd heard by this fine pianist, I'd have almost forgotten it. It made no lasting impression. All these years later, I haven't forgotten Claudio Arrau's concerts.

Finally, I must mention Menahem Pressler. This special artist, who concentrated mostly on chamber music, was one of the greatest I've ever encountered. The performances of the Beaux Arts Trio that I heard were magnificent. Pressler has been the lynchpin of this trio for over 50 years. I believe he has just recently retired from this ensemble. The Mozart and Beethoven trios that I heard him perform were on another level of artistry from all but perhaps a handful of musicians. His energy, his ebullience, and his focus were beautiful to behold. Mozart and Beethoven sparkled with such joy and depth under his unerring technique. Every line seemed alive with meaning. His delineation of voices and his feeling for each phrase never felt ordinary, forced, or false. The music unfolded under his fingers with such a joyful understanding of these great composers, that I can truly use the word elevated to describe my state of being all three times that I was lucky enough to catch him perform. On one occasion, I heard the ensemble perform Schubert's E-flat Trio. Once more, I was entranced by Mr. Pressler's uplifting artistry. The rhythmic focus of the haunting slow movement couldn't have been more captivating. And the drive and merriment of the finale swept me along in high jubilation. His playing was alive, incisive, and profoundly genuine. To Mr. Pressler, who is now 87 years of age, I offer my humble and heartfelt thanks.

Before concluding, I would like to stress that there are many worthy pianists who don't have huge careers and are not heard in the large cities of the world. There are thousands of them. Not so surprisingly, some of the most affecting and intimate performances I have heard have come from relatively anonymous musicians. Some of these have touched me as deeply as those by Gilels, Rubinstein, or anyone else.

I remember a student at Ithaca named Laurie, a very deep, spiritual, fiercely independent and talented young woman, play Liszt's etude *La Campanella*, in a large classroom full of other piano students. It was mesmerizing. I haven't forgotten it, nearly 40 years later.

Music is not something reserved for the 50 or so virtuosi that can make a living by touring the world playing concerts. Anyone with talent, ardor, and a willingness to work hard may play great music. The extra ingredient that must be added to this mix is sincerity. The pianist who can really touch the listener must be himself, authentic, with something genuinely individual to say. I once heard Rubinstein tell an interviewer that there is no such thing as "the greatest." No greatest pianist or greatest composer. An artist, he said, can only be different, unique. "If someone says that a young pianist is the second Paderewski, or the second Rachmaninoff, you know he's already in trouble." He explained that an artist must be himself, not an imitator of anyone else.

I spent three weeks in the summer of 2010 visiting two good friends of mine in Germany. While in Düsseldorf with my friend Helmut, we visited the Robert Schumann Hochschule Für Musik, named after the great composer who once lived in this town. We attended a concert given by some of the school's students. We heard two pianists, and three singers perform. One young Asian boy, perhaps 19 years old, played a late Beethoven sonata, the one in A Major, Opus 101. He played with beauty and true understanding. This young, slight, wispy, unassuming figure settled himself quietly at the piano and began playing with an assured, calm focus. He avoided dramatic facial expressions or bodily gestures. With minimal physical movement he played Beethoven's complex sonata with an insight that belied his youth. I remember exchanging a knowing glance with Helmut, my music loving friend, and inwardly thinking, "This boy has it-this is a real musician. This is authentic."

After completing the sonata, this youngster bowed slightly without any outward show of emotion. Then he walked stoically over to his seat in the audience. He managed a shy smile when his fellow conservatory students came over to congratulate him.

I don't know if this young musician will have a successful career as a pianist. I don't even remember his name. It is not important to me. What I do know is that he is a true musician and that he gave me a beautiful 20 minutes of Beethoven. This performance, given in a small *saal* at the Düsseldorf conservatory before an audience of perhaps 65 persons, touched me as deeply as any performance given by Serkin, Horowitz, or anyone else I've ever heard. It was the real thing. Beethoven had composed this sonata with sincerity and genius. A talented young pianist had understood, and had played it with sincerity and commitment. I listened with receptivity and was struck. Struck by the life-affirming force of music.

# MUSIC MUSIC EVERYWHERE,
## BUT WHO'S LISTENING?

I love music. But not all the time! As with everything else, quality, moderation, and balance have importance. I also love people, but solitude is still precious, and I can't pursue close friendships with everyone. So it is with music. In saying that I love music, it is not all music but rather only some music of which this statement holds true. There does exist much music in this world which just doesn't interest me. And then too, is there music which I find downright grating.

I have spent many hours of my life listening to music, playing it, studying it, hearing it inwardly, teaching it, and thinking about it. Sometimes I need a break. In fact, at times I have the desire to flee from music completely. How wonderfully refreshing it can be to rest amidst the sounds of nature's flowing rivers, warbling birds, or the soothing harmony of a spring shower. Music at times, can be an unwelcome intruder.

Increasingly it has become difficult to avoid music when one is out in the public sphere. This brings me to my point. Music is heard almost everywhere, yet it is listened to but rarely.

One can encounter music at a restaurant, in a department store, the baseball park, the barber shop, the beach, almost anywhere where human beings congregate. This ubiquitous music serves as a background, not as a foreground. It is not intended to be listened to attentively. People hear the sound, but barely register the beauty. We are thus becoming jaded to music's beauty by the incessant barrage of the omnipresent speakers, pouring forth a relentless stream of myriad tones. One can walk into a restaurant, pub, or café, and be immediately engulfed by some kind of music, usually piped in electronically. It could be Ella Fitzgerald singing jazz with great verve, a searching, heartfelt Mahler Adagio, a raucous, hard-driving rock tune, a Christmas carol, a plaintive folk song with contemplative lyrics, pulsating hip hop, a delicate, melancholy Chopin nocturne. It might be Pavarotti's Golden Tenor, ardently singing *Nessun Dorma,*, Sinatra's reed like tones proclaiming *The Lady is a Tramp*, Elvis's rocking accusation that *You Ain't Nothin but a Hound Dog*, Dylan's jagged voice crackling, *The Times They Are A'changing*, or the Beatles tunefully suggesting to simply *Let it Be*. What's the difference? No one's paying attention anyway. Everyone is eating, typing, reading, talking, checking email, texting, or thinking an array of thoughts which preclude the possibility of paying real attention to any of the musical samples I've just cited. This music is given no respect.

From Bach and Beethoven,to the Beatles and beyond, musicians have put great effort and lots of soul into trying to communicate something special to their fellows. They are trying to reach us and touch us. All of this ubiquitous background music isn't touching people much. In fact, I submit that it jades us to music's real power. We're actually being trained to take music's presence for granted. We're learning how to put it aside as a backdrop. Lucid alertness is not being promoted by this musical battering. On the contrary, numbness is being cultivated.

It seems that most men, women, and children, though not all, have learned to tune this ambient music out. Not me. Consequently, I have a problem. I can't *tune out* music so easily. It means too much to me. It is too present to ignore. Every note that wafts through a restaurant or a hardware store seems to find its way to my ears and on into the part of the brain that recognizes and discerns pitches, timbres, and rhythms. For me, there's no escape. Though I protest, my friends tell me, "Just tune it out, try to ignore it."

I suppose I could work harder to learn how to tune it out. But should I? Should we learn how to tune out music? What else might we tune out? The sound of wind rustling the leaves? The beauty of a sunset? The despair of someone in pain? Should we tune out our emotions? Maybe we've done enough of tuning out, and need to better learn to tune in. Perhaps our hyper-stimulated society is robbing us from life's most elemental and precious beauties.

One final point on this subject. Do I have any say over whether there will be music in some public space? Or which type of music it will be? Or am I to understand that music will accost me as I enter a grocery store, regardless of my wishes? We're given choices when dining at a restaurant. There's the choice of which dish to order, the choice to drink wine or not, the particular wine to drink if partaking in wine, a choice of beverages, desserts, etc, are given. But who ever asks if a guest prefers music or not, and if a guest answers in the affirmative, is he ever asked to choose the type of music that should be played? At best, a guest may request to lower the music. This is what I often do, and sometimes my request is granted. When background music is especially loud and abrasive, and is not lowered upon request, I leave. That of course is still a choice left to me.

At the cinema, one may choose to buy popcorn or not. It is possible to watch a film with or without popcorn. No plastic tube drops automatically from the ceiling, and funnels a carefully measured-out portion of popcorn into the moviegoer's mouth. We're probably not yet ready to accept that. But music of almost any type, pumped into the air, without having been requested, is accepted, or at least tolerated by most people. That is because it is not considered very important. It's just music. It can easily be tuned out and relegated to white noise by the majority of modern men and women.

Fortunately, I am getting better at withstanding this tonal nemesis of mine. I am learning to accept that though I cannot completely ignore background music, it won't kill me. True, my concentration will be diffused. This reality can be observed and accepted. Like with everyone else, my musical sensitivities will be somewhat hardened. I avoid what I can, and just try to take the hectic stimuli of modern life with mindfulness, and hopefully a measure of equanimity. I try. I am improving, but I will now relate a story which illustrates how I formerly reacted to this personal scourge.

Catherine and I were out walking one lovely spring afternoon in downtown Seattle. Catherine Treadgold is a wonderful friend. She is an excellent mezzo-soprano, and we have given several concerts together. Our relationship began 16 years ago as an exciting romance, and then settled two years later into a wonderful and abiding friendship that endures to this day. Catherine is thin, athletic, and energetic. She has beautiful blue eyes and shoulder-length blonde hair. She is attractive and possesses a lively intelligence and a terrific sense of humor. No wonder I liked her instantly.

On this particular day, we were both in high spirits and enjoying our city jaunt. We were getting hungry, and came across a café-restaurant that had an appealing European look to it. Upon entering, we were confronted with the Rolling Stones, blaring at quite high volume. This struck me as incongruous; the loud rock music in this otherwise quaint setting, with colorful frescoes on the walls.

Catherine knows me all too well. She looked at me dubiously. "Let's just see if they'll turn it down," I ventured. I'm not a Rolling Stones fan but I don't hate their music. "Look, if they agree to turn the music down, I'd like to have lunch here," I told Catherine. "Ask nicely," she suggested.

I told someone at the cash register that the two of us would like to have lunch, but it would depend on the music being turned to a low level. "No problem," came the response. The man at the register yelled out to someone in the kitchen to lower the music. Within a couple of seconds, the blaring rock music was transformed to a quieter, much less intrusive presence. "Thank you very much," I told the employee. "That was really nice of you." Catherine and I took a table and ordered lunch. I was so pleased with this café's consideration in honoring my request, that I walked over to the kitchen counter where I had spied a glass bowl that served as a tip jar. I put a few dollar bills into the jar. I sat back down at our table, happily ensconced in this pleasant café, which my charming companion, awaiting a grilled eggplant panino.

It is true, that from my point of view, no background music is preferable to any. Still, Rolling Stones played *sotto voce* is a great improvement over Rolling Stones played *fortissimo* when enjoying a cozy, intimate lunch date. However, to my extreme dismay, this peaceable atmosphere was not to last. Halfway through a very tasty sandwich, the music suddenly surged to a volume at least as loud as what it had been when we arrived, perhaps even louder. My nervous system received a rude jolt. The Stones were back to *forte* with a vengeance, as rough, rebellious, and in-your-face as ever. When it comes to my efforts to negotiate the peace with unwanted, relentless loud music, I generally fare poorly. As Mick Jagger himself once lamented in a well-known lyric, "I can't get no satisfaction."

My blood pressure shot up. The shock of this drastic change in my situation took hold of me. "No!" I yelled. "You told me the music would be lower!" I hollered to the waiter and cashier. Catherine put her hand on my arm in a futile attempt to get me to calm down. She looked at me with an expression that was both slightly mortified but also menacing. It was her "don't make a scene" expression. Alas, I would not be pacified. Having been betrayed with music was too much for me.

"I wouldn't have ordered lunch if I hadn't been promised the music would be kept low," I bellowed. "I'm sorry," shrugged the fellow at the register. "They really want the music going strong," he said, motioning toward the kitchen. "Fred," Catherine now implored me. "Don't make a scene."

Make a scene? Is that all she cared about? I looked at Catherine impatiently. "I'm at least going to retrieve my tip," I told her. With that, I stomped over to the tip jar and began reaching my hand in to reclaim the dollar bills I had just placed there 10 minutes earlier, when I had been in the best of spirits. This piece of deceitful knavery would not go rewarded by a tip. Unfortunately, I had difficulty in executing my design quickly and elegantly. My hand wouldn't fit through the neck of the jar. This only increased my agitation. I took the jar, turned it over, and angrily shook all the bills and coins out. "I just want my money!" I announced. No one said a word. I extricated my three dollars then carefully returned the rest of the money to the jar. I looked at Catherine whose facial expression told me she was not sympathetic to my performance. "I'm leaving this place," I said. I walked out on to the sidewalk where that cursed music, which I had been assured would not impede on our lunch, could be left behind. The city sounds of car traffic and wisps of conversation from passing pedestrians made for a satisfying antidote to that bloody, blaring background music.

In retrospect, with the benefit of tranquil reflection, I understand that the fellow in the kitchen must have found it just as frustrating and enervating to go about his work without the aid of a loud, driving rock beat as it was for me to enjoy lunch and Catherine's conversation with it. It seems we were at loggerheads.

Catherine joined me out on the sidewalk with daggers in her eyes. We were both furious, albeit for different reasons. She was furious at me for my behavior. I was furious at several things; having been deceived by the restaurant, having a pleasant, quiet lunch ruined, and also by Catherine's main interest in mollifying my anger, and choosing social propriety over taking my side. I was really angry at everything, and as I analyze it now, what I was most piqued by was my inability to bend things to my will. I wanted what I wanted! The world refused to cooperate.

My irascibility having subsided some, I devoted my energies to mollifying Catherine's. Fortunately it didn't take long to win her forgiveness. I only had to remind her of the years that she had spent living in New York. "I know I embarrassed you," I told her. "But come on. In New York, no one would have paid any attention to a little scene like this." She laughed at that. I was soon apologizing for my little tantrum. It was a small window of insight into my own complicity of having allowed some loud rock and roll to buffet my equanimity.

So I've gotten somewhat better at handling unwanted sound, music, and noise. This is not to say that I consider the preponderance of ambient music to be harmless. I continue to hold to the view that it jades human beings to music's true beauty and power.

I have heard the advice given that we ought to slow down and "smell the coffee." This can only work if we enjoy coffee in some moderation. Go to a coffee shop and drink eight cups of coffee over a couple of hours, and I believe you will find the pleasure of drinking and smelling coffee to be reduced. Too much of a good thing ruins it.

It is a proper balance that I appeal to. Maybe losing my temper that day with Catherine wasn't my finest hour. But I know a wonderful old gentleman named Paul, who once took matters into his own hands at a restaurant, by disconnecting the wires from the offending speakers. Paul, who passed away this year at the age of 89, was a man after my own heart. I can only tip my hat at his audacity.

Music is a beautiful art. It is not a cheap throw-away toy. It deserves our attention. If it were heard a bit less, it would actually be *listened* to more, and understood more deeply. So let me appeal to the good citizens of the world to stand united against tyranny, racism, violence, plutocracy; and yes, the ceaseless, numbing oral stimuli buzzing about us and sucking a portion of sensitivity and alertness right out of our skins. The constantly besieged, distracted mind cannot be reflective. Such a mind lacks the peace and clarity to attain insight, or perceive beauty.

And what shall we stand for? I suggest democracy, brotherhood, kindness, and peace. *Peace and quiet.* The world could always use more peace, and it could also benefit from a little more quiet. And if anyone reads these words while music is playing, turn it off!

# BACK TO WORK

It's been cold and clear this week. A respite from the grey, drizzly mist of a Seattle December. The holiday season is in full swing. There have been fewer lessons to teach the past two weeks. More time to devote to fine tuning my piano pieces for January's upcoming recital.

I'm writing these lines at Picolino's restaurant/café in Seattle's Ballard neighborhood, where I await a rendezvous with my friend Charles. I'm early and feeling in the best of moods. After the usual playful banter with Allie, the witty and beautiful young barista, I take my seat at a favorite table.

This morning's work on Chopin's great Fourth Ballade still resonates in my mind, in my ear, and on down into my fingers. It's taken some time, but now I'm making headway. The piece is finally starting to yield its haunting beauty to my persistent wooing. I'll get another crack at practicing some more this afternoon. The closer I come to gaining mastery of a great work of music, the more of a man on a mission I become.

I know I am not as gifted as some musicians. Moreover, crucial years of childhood, when musical ability is most readily developed, were partially squandered in my case. Whatever musical bounty nature presented me with, it was not as fully cultivated as it might have been during those precious, impressionable years. My sight-reading is certainly not exceptional, and I don't memorize a work in a mere matter of days as certain prodigious talents do. But I trust in my musical ability. Being around so many musicians, as well as teaching so many students these past 35 years, has revealed to me that I have my share of what is rightly called musical talent. I know I have a fine ear; perfect pitch, and a gift for improvisation and playing by ear. In measuring artistic talent, there is also a wild card that must be considered. How deeply does a performing musician penetrate into musical creation? Does he have something unique and genuine to say? Can he or she connect with an audience and profoundly move the listener? This extra dimension is not easily measured, but is central to the creation of real art. Einstein once said, "Not everything that counts can be counted, and not everything that can be counted counts." This seems to apply to music and to art in general.

The musical performer must have discernible, obvious gifts, of course, but also that extra intangible ingredient— the knowing, receptive soul. To perform a Chopin ballade or a Beethoven sonata before an audience, a pianist must possess conviction, technique, intelligence, and sincerity. He must have something all his own to say. This final point; this distinct, individualistic insight and love, is what separates a respectable performance from a special one.

I am resigned to the fact that I cannot learn scores as effortlessly as some with superior talents. There will always be those with greater and lesser abilities. A musician will inevitably question his own gifts, and compare them to those of his colleagues. This is natural since it is simply undeniable that one must possess talent— raw talent— to become an excellent pianist and musician. Do I have what it takes? How do I stack up? These questions will gnaw at any aspiring musician.

I have answered them to my own satisfaction. I have as much natural ability as I have. No more and no less. It is acceptable to me that some pianists own more impressive talents. I am fortunate to have whatever musical gifts have been allotted me. I feel sufficiently blessed.

And so I continue to court the beautiful f minor Ballade. Though I can't learn it in a week or two, I'm not deterred. It's been four months of on and off practice, but now it is gelling. A special relationship is forming. As with any great work of art, it will be a relationship that shall evolve, grow, and endure over time. I am not the first pianist, nor shall I be the last to enter into a love affair with this sublime, dramatic ballade. She has had many lovers, and gives her soulful beauty to any who approach with a receptive heart. She is beloved by many and avail-

able to many. For this truth, I suffer no pangs of jealousy. My relationship with this enchantress shall be my very own; unique from all others.

I have grown accustomed to the way Chopin's deeply personal
creation twists, turns, and dances; grown accustomed to its enveloping harmonic mist, its seductive melodies and exquisite arabesques. I
live with its oscillating moods; from heartrending melancholy to serene
innocence, from despair to hope, from passionate love to wild, unbridled
fury. The formidable difficulties of this work only heighten my hunger
to achieve a sympathetic union. I am hooked.

Since returning from my summer hiking in Alberta, I've been back in
my satisfying routine. Recently I made a first trip to my student Henry's
fifth grade class. I had never been with this group of ten-year-olds
before, and I started them off with Mozart. "Mozart was born in 1756.
Was the United States a country then?" I asked. They were all ready with
the answer. "No, no!– colonies, yeah, colonies!" came a chorus of young
voices. "When he died at the young age of 35, in 1791, was the United
States a country then?" They were ready for that one too. A near unani-
mous wave of affirmative responses washed through the classroom.

I turned to their teacher, Ms. Roth, and asked, "Have they learned
about the French Revolution?" She told me they had not, but several
bright-eyed students having overheard our exchange broke in eagerly
to assure me that they knew all about it. "You see," I said. "During
Mozart's short lifetime, both the American Revolution and the French
Revolution had occurred." The boy sitting just next to my student
Henry instantly shot up his arm. I called on him and he proudly
proclaimed "But the war of 1812 hadn't happened!" At that, Henry
jumped in, "Hey, what was the war of 1812 about anyway?"

Ms. Roth quickly stepped in and asserted her authority to dissuade
any further analysis of this and future historical upheavals. I chose to
refrain from exploring either the British-American conflict of 1812, or
the Napoleonic War in Russia, tempting though it was to segue right
into Tchaikovsky's 1812 Overture. Mozart was the day's subject and I
was determined to stay on point.

The kids remained alert and engaged throughout the remainder of our time together. They were extremely quiet and attentive during the musical interludes I played on the piano. Just before leaving, I told them, "Mozart wrote over 600 compositions. His music is now over 220 years old, and you know—people all over the world listen, play, and love his music. Every time the clock ticks, hundreds of thousands of people somewhere in the world, on differnt continents, are involved with and inspired by Mozart. When we're asleep in North America, hundreds of thousands of people in Europe and Asia are practicing Mozart on their instruments, or listening to performances of his music." The students looked back at me wearing pensive faces. "Just think," I continued. "Day after day, every single second, year after year, Mozart's music is perpetually playing all over the world!" Finally one boy raised his hand and inquired, "What about Antarctica? Is Mozart playing in Antarctica?"

Ah! Charles has arrived. He appears with his customary folded copy of the New York Times tucked under his right arm. He joins me at my table and we exchange pleasant greetings. "What's in the paper today Charles?" He explains that the Times is filled with only partial truths, and omits some very basic, salient truths. That starts us off on an analysis of the mainstream media. We easily reach agreement that the media is a "presentation," subject to bias and beholden to moneyed interests. "But beyond that Charles, I bet I can tell you what's in that newspaper—stories of avarice, injustice, violence, aspiration, hope, conflict—what am I leaving out?" "If you already know so much about what's in the paper," Charles responds, "I'm not going to give it to you." Charles often passes his copy of the paper to me after having finished reading it.

That moves us away from the New York Times and into a consideration of other things. I enjoy these meetings with my friend. Charles is in his sixties and semi-retired from a career in editing. We share an appreciation for simple pleasures, and seek to avoid much of the frenzied, frenetic energy found swirling madly about our modern society.

Later that afternoon after a short but concentrated practice session, Dani arrives for her lesson. Daniela Schulman has been my piano student for nearly nine years. As a five and a half year old, she had plenty of spirit and energy, but a short fall of calm focus. Ah, Dani was a little spitfire in those days. She was moody, easily frustrated, and in perpetual motion. Just getting her to sit still on the piano bench took some doing. "Don't stand up sweetheart," her father Andrew, present at all those early lessons, would often advise. "Daddy!" she would wheel around to face her father. "I know what I'm doing!" Dani could be a handful in those days. But she was a jewel. She was clearly intelligent, extremely sensitive, vibrant, and best of all to my view, possessed a precious, almost beatific smile when playing the piano. On those occasions when her active, percolating brain would settle into sustained concentration, and as she gained control over a scale, an arpeggio, or a short piece of music, that priceless smile would appear.

There were those lessons at which she was really prepared, confident, and focused. As she'd ready herself to play her piece, Andrew would gently remind her, "Now Dani, remember not to play too fast." This would usually provoke a swift rebuke from his temperamental daughter. "Daddy! I know what I'm doing!" Then she would compose herself and begin playing. With the sounding of the first note, that beautiful smile would spread across her face. She was engaged in making music and the joy of it all was transparent. The lovely little smile would remain in place until she hit her first mistake. The first wrong note would wipe it away instantly.

Now that Dani is 14, her boastful proclamations are rare. She is far more even-tempered, but still a vibrant, intelligent, lovely girl. I have become friends with her parents Andrew and Betsy. In fact, the whole clan, all three, joined my second tour to Vienna. Last year, as she turned 13, I attended her bat mitzvah.

On this particular December day, she settles herself calmly at the piano and begins to play Mozart's Fantasy in d minor. The introductory arpeggios roll up the piano with color and feeling. The ensuing adagio is given with an appropriately plaintive, sensitive quality. Her balance is good. Her phrasing is intelligent. Her tone is rich and communicative. Dani understands this music. That wonderful smile appears and blooms on her now adolescent face.

Dani has matured. She's still her own toughest critic and given to frustration when things don't go smoothly, but she's gained a good measure of self control. Dani will always be demanding of herself.

Her interest in the piano has increased over the past year or two. She seems poised to make large strides as a musician. Our lessons have become great fun. Among her many gifts is a quick wit and a devilish, mischievous sense of humor.

She knows I'm writing a book and has asked me if she's to be mentioned in it. "Dani, you're in my book" I tell her near the end of our lesson. She's in excellent spirits, having played Mozart and Granados beautifully. "You'll probably say that I'm prone to temper tantrums" she announces, then laughs." It's true, I can't deny it".

I read her what I've written and she laughs, blushes a bit , then thanks me for the complimentary words. "It's okay, it's true that I'm hard on myself, too moody and too hard on myself". A sassy smirk is followed by a natural, relaxed smile. Dani has developed some real self awareness for a fourteen year old. We conclude the lesson with a Chopin mazurka that she has just begun to learn. Already she grasps this music and is taking to it. Oh, how it gladdens me when young people delight in great music.

Madeleine's lesson follows Dani's on this day. Madeleine, a woman of perhaps forty, a fine pianist and a student of long standing, has overheard Dani proclaim her pleasure at being included in my little book. An accomplished, intelligent, multi talented person, she catches me by surprise, asking "what about me Fred? Am I in your book? I'm pretty interesting, don't you think?" She smiles sheepishly.

"You are interesting Madeleine, very interesting" I reply. Suddenly it dawns on me that any student that goes unmentioned in this diary might feel slighted. An unforeseen problem! Madeleine quickly collects herself and assumes a mature, adult persona. She assures me that there is really no need to write about her— Too late! I'm happy to reflect on what a fine pianist and person she is.

Madeleine first became my student some fourteen years ago while she was working at Microsoft. Already a competent pianist, I enjoyed our lessons from the start. Eventually she left for California to attend the Monterrey Institute of International Studies. Since finishing up her diploma there she has been employed by Catholic Relief Services, and has lived and worked in Madagascar, India, Zambia, Tanzania and Montenegro. Despite the many enriching experiences this life has brought her, there remained two things about life in the United States that she greatly missed; her family, and as you may have guessed, her piano.

Madeleine's back in Seattle now. She has bought a little house here and though her profession still requires her to travel frequently, she is back to practicing and regular lessons. Today she regales me with three movements from a Bach French suite, played with style and beauty. Unfortunately, she must intermittently disappear from regular lessons to travel to Africa. This slows her momentum on the piano. And yet she persists as a musician. She has talent and loves music. Though it took a whole year due to the irregularity of her practice schedule, she recently gave me a lovely performance of Rachmaninoff's D Major Prelude from opus 32; a truly splendid performance!

Additionally, Madeleine is a friend, and currently serves on the board of Musical Experiences. She has shared with me many of her observations and experiences gleaned from her far flung travels. One that impressed me greatly and has stuck in my mind is her description of the ease with which people make music in Madagascar. "Fred, in the villages it is really something to see", she has told me. "Everyone, and I mean *everyone* sings and dances. They are poor. They don't have stereos, televisions or I pods. They can't push some button or turn a knob to produce music. So they can't be musically passive. But they all make music. They sing beautifully, and they *all* sing".

This set me thinking. Music is something very basic, something we have in us. It exists where ever human beings do. Whether villagers in Madagascar, a concert pianist in Berlin, a gospel choir in Atlanta, a lone flautist on a Japanese hillside, a sitar master in Delhi, or a fiery flamenco guitarist in Andalucia; be it a sultry tango in a Buenos Aires plaza, the soulful chant of an Arabic song, the bluesy rasps of a sax riff filling a New York jazz club, or a rustic, rousing Ukranian folk song at an open air wedding, a constant diversity of music ever sweeps through the family of humankind.

When Madeleine first painted the picture of the plebian musicians of Madagascar for me, it inspired me instantly.

After my evening lessons finish, I prepare to do a little reading. However, hardly had I opened my book when the telephone's ring interrupted me. Jess Smith, my old boss from the Brooklyn Conservatory was on the line, an unexpected pleasure. Jess, who has now reached the advanced age of 87 once hired me to teach piano. That was back in 1979, in New York. I still vividly remember the interview he conducted before offering me the job. He had asked me about my repertoire, and when I mentioned Chopin études he wanted to know which ones I had studied. I named them, referring to the keys that they're written in. "I appreciate that you name them by their keys," I remember him saying. Somehow we clicked right away, and soon became friends. Nonetheless, Jess Smith was my boss all the years that I taught at the conservatory and I referred to him respectfully as Mr. Smith, never Jess. He would remain Mr. Smith to me for many more years. It was only after I moved to Seattle, and he had retired from his post at the conservatory that he insisted I call him Jess. "Fred, Mr. Smith is dead," he declared. My friend was asserting his liberty, glad to be freed from playing the roles of administrator and boss.

Today, Jess Smith is living on the Oregon coast, just south of the town of Newport, with his longtime partner. "Fred, I've been thinking about you," he tells me through the phone. "You know, I'm playing some impromptus by Fauré, and I distinctly remember you once telling me that Fauré's music was influenced by Chopin. I felt I just had to talk to you." "Really? Did I say that?" I replied. I could not remember. "Well, Fauré does seem to owe a lot to Chopin, but his piano music is less pianistic. It has more awkward and wider intervals for the left hand, wouldn't you say?"

With that, we were off on a stimulating discussion of Gabriel Fauré, the refined master of late French Romanticism. I hadn't spoken with

Jess in many months, perhaps a year, but we were quickly locked in a sympathetic and scintillating exploration of music. This is what happens with kindred spirits.

"Jess, remember that the seeds of impressionism can be found in Fauré. Think of his harmonic progressions, the planing of seventh chords for example." "Yes that is true, his harmonies are fascinating," added Jess. "Remember, Fauré was Ravel's teacher in Paris."

Though I hadn't spoken with Jess in quite some time, he dispensed with any idle introductory remarks— no "how have you been" or "what's new." With us, there's never any small talk. We seem to understand something elemental about one another. Though music is our bond and provides an entrée to our relationship, our thoughts spiral out into other realms as well. On this winter's eve, we talk about Fauré, Rachmaninoff, Jess's eight students in his "retirement" on the coast, the aging process, the learning process, consciousness, and even death. At the ripe old age of 87, Jess is not ready to fully withdraw from either playing or teaching the piano. It is hard for true musicians to retire. General Douglas MacArthur once famously said, "Old soldiers never die, they just fade away." It seems that true musicians need to be officially and unequivocally pronounced dead for it to be said that they are retired. As for me, I hope to follow in Jess's footsteps, teaching and playing music well into my golden years.

Jess Smith grew up in Tacoma, Washington. As a young man, he served in England during the Second World War. After the war, he did what so many aspiring young musicians had done before him, and have done after him. He found his way to New York. Jess studied in the great metropolis with the renowned pianist and pedagogue Rosina Lhevine. The pressures of making a living led him to accept a position as the director of the Brooklyn Conservatory of Music. It was a good job, but it was also a compromise. Jess became an administrator and he managed the direction and growth of this institution. It meant that practicing and performing would be limited by his professional responsibilities. Fortunately, Jess was still able to do some teaching which he's always loved.

As a young man living in the "Big Apple," Jess Smith knew what it was to fall in love with the piano. He once told me his routine in those years. Practicing five hours every day, and then taking the subway to an accounting job on Wall Street where he'd work at a large bank from five in the afternoon until midnight. He understands me. "Fred, I envy you. You've never given in. You've kept your playing up over the years. You've kept improving as an artist. You are a superb pianist. I let my playing languish. You are so lucky." He's said this to me on more than one occasion. Jess certainly appreciated the life he had in New York. His position at the conservatory afforded him the opportunity to meet many fascinating people, including some shining lights of the music and art community. And yet, he had to put his own artistic aspirations on hold. This regret, at not having followed the musician's precarious path seems to gently haunt him. "You've stayed the course Fred," he's told me several times. "You have a freedom which I do not." Jess is yet a very fine pianist, a truly accomplished professional. But he knows he might have been even better.

I wonder if Jess romanticizes. It's easy to imagine the fruits of another's life while undervaluing one's own. Each of us has a different story, and the individual course one navigates unfolds mysteriously. Many are the influences that steer our barks.

I've stuck it out as a musician. I'm not sure how or why, it just happened that way. I loved music since I was little. I have some aptitude for it. I've learned to love teaching.

I never try to convince any of my students to pursue music as a profession. Those who feel they absolutely must follow its melodious siren should do so. Those who can't imagine any other calling; those who would feel unsatisfied or cheated in any other profession; only those students do I encourage to consider music as a profession. Hardly had I finished my phone conversation with Jess, that the phone rang again and Jackson, my erstwhile student was on the line; another delightful surprise. Jackson is home on holiday from Interlochen School of Music and Art. We set up a rendezvous at Peet's Café on Green Lake for the following day. Ah, I will soon learn all about my precocious 16 year old friend's first semester living away from home at boarding school. Jackson seems to be one of those souls who simply *must* see through his desire to follow the musician's path. Time will tell where his sojourn will take him. Tomorrow, at least, it will be to Green Lake, for what promises to be a lively conversation and a vigorous ramble around the lake with his old teacher.

Reading is just not meant to be this particular evening. I turn in shortly before ten. I'll be up early in the morning. The Chopin f minor Ballade will be waiting on my old Chickering's music stand, its well-worn pages marked by the master's instructions. I'll be there, striving once again to make this music live anew. The call of a more compelling voice has yet to draw me from my piano. So yes— I'll be there, bright and early in the morning.

# CODA: PEARL'S SONG

I awake this morning with a slight headache, in a haze, feeling logy. It's the 30th day of December. Another year dwindles away. A light, steady rain falls outside. Tomorrow I begin a little two and a half day holiday. I really ought to be in fine form. It's been nearly five months since I've allowed myself a vacation, working steadily six days a week, sometimes seven. Here I am, standing on the precipice of not two, but two and a half days where I need not be present to teach piano lessons. The thought that I might be coming down with a cold annoys me. "No, please not now!" I think.

My little holiday does not involve plans to go anywhere. It will merely be a break from the responsibilities of teaching, and having my schedule tethered to the calendar of my lesson book. There will be no break from practicing. My upcoming recital looms portentously, four weeks hence. I want to be ready!

An extra potent dose of vitamin C accompanies my breakfast. Afterwards, I make coffee , then sip it appreciatively without a newspaper or a radio to occupy my thoughts. I muse on the winding down of the year. After finishing my coffee, I take 20 minutes or so to sit quietly. Then I go to the piano. It's not long before my mind is absorbed by the Scarlatti d minor Sonata. Two Bach preludes and fugues follow the Scarlatti and their well-learned sequence of notes seems to play by itself. These pieces are well-memorized and there is no need to open a book.

The recital I'm preparing for next month includes works by Scarlatti, Bach, Beethoven, Mendelssohn, and Chopin. The f minor Ballade is the big new piece which casts the largest shadow over my piano these days.

It comes next this fine morning. I spend just under an hour practicing it.

My two and a half day holiday could easily have been extended to three days, but a few students voiced their concerns about missing their weekly lessons. I found it hard to say no to them. Consequently, Yann, Krithi, and Yurina will be along for lessons this morning. They are more than worthy of my time.

Yann arrives at 9:30 with his mother Catherine. Catherine is French and has been living in Seattle for at least 12 years now. She was my French tutor some years back, and that is how I first met her son Yann, then seven years old. By the time Yann turned eight, he had become my piano student. "Bonjour, comment ca va," we greet each other as they enter the house. Both Yann and Catherine indulge me with patience, allowing me to speak French with them. Yann, now 14, is full of *joie de vivre*. He loves music; also biology, soccer, his two cats, his friends, political discourse, and science fiction. His eclectic tastes apply to his musical life where his passions range from Bach, Chopin, and Prokofiev, to Yves Montand, Jacques Brel, Bob Dylan, Louis Armstrong, Duke Ellington, and John Coltrane. When he sings a *chanson* from the world of French cabaret, he takes on the aura of the suave, Gallic, charmer. I believe both Yves Montand and Maurice Chevalier would be proud.

Today he plays the Chopin b minor Waltz with verve and feeling. Yann's body moves subtly, rhythmically to the music. His head, crowned with blond-brown hair is bowed slightly, complete absorption showing on his face. He struggles with his memory on Prokofiev's Vision Fugitive Number 8, which he's in the midst of learning. His face takes on a gloomy air, as he tells me, "I've been overloaded with homework this week and it cut into my practice time." Yann is too stretched thin to become the pianist he could be. He sings in a choir, plays the clarinet and alto sax, and has recently picked up the ukulele. "Don't worry," I tell him. "You're getting it. The memory will firm up." "I know," he replies. "I'll do it. I just need more time." Yann loves Prokofiev and I'm confident he'll soon attain a fine performance of this short, evocative piece. "Yann, do the best you can," I say. "You know, you can't do justice to Chopin and Prokofiev without sufficient practice. You have to choose your priorities and manage your time." Every time I've spoken like this to him in the past, it has resulted in an excellent lesson the following week. Yann will play and love music for years to come.

Krithi, my next student is also 14. She appears with her mother, Kavita. Krithi, along with her parents and older sister, arrived here from India when she was just seven years old. Both Krithi and her sister Kavya began lessons with me five years ago. Kavya eventually lost interest, but Krithi loved the piano from the very first lesson. I still recall how much affinity she showed that very first day. Her attention span was good, her musical aptitude evident, her joy palpable. She is an excellent student, highly motivated and disciplined. In response to her own initiative, I have enrolled her in the Seattle Young Artist's Festival this upcoming March. Krithi will play the Chopin E-Flat Nocturne in front of an adjudicator. She'll be ready.

"Krithi, this piece is really improving now," I tell her after she plays it through for me. "Now I'm starting to really hear a satisfying balance." It's taken some work for Krithi to confidently sing out the right hand melodic line with an appropriate penetrating tone, while letting the chords in the bass provide a gentle, reassuring anchor. It is no small feat to play this piece with control and skill. "And your shaping, Krithi, you're starting to show me some real color!" "I'm trying," she replies. Shaping the melodic line takes practice, a sensitive ear, and taste. The more ingrained this nocturne seeps into Krithi's memory, the freer she becomes in spinning out the more refined and subtle nuances of the music.

Krithi is sweet, mild, and personable, but also strong, determined, and competitive. Her long, lovely dark hair, her slender, slight frame, and her gentle smile may give the impression of fragility, but a steely strength and indomitable spirit lurks within. When her mother, who watches her daughter's lesson on this day, attempts to engage me in friendly conversation, Krithi glares at her, then barks "Mom! This is my lesson time now. It's my time!" She's all business at the piano.

She plays a Schubert impromptu and a movement from a Bach suite after we put the nocturne aside. When we finish, she tells me she had never even seen a piano as a little girl in India. Now she loves it and is learning to play it with artistic finish.

One more student and my little "holiday" shall commence. Six and a half year old Yurina is right on time. She's been my student for eight months and has really taken to playing the piano. Yurina's parents Genta and Rie, both born in Japan, alternate in bringing her each week, and observing our lessons.

Yurina's brown eyes open wide when she plays the piano. She concentrates well. She listens, absorbs, catches on quickly, and with her parents' help, shows clear improvement most every week. "Yurina, how is Pearl doing?" I ask. Pearl is her dog, a beagle. Though I've never met Pearl, I've heard about her from Yurina. "She's okay," she tells me. She smiles shyly and casts a quick, furtive glance at her mother who returns the smile. "Can you still play Pearl's Song?" I wonder. "Um- maybe," she responds. Three months ago, the two of us, Yurina and I, wrote a song about Pearl. I suppose I did most, though not entirely all, of the musical composition. Yurina had some say in the choice of melodic intervals and a large hand in the lyrics that went along with it. Pearl's Song comes replete with chordal harmonies in the left hand, and Yurina has performed it adroitly at one of my student playing classes. "The thing is," she says, "Well- I haven't played it much lately." "I know, it hasn't been part of this week's assignment," I remark. "Let's play your other songs first, then at the end of our lesson, we'll review Pearl's Song. Let's see if you'll remember it."

She plays her exercises and scales with confidence. Though shy and taciturn during our lessons, her playing is crisp and purposeful. She exudes sanguine pleasure making the piano come to life. Her perform-ance of Thompson's *The Cukoo* pleases me. Yurina breezes through it happily, utilizing the *drop-roll* touch with fine style. This touch, which my volatile old teacher Mr. Brent once coached me on long ago, is now being mastered by six year old Yurina. It will profit her on her insipient musical odyssey for many years to come.

She doesn't say anything after I praise her *drop-roll* touch, but she can't suppress a lovely smile, and then shoots a proud glance at her mom.

Yurina is learning to read music well. We also work on playing by ear. That is how she's learned to play versions of *Greensleeves* and *Do a Deer*. On this rainy morning, she gleefully knocks out *Do a Deer* with nary a moment's hesitation. I've taught it to her with harmony in the left hand, and even some varied accompaniment.

By the time we get around to reviewing Pearl's Song, I notice that the headache I woke up with has completely vanished. The morning fog has lifted. I'm in clear blue sky. With help from Rie, we piece together the lyrics of our song.

I have a dog named Pearl
She's a friend of mine
She can bark at times
She's a friend of mine

Pearl's song is written in D Major, but features a contrasting middle section in d minor. It's here, in the minor mode, that the lyrics change and lament the sadness Pearl feels when the family leaves her all alone in the house. The triumphant return to the main theme in Major, revels in the joy of reunification, and brings the song to a happy conclusion. Yurina plays it for me. If truth be told, I believe she's already outgrown it and is tiring of it. She plays it more dutifully than anything else, indulging the wishes of her teacher and her mother.

"She's so quiet here," her mother tells me. "You should see her at home, or when she visits her friends. She never stops talking." I would have been hard-pressed to have predicted what happened next. Rie's cell phone rings and she informs me that she must take the call, and then steps out into the living room for a few minutes. Yurina and I are now left alone, and lo and behold, she strikes up a small conversation. "Pearl is 12 years old. - Tomorrow is her birthday," she tells me. I'm surprised, all this time I pictured Pearl as being a younger dog. "That's getting fairly old," I say. "It's about the same as 70 for a person," she explains. "Do you have any other pets?" I ask. "No, my mom says we shouldn't get another puppy because the puppy would be too sad when Pearl eventually dies." With that, Yurina turns to face the keyboard and waits, poised to resume the piano lesson.

Our little dialogue might not sound like much, but it gladdened me. I sensed it was a harbinger of lengthier ones to come. I, m happy that Yurina didn't want to miss her lesson this holiday week, and that she enjoys playing the piano. I look forward in continuing to share a small portion of this beautiful girl's unfolding journey.

In just eight months of weekly lessons, we've related on a not inconsequential level. We've collaborated on composing a song. She's picked up the *drop-roll* touch. In fact, she's becoming a musician. As for me, well, my headache is gone, I've learned more about a dog named Pearl, and sharing music with Yurina has made the past 35 minutes just fly by. She has helped me to do what I'm meant to do and what makes me feel most happily myself. The noise of the world has remained well outside the confines of the piano studio. As I walk Yurina and Rie to the door, we wish each other a happy new year. It's a fine thing being well used; like a drinking vessel that can hold and pour cool, clear, water. I know how lucky I am.

It is here that I shall drop the curtain, and bring this set of Piano Variations to a close. There will be no sparkling cadenza to traverse. I don't have any driving, fortissimo chords to offer either. Just a few more phrases, winding down to a last cadence. They may be played *mezzo-piano, poco ritardando*.

I'm officially on break now. It's off to Green Lake to see Jackson. Over the coming days I will get together with some good friends. It should be relaxing. But whatever pleasures the next few days may bring, nothing is likely to surpass in deep, well-rounded joy, the morning I have just known. I throw on my Gore-Tex jacket and head out into the rain. The beautiful, life giving rain. Jackson and I will have much to discuss. As the old year ebbs away, I prepare to greet the dawning of the one to come.

# ENDNOTES

1    THE ART SPIRIT…..Robert Henri……Basic Books….page 4.
2    Ibid…..page 7

Made in the USA
San Bernardino, CA
22 July 2014